THE HARROWSMITH BOOK OF

FRUIT TREES

CAMDEN
•HOUSE•
PUBLISHING

Canadian Cataloguing in Publication Data

Bennett, Jennifer
    The Harrowsmith book of fruit trees

Includes index.
ISBN 0-921820-33-X

1. Fruit trees—Canada.   2. Orchards—Canada.
I. Title.

SB354.6.C2B4 1991   634'.0971   C91-094362-1

Trade distribution by
Firefly Books
250 Sparks Avenue
Willowdale, Ontario
Canada M2H 2S4

Printed and bound in Canada by
D.W. Friesen & Sons Ltd.
Altona, Manitoba, for
Camden House Publishing
(a division of Telemedia Publishing Inc.)
7 Queen Victoria Road
Camden East, Ontario
K0K 1J0

Design by
Andrew McLachlan

Cover photograph by
Pablo Rivera, Superstock

Backcover photograph by
Superstock/Four By Five

Colour separations by
Hadwen Graphics
Ottawa, Ontario

Printed on acid-free paper

For John, as we plant a new orchard

The Harrowsmith Book of Fruit Trees
required the work of many people. First,
thanks to the experts who described their
favourite varieties and to the scientists at
various experimental stations who gave gen-
erously of their time and knowledge. At
Camden House, my thanks go to editor Tracy
C. Read, production manager Susan Dickin-
son, designer Andrew McLachlan, typesetter
Patricia Denard-Hinch, chief copy editor
Catherine DeLury, assistant copy editor
Christine Kulyk, editorial assistant Jane Good
and associates Laurel Aziz, Lois Casselman,
Charlotte DuChene, Laura Elston, Kathryn
MacDonald, Mary Patton and Eileen Whitney.

Contents

The visual value of fruit trees in the landscape is most apparent at blossom time, when they are as much at home in a flower garden as a flock of narcissus.

PARADISE RECLAIMED

"What was Paradise but a garden,
an orchard full of trees and herbs,
full of pleasures and nothing
there but delights."

—WILLIAM LAWSON, *A New Orchard and Garden*, 1683

Fruit trees offer beauty of blossom and shade to the landscape, as well as their more obvious contribution of an edible harvest. This is a crab apple, a type of tree fruit that can be grown in almost any location, rural or urban, in Canada and the northern United States.

Fruit trees in the landscape

Fruit is the stuff of paradise. According to legend, fruit was the first food given to humanity, whose dabbling with the apples of the Tree of Knowledge was to change the culinary picture drastically. There is still something magical, almost Edenlike, about trees that bear flowers and edible fruits, some as big as your fist. In a garden, their summer generosity and fall bounty are perfectly at home.

All the common northern fruit trees are members of the rose family, a family rich with legends of its own. Their blossoms are beautiful and fragrant, their fruits attractive, sometimes scented and occasionally produced by the bushel. Windfalls, damsons, russets, pippins, clingstones—all are words that have tripped deliciously off the tongues of English-speaking people for centuries. Fruit trees are best considered part of the rhythm of the living garden, not merely utilitarian objects or as inanimate as fenceposts.

In a time when building lots are small and costly and when the best way to ensure that your food is free from harmful sprays is to grow it yourself, it makes sense to plant trees that bear edible fruit instead of those that are ornamental only—a couple of apples rather than a maple, a cherry plum rather than a lilac. Although it is now known as edible landscaping, or permaculture, the practice is very old. For centuries, the Chinese have considered the beauty of fruit-tree blossoms essential in the landscape, an aesthetic priority borrowed by the Japanese. In Europe, fruit trees were vital to the family food supply. Richard Jefferies describes a typical cottage garden of the last century: "The garden stretches in a long strip from the door, one mass of green. It is enclosed by thick hedges, over which the dog-rose grows, and the wild convolvulus will blossom in the autumn. Trees fill up every available space and corner—apple trees, pear trees, damsons, plums, bullaces—all varieties. The cottages seem to like to have at least one tree of every sort. These trees look very nice in the spring when the apple blossom is out and again in the autumn when the fruit is ripe. Under the trees are gooseberry bushes, raspberries and numbers of currants."

Underneath fruit trees, it is also possible to grow shade-tolerant ornamentals, such as hostas, pansies, periwinkles, alyssum and junipers, but nothing so tall that it will be obscured in the branches nor anything that will offer too much competition to the tree roots. In Elizabethan England, Francis Bacon

recommended that "the borders wherein you plant your fruit trees be fair and large, and low and not steep; and set with fine flowers, but thin and sparingly, lest they deceive the trees."

Four of my own fruit trees—a 'Royalty' crab apple, a seedling pear and two European plums—grow within flowerbeds that have curving borders, a style borrowed from English country gardens. In a couple of cases, the flowerbeds were already in place and I planted the trees afterward. The remaining two trees were originally surrounded by lawn, but I later extended nearby flowerbeds to encircle the trees, peeling away the sod and replacing it with a mixture of topsoil and compost that could support a variety of annual and perennial flowers. This marriage of fruit trees and flowerbeds gives the garden a satisfying, unified appearance, with everything connected to everything else. Louise Beebe Wilder, celebrated turn-of-the-century American garden writer, wrote that she was inspired to plant a fruit tree in her flower garden after seeing "an ancient Apple tree that seemed, with every twig wreathed in fragrant bloom, to stand lost in an ecstatic dream of its departed youth. Beneath it in the fresh grass, crowding

between the crimson Peony shoots, were swaying hosts of little scarlet Tulips."

Grown this way, fruit trees are perceived as tall design elements in the landscape. The surrounding flowerbeds should be narrow enough to allow easy access to the tree for tending and harvesting but wide enough to include a satisfying spread of flowers. Gertrude Jekyll, one of the most influential garden designers of the late 19th century, described a beautiful fruit garden of ambitious proportions: " . . . a walled enclosure of about an acre and a half, longer than wide. The wall has trained fruit trees—peaches spreading their goodly fans, pears showing long, level lines and including hardy grape vines. Next to the wall is a space six feet wide for ample access to the fruit trees, their pruning, training and root-management; then a 14-foot plant border, wholly for beauty; and a path eight feet wide." Jekyll describes crosswise rows of additional fruit trees; she suggests apples and pears for the cooler parts of England. The borders surrounding the trees can include ornamental shrubs and perennials such as peonies, hollyhocks, dahlias, hydrangeas, irises, forsythias, spiraeas, roses and hostas. "Surely my fruit garden would be not only a place of beauty, of pleasant sight and pleasant thought, but of leisurely repose, a repose broken only faintly and in welcome fashion by its own interests—in July, August and September a goodly place in which to wander and find luscious fruits in quantity that can be gathered and eaten straight from the tree. There is a pleasure in searching for and eating fruit in this way that is far better than having it picked by the gardener and brought in and set before one on a dish in a tame room."

Jekyll's enclosed fruit garden would lead to an orchard with rows of plums, apples and quinces. My own remaining fruit trees—two apples, two cherry plums, an apricot, a sour cherry and a pear—grow behind the house in a stretch of grass beside the vegetable garden. This setting, which is more orchard than garden—although it is too small and my attitude too laissez-faire (there are no rows) for me to call it an orchard—is just as attractive in its own way as the flower garden with its attendant fruits; but this space is more utilitarian, less deliberately decorative, and here, there is room for a firepit and for summer croquet games and picnics.

Because building lots are costly and the surest way to obtain pesticide-free fruit is to grow it at home, a sensible approach to landscaping involves making the best use of available space by planting trees that bear edible fruit instead of those that are ornamental only.

Fruit trees in the landscape

If I were short of space, which I am not, I might consider some espalier trees—like the walled peaches and pears Jekyll describes—although I would avoid her peaches, which are not hardy enough for my eastern Ontario garden. I am not the type of gardener, however, who can be counted on to turn to my appointed tasks with the precision that espalier requires. Espalier is made up of equal parts of biology and motivation. In that sense, it is the Western equivalent of bonsai, a far more extreme dwarfing and training technique which can also be used on fruit trees. Gardeners who do not like to fuss should avoid both of these severe pruning techniques, but those who are willing to invest the necessary time and energy can achieve some striking results. (Basic directions can be found on page 25.)

In considering fruit trees for the landscape, remember that they are not like the annual or even perennial flowers which surround them. Once planted, they will, with luck, stay in place through winter, summer, drought and flood for years, perhaps generations. Do not be hasty about deciding what tree to buy or where to plant it—a dying tree is a tragic creature. Bob Osborne, owner of Corn Hill Nursery, in New Brunswick, says: "It seems to me that choice of variety is the key to truly successful fruit growing, whether it be in the backyard or a commercial plot. My bias is toward those varieties that exhibit good disease resistance, hardiness and, of course, taste."

Cold hardiness should be the first priority of northerners. British gardeners wax enthusiastic about walled gardens, like Jekyll's, in which fruit trees are trained to grow flat or espaliered. "A south-facing wall is an invitation to plant a peach or, better still, a nectarine to train as a fan," writes Englishman Hugh Johnson in his encyclopaedic work *The Principles of Gardening*. For most of us, this is the stuff

Fruit trees are best considered as vertical design elements within the landscape. In the author's garden, a 'Royalty' crab is one of several fruit trees that grow within flowerbeds that have curving borders.

of dreams. European design techniques can be modified and used anywhere, but the fruit species and cultivars must be suitable for the particular garden. Peaches and nectarines can be grown only in the mildest places—climatic zone 6 or warmer. Any tree too tender may not make it through the first winter; it may be damaged every year until an especially severe "test winter" does it in; or it may thrive but never bear fruit because the blossoms are killed every year. Many a so-called male tree is caught in exactly that situation. Suitability for your area is a similar priority. You might like 'Granny Smith' apples, but chances are they will not mature in your garden—northern summers are simply not long enough. Also, the cooler the climate, the slower maturation will be. 'Redhaven' peaches ripen about August 17 around the southern Great Lakes, but the few parts of the Atlantic Provinces warm enough to ripen peaches at all will not harvest 'Redhavens' until about September 1.

Once you have chosen your fruit variety—and all the chapters in this book will be of help—you must decide whether you can offer the tree the conditions it needs. Growing healthy trees is especially important if you want to garden organically, which is a priority of mine. Because a tree is in place for the long haul, its basic requirements must be respected from the outset: sun most of the day; reasonably good, well-drained soil; and no other tree close enough to compete. The tree may require a partner for pollination, in which case, you will need even more space for at least two trees, or there must be a compatible pollinator within 100 feet, perhaps in the garden next door or across the street. You may want to try grafting a branch of a pollinator onto the tree (described on page 23). Wild fruit trees such as crab apples or pin cherries nearby may help with pollination, but they can also be the source of disease. The trees that do not require partners, described in the following chapters, are often the best choices for city gardens.

What about dwarfs? Some trees are naturally small, even shrublike, as is the case with native plums and cherries and Manchurian apricots. These are, naturally enough, easier to place in the landscape than 20- or 30-foot standard trees. In harsh conditions, trees may be dwarfs even though they are genetically predisposed to reaching a large size. Other fruit trees can be had in various sizes, depending on the roots upon which they grow. Every fruit tree you buy will be grafted, with the

top almost always a different variety from the roots. Sometimes, the rootstock is an entirely different species. Grafting is both a quicker and a more dependable way to multiply fruit trees than growing them from seed. The rootstock influences not only the tree's size but also its hardiness, its disease resistance and even its budding schedule and the colour and size of its fruit. In other words, both ends of the tree are equally important.

Dwarfing rootstocks—those which result in a tree about half-size or less—are available primarily for apples, although there are some size-controlling stocks for other trees. Most dwarfing stocks will create a less winter-hardy tree. Certainly, it will be less "vigorous," the word used to describe the ability of a tree to grow big and quickly. Bart Hall-Beyer writes in the catalogue of Sursum Corda, his zone-4 Quebec nursery: "The last thing to do to a tree in a harsh climate is to reduce its vigour." Furthermore, in really tough places, trees are apt to be smaller than usual, whether or not they have dwarfing rootstocks.

On the other hand, where conditions are more forgiving, Roger Way, a fruit breeder in Geneva, New York, recommends that "dwarf trees are definitely the way for a home gardener." Most small gardens are in cities, and a city creates its own climate, which will be somewhat—or dramatically—warmer than the surrounding countryside. Also, city gardens tend to be small, and small gardens have nearby walls, garages and fences that break the wind and collect snow, which has an insulating effect on roots. Way recommends dwarf trees because they take up less space and are easier to pick and tend yet produce full-sized, sometimes even larger-than-average-sized, fruit. The smaller harvest, which comes earlier than that of other trees, may be perfect for a family that wants less fruit. The trees will probably not live as long, but that, too, is not necessarily detrimental. As far as aesthetics go, small trees are more compatible with small spaces.

Before planting, look at as many pictures as you can find of gardens that incorporate fruit trees. The graceful Japanese garden traditionally includes large stones and reflective pools of water. English cottage gardens may feature trellises and archways. The French have perfected the art of growing small trees in pots. If possible, look at the living tree—or, at least, a picture of one—fully grown so that you can visualize it in your garden. Decide whether you can provide the necessary growing conditions and the time needed every year for pruning, perhaps for spraying and, if nature is kind, for harvesting. Fruit trees are a responsibility, but like all living things, they have the potential to repay the debt countless times over. If you do a little work now, it can mean the creation of a small paradise that will give you a lifetime of respite from the fast-paced world beyond the garden.

The 17th-century quotation at the beginning of this chapter continues: "The gods of the earth, resembling the great God of heaven in their authority, majesty and abundance of all things, wherein is their most delight? And whither do they withdraw themselves from the troublesome affairs of their estate, being tired with the hearing and judging of litigious controversies? Whither but into their orchards, made and prepared, dressed and destined for that purpose to renew and refresh their senses and to call home their over-wearied spirits.

"What can your eye desire to see, your ears to hear, your mouth to taste or your nose to smell that is not to be had in an orchard with abundance and variety?"

Fruit trees in the landscape

A fruit tree in the front yard may be surrounded by flowerbeds, or it may stand alone as a focal point. A sweet cherry, left, is not only ornamental and productive but also cools a nearby house in summer and shelters shade-loving shrubs such as azaleas.

WONDROUS LIFE

"What wondrous life is this I lead!
Rich apples drop about my head.
The luscious clusters of the vine
Upon my mouth do crush their wine.
The nectarine and curious peach
Into my hands themselves do reach."

—ANDREW MARVELL, *The Garden*, 1681

The perfect tree in the perfect place, such as this sweetly scented 'Bechtal's' crab apple in an Ontario garden, is the result of choosing both site and cultivar wisely, then planting correctly and tending faithfully. Note that no branches should be allowed to grow on the bottom 18 inches of the trunk.

At the tail end of summer, most of the apple trees at the New York Agricultural Experiment Station in Geneva are still bright with red, yellow and green fruit, while other trees overshadow puddles of fallen fruit. In a field close by, branches hang heavy with purple plums, but the "curious" peaches, as Marvell would have it, are bare, as are the nectarines, which, to my mind, are far more curious. Some of the harvest has gone to the offices of the station scientists, who are looking for improved varieties with better taste, better appearance and better disease resistance. This is, after all, the experimental station that has turned out the 'Jonagold' apple, the 'Stanley' plum and scores more well-known names. The scientists here, like their colleagues around the world, seek to add to the hundreds of different varieties of each kind of fruit that already exist, tributes to generations of appreciation and selection.

Gardeners who live in a climatic area similar to that of Geneva, New York, which is classified as being within the United States Department of Agriculture (USDA) climatic zone 5b, can expect that fruit trees developed here will likely succeed for them. The USDA defines zone 5b as a place where lowest winter temperatures fall in the range of minus 20 to minus 10 degrees F (-29° to -23°C). Agriculture Canada has more complex standards for its definition of hardiness zones. (See the maps on pages 140 and 141.)

When choosing fruit trees, the top priorities are hardiness and suitability for your climate, and the best way to find trees that meet those requirements is to look for varieties developed in a climatic area similar to yours. Nurseries that grow their own trees in a zone the same as, or colder than, yours are a good place to start. Mail-order nurseries issue catalogues, so potential buyers can take their time shopping at home, a method that I have found discourages impulse buying and makes for a better long-term decision. The sort of fall Andrew Marvell describes at the beginning of this chapter is possible for everyone—with modifications in keeping with the climate—but only if you choose wisely before putting spade to soil.

Wisdom is needed, too, in choosing when and where to put spade to soil. Most northern companies will ship only during early spring. This is not simply because trees ship much more safely when dormant—that is, before their buds begin to swell—but also be-

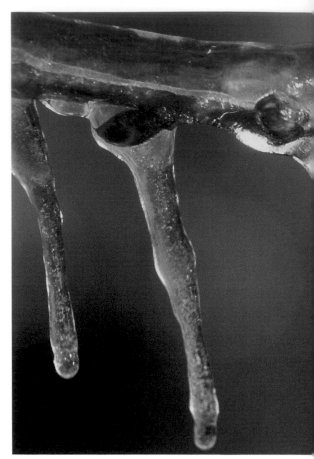

cause the trees should be planted as soon as possible after the ground thaws. When the buds swell, the chance of transplant shock increases. Trees just a year old, called maidens or, more descriptively, whips, will suffer the least trauma when moved from nursery to garden, but not all nurseries sell them. Larger trees will adapt to the move too, if planted right away and tended well, but do not be beguiled by a large supermarket tree if a smaller one is available.

If you can, plant the tree as soon as you obtain it; some frost in the ground will not harm it. If immediate planting is not possible, leave the tree outdoors in a shady place or in a dark cellar, garage or shed that is cool but not freezing. The roots must be kept damp and never exposed to the air. Potted trees should be watered thoroughly whenever the top inch of soil dries. Unwrap bare-root trees (those not in pots), and set them into a trench outdoors at an angle. Cover the roots with damp peat moss, sawdust or shredded paper, and top with a layer of moist soil until planting time. This process is called heeling in. Firm the soil lightly, and wrap the trunks with foil or plastic guards to protect them from rodents.

Winter cold and frost damage are the two most severe limitations to growing fruit trees in the north. At the outset, tree species and cultivars must be selected with climate in mind. Then, tree position in the landscape and cultural practices can minimize winter's harm.

SITUATING

Have the planting hole ready before the tree arrives so that you can situate the hole carefully without feeling pressured by a tree in need of planting. Take into account the basic requirements of the tree—sunlight, deep, well-drained soil, sufficient space and shelter—and remember that trees far from the house may be "out of sight, out of mind." I once lost a young pear that had been used as a cat scratching post until the lower bark was entirely stripped; I did not notice the damage in time.

Deep, well-drained soil is necessary for fruit trees. William Craig, tree-fruit specialist for Agriculture Canada in Nova Scotia, says that one of the problems Atlantic growers have is lack of good soil. "Soils can be shallow or poorly drained, which results in poor tree growth or tree mortality. A good soil would be about three feet in depth and free of restrictions to root growth." If you cannot offer this much depth, it is possible to raise the soil level as much as a foot with compost and topsoil. This works well, for instance, if you are planting your trees within flower-

beds, as described in the previous chapter.

Raising the bed also has the advantage of giving at least the upper roots good drainage. Another way to ensure that the soil is well drained is to choose slightly sloping land, which offers the added advantage that frost will move down the slope away from the trees. Most backyard gardeners have little choice in such matters, but fruit trees must not be subjected to "wet feet," or they will not survive. Consider not only the backyard but also the front, where light exposure and soil conditions may be better. Roger Way, a scientist at the experimental station in Geneva, New York, says: "The soil must be fairly well drained. If it is a swamp, there is no point in planting any sort of fruit tree." If all else fails, you can always grow the smallest trees in large pots, as described on pages 118 to 123.

All fruit trees require sunshine. Watch for shadows from buildings and fences and for competition from surrounding trees, some of which may not yet be mature. "Fruit trees must have full sun," says Way. "We have that problem ourselves at Geneva. There are woods 60 feet from the trees at the edge of the orchard, and because of the shade in late after-

The object of pruning, here performed on a 'Mount Royal' plum by the author, is to produce and maintain a tree that admits plenty of light and air and has a maximum of fruiting wood within easy reach of the picker.

noons, especially in fall, the edge trees don't perform like the ones at the centre of the orchard. We might get some fruit, but it's not optimal." Keep all fruit trees at least 20 feet from other trees to avoid shade and root competition. On the other hand, some shelter from the prevailing wind is good, such as a wall about 10 feet away—closer, of course, for espalier—or a windbreak 20 feet away or farther on the windward side. If you are growing your trees in rows, try to orient them north-south.

In situating the tree, take its mature size into account. Watch for low overhead wires or a nearby pathway or driveway that the tree may crowd. The size of the mature tree will depend on species, rootstock and growing conditions (trees grow larger when given more space), but the general rule is to leave enough space around each tree for plenty of sun exposure and good air circulation. Pears, apricots, peaches, plums, sweet cherries and standard apples should be at least 20 feet from other fruit trees; sour cherries and cherry plums need 15 feet. Allow about half that distance from driveways, roads, pathways and walls, unless you particularly want closeness. Dwarf apples, pears on quince rootstocks and other small trees need the least space of all.

PLANTING

Dig a hole about twice as deep and twice as wide as the size of the rootball. If the tree has not yet arrived, you will be reasonably safe in digging a hole about two feet deep and wide. Bart Hall-Beyer of Sursum Corda nursery in Quebec has a succinct piece of advice: "Putting a $1 tree in a $15 hole gives better results than the other way around." Set the topsoil aside, and mix it half-and-half with compost. Push the spade into the bottom of the hole to break up the subsoil, and insert a stake firmly in the ground. Stakes are necessary for dwarf trees throughout their lives and are a good idea for all trees in their first year to help the roots become firmly established.

The planting depth will depend in part upon the eventual position of the graft union, visible as a swelling on the trunk. If the union is below the soil surface, roots may extend from above the graft; the roots, then, come from the scion, the top part of the tree. Sometimes this is desirable, especially with pear, plum and other trees on seedling rootstocks in gardens where conditions are harsh, such as on the prairies or in the Far North. In these cases, the graft goes about two inches *below* the soil surface. Usually, however, you want only the rootstock to take root. If you are growing a tree on a size-controlling rootstock, rooting from the scion will result in a full-sized tree. In general, ensure that the graft union is two or three inches *above* the ground. Studies have shown that the higher a rootstock graft is above the ground, the more influence the rootstock has on the tree; this influence may include dwarfing, cold hardiness or any other quality. The third planting situation involves a tree with an interstem. Interstem trees, usually apples, are made up of rootstock on the bottom, interstem in the middle and scion at the top, so they have two graft unions on the trunk. The tree should be planted so that *half the interstem is underground* to reduce sucker growth.

Backfill the hole with the soil mixture so that the tree is at the proper depth with all roots covered. Be sure that it is vertical, with the stake in place about six inches from the tree. This job is easier when done by two people. Fill in around the roots with the remain-

ing topsoil mixture, pushing soil between the roots and tamping it firmly in place as you go. At the surface, leave the soil firmed and slightly dished, and then water thoroughly, at least one bucket per tree. Tie the trunk loosely to the stake with loops of soft fabric or old garden hose. Some motion of the tree in the wind should be allowed, as it helps strengthen the trunk at the base. If you are creating an espalier, as described on page 25, you will begin now to tie the tree to its wall or trellis.

Under each tree, leave a circle of clear ground extending outward one or two feet from the trunk. To slow weed growth, this space can be mulched with four sheets of newspaper, held in place and made more attractive by adding wood chips, hay, sawdust or gravel. When weeds eventually grow within this circle, cultivate shallowly—only two or three inches deep—so that tree roots are not injured. Between the trees, a cover crop such as lawn grass or flowers helps the roots harden in fall by absorbing nutrients and water and provides some protection in winter by collecting snow and acting as insulation.

Should you wish to move a fruit tree—a procedure to be avoided if at all possible—your chances for success will be better the smaller and younger the tree. Cut around the sides of the rootball as soon as the soil thaws in spring. After leaf drop the following fall or in spring before the buds swell, dig up the tree, keeping as much soil as possible around the roots, and transplant it at the same depth as soon as you can, watering it thoroughly. Watch for and cut off any dead branches the following spring.

PRUNING

The object of pruning is to produce and maintain a tree that admits plenty of light and

A selection of sharp, good-quality tools such as regular garden secateurs and long-handled pruning shears helps make the job of pruning easy and pleasant.

Branches with wide crotch angles are the best, as they are the strongest and are capable of bearing the most fruit. Here, a pear branch is trained into a nearly horizontal position with a wooden spreader.

air, has a maximum of healthy, fruiting wood and bears its fruit fairly evenly and within easy reach of the picker (although a ladder may eventually be required for harvesting standard trees). Paul Olsen, who owns Roseberry Gardens in Thunder Bay, Ontario, says: "Fruit trees in cold climates are rarely pruned. This is unfortunate, because pruning is essential for the health of the tree and for high-quality fruit. Most people are intimidated by the pruning process, so they do not do any at all. The steps to pruning are simple, and it just takes some experience with it to become confident."

Richard Layne of the Agriculture Canada Research Station in Harrow, Ontario, recommends that all home fruit trees be pruned according to the modified central leader system. The name sounds complicated, but it just refers to the modification—cutting back—of the central leader, which is the highest point of the tree, often the central stem or trunk.

The first year, if you are planting a year-old whip, remove all branches, and head back the leader to about a foot above where you want the lowest scaffold branch, normally about 18 inches off the ground, meaning that you will be topping the young tree to a height of about 2½ feet. The second year—or, if the tree is more than a year old, as soon as it is planted—after the coldest winter weather has passed, remove all branches except three or four well-spaced scaffolds that have wide crotch angles and point in different compass directions. They should be six to eight inches apart on the trunk. Head the leader back to about a foot above where the next set of scaffold limbs is desired. The third year, repeat the procedure of the second year. By now, the tree should have assumed its basic structure, with scaffold branches situated around the leader like the steps on a spiral staircase. If necessary, choose additional new scaffolds the fourth spring, for a total of six to eight. Cut the leader back to just above a weak branch. This year and henceforth, thin side branches from the scaffold limbs, removing branches that grow downward or upward into the tree. The middle of the tree will seldom be densely branched and should require little thinning.

Remember that branches now the size of knitting needles may eventually be as thick as your arm and must be spaced accordingly. Olsen writes, "When fruit trees are planted, it is important to train the branches well to prevent problems later on." An important principle of pruning is to keep the branches as close to horizontal as possible. Horizontal branches are stronger, more likely to bear fruit and less likely to suffer from a type of winter damage called crotch injury, which may lead to broken branches when the tree is heavy with fruit. Trees have a natural tendency to grow upward—they are "rather contrary creatures," says Wayne Still, who owns an organic orchard in British Columbia. Remove branches that grow at an angle of less than 35 degrees from the vertical, or train them into a more horizontal position with clothespins attached to the trunk. Larger branches can be wedged into position with wooden posts, or they can be weighted with anything reasonably heavy, such as small bags of sand. When the tree begins to bear, the weight of the fruit will help pull down the branches. If the tip of a branch becomes lower than any other part of the branch, it will lose its vigour and must then be tied or propped up.

When cutting off branches, do not leave stubs. Nor should you cut branches flush with the larger branches from which they grow, as was formerly recommended. Instead, cut at the outward edge of the raised collar at the

Pruning is an easily
mastered skill that is
essential for the health of
the tree and for high-quality
fruit. Clean shears between
cuts in a disease-reducing
solution of one part
household bleach in
nine parts water.

base of the branch. USDA researchers have found that this practice encourages wounds to heal rapidly and without infection.

Tree dressings are not necessary. Traditionally, tree wounds have been painted with substances such as tar or paint; but recently, it has been shown that unlike humans, trees seal off the wounded portion and produce ethylene to enhance growth in the surrounding tissue. A chemical barrier limits the spread of decay from the wound to healthy tissues nearby, then the cambium forms a wall to protect the new growth. This process is faster in some trees than in others, but in no cases have wound dressings been found to facilitate it.

Normal pruning should always be done with a light hand; heavy pruning disrupts the balance of roots to foliage and retards the year of first fruiting. "As soon as you put pruning shears to the tree, you have interrupted the fruiting system," cautions John C. Sanford, a professor of pomology at Cornell University. This does not mean that pruning should be avoided. Check the tree every year, and remove unwanted growth when small. Dormant pruning, done in early spring just before the buds swell, stimulates vegetative growth as the tree strives to utilize a root supply too great for the amount of aboveground growth. Severe dormant pruning can result in a crop of rapidly growing vertical shoots called water sprouts, which arise just behind the pruning cuts. These shoots increase the likelihood of

infection by certain diseases such as fire blight and peach canker, are vulnerable to winter injury and must be either pruned off or trained downward to form useful branches. Summer pruning, on the other hand, slows growth and can have a dwarfing effect on the tree by removing its food-manufacturing parts. Richard Layne advises that vigorous water sprouts be removed during the summer to prevent their regrowth. West Coast gardeners should do summer pruning two or three weeks before the harvest for the greatest benefit, but in colder areas, there should be no summer pruning within a month before the first fall frost.

The exception regarding pruning occurs with apricots, peaches and nectarines, which should not be pruned before they bloom, because pruning at that time will encourage earlier blooming. Pruning can be done anytime from bloom until June, but no later than June, so that winter-tender growth is not encouraged.

Maintenance pruning on all fruit trees includes the removal of dead branches and one of any two neighbouring branches that rub together. It also may be necessary to cut away diseased areas, as described in the next chapter.

For pruning, I like to have a variety of implements on hand. Regular garden secateurs will remove water sprouts and small branches within reach. Larger branches and those a lit-

Just as branches that are too vertical will not bear well, so those that dip below horizontal will cease bearing. These peach branches have been propped up for good cropping and to help support the load of ripe fruit.

tle farther away can be removed with long-handled pruning shears, which give greater leverage and so provide better cutting power. Pruning shears operated by a string-and-pulley system will handle branches even farther away. You may need to use a ladder as the tree grows. Having the appropriate equipment on hand makes the job much easier and therefore more enjoyable.

CARETAKING

It may seem that little is going on with a newly planted tree. Hugh Johnson, British gardener and author, mentions "the three-year rule: for three years, not much happens." During this time, however, roots are growing, and the groundwork is being laid for a lifetime of harvests. Watering now is most important. Trees tend to look self-sufficient because they have woody stems and do not wilt as readily as flowers or vegetables; but before the roots have had a chance to grow, trees are as vulnerable to drought damage as any other plants. I almost lost the first fruit trees I planted because I did not water them during their first summer, a dry one. The trees were so weakened

that they suffered severe winter damage, but they managed to rally the following year when I did water them, and they were growing normally by their third year. Unless there are heavy rains, give each tree a bucket of water weekly until around August, then water sparingly or not at all to allow the trees to harden for winter.

Tree growth begins in May and reaches its peak around July, when the fruit is developing quickly. If the trees are healthy and not excessively pruned, they should come into bearing in three to eight years: the shorter duration for peaches, as well as apples and pears on dwarfing rootstocks, the longer for some apples and pears. Plums and cherries take about five years, although cherry plums and native cherries may bear fruit the year after planting.

Do not fertilize newly planted trees. If they have been planted in reasonably decent compost-enhanced, well-drained soil, they should have no severe nutrient problems, whereas fertilizing can cause more difficulties than it solves. Too much nitrogen, for instance, whether in chemical fertilizers or manure, can cause a calcium deficiency, which leaves trees soft, attractive to pests such as aphids and pear psylla and unable to withstand winter cold and disease infestations. Organic orchardist Wayne Still says: "The first year, I put turkey manure down, and the following year, I got more growth and bitterpit and aphid problems. It took about eight years for the trees to settle down." Trees that are left unfertilized grow slowly and are better equipped to deal with diseases, pests and harsh winters. After fruiting begins, the application of a soil conditioner, such as an inch of compost under the mulch around the trunk in May, will help provide an ongoing supply of necessary nutrients.

Soil that is too acidic or too alkaline should be corrected, if it can support fruit trees at all. A soil test, available inexpensively from your provincial department of agriculture or state extension service, will determine the soil's pH—its acidity or alkalinity. In the pH scale of measurement, 7 means neutral (neither acidic nor alkaline); increasing acidity is designated by lower numbers and increasing alkalinity with higher ones. In soil with a pH below about 6 or above 8, nutrients may be present in the soil but simply not available to the roots. For instance, the alkaline soils of the prairies may cause an iron deficiency that turns leaves yellow or whitish. Rather than needing iron, the soil requires acidification with sulphur, which will make the soil's iron available to plants. Acidic soils, on the other hand, may require an application of calcitic or dolomitic lime. If fruit trees thrive in your area, you can fairly safely assume that the pH of your soil is acceptable.

Winter Preparation

Preparing for winter is part of the annual routine for growers of northern fruit trees. After trees become dormant in fall, they are much better able to withstand cold weather. The external sign that dormancy has occurred is leaf fall. Thereafter, trees continue to grow but very slowly. They are, in a sense, marking time until spring; all northern trees need a certain period of chilling in order to produce large crops of good fruit—the reason few of these fruits do well in the Deep South. This chilling must be at a temperature below 45 degrees F (7°C). Just how much chilling the tree requires varies—apples need between 300 and 1,700 hours, depending upon cultivar, whereas most peaches and apricots need less.

While the tree is dormant, it will not begin to grow even if the weather warms above 45 degrees, but as soon as the chilling requirement has been satisfied, the tree will respond to higher temperatures with swelling buds. Trees that have begun to grow can be damaged if cold temperatures return; the buds will sustain the worst damage.

Clearly, then, it is important to grow trees which are hardy in one's own climatic area and which do not bloom before the last heavy frost. But even suitable cultivars may suffer winter damage if they have been improperly tended. Trees are best able to withstand winter weather if they have not been fertilized since spring (if at all), if they have borne only a moderate crop of fruit, if they have not been defoliated by insects or diseases and if they are not weakened by drought or excessive soil wetness. Although they have been healthy all season, trees that grow near the limits of their area of hardiness may suffer from tip dieback, which is evident in spring when branch ends shrivel because they did not harden sufficiently. Winter injury is cumulative, so damage may show up after a winter that was not particularly harsh.

There are several ways to lessen the possibility of winter damage. If there is a depression in the soil at the base of the tree, fill it in in the fall, or else it will collect water during winter thaws that will contract when it freezes, constricting the trunk. Wrap the trunk to prevent rodent damage: foil can be used for young, slender trees, while plastic guards or quarter-inch wire netting are the usual choices for larger ones. Pile soil or gravel around the base of the tree to cover the bottom edge of the guard.

Southwest injury is another potential problem. It occurs on sunny winter days, especially if there is snow on the ground. The bark on

Heavy fertilization of fruit trees will do more harm than good, but once fruiting begins, an inch of compost applied around the trunk in May will help to provide a mild, ongoing supply of necessary nutrients.

the sunny (southwest) side warms up, but when the sun sets or goes behind a cloud, it cools so rapidly that a section may be killed. The dead bark then dries and peels back during the growing season. To prevent southwest injury, mix one part white latex paint with four parts water, and soon after the first fall frost, paint the trunk, branch crotches and lower scaffold limbs to about six inches out from the trunk. The paint reflects the winter sun, cooling the tree sufficiently to avoid injury, which is worst in trees three to seven years old. Besides suffering from southwest injury, the bark may split during frigid winter weather. Painting the tree not only protects the bark from winter damage but also helps delay blooming, an advantage in most northern gardens. A white tree wrap is available that protects against rodents, southwest injury and borers.

When frosts threaten blossoms or young fruit, commercial growers employ a variety of techniques to raise the temperature around the trees. One is to burn small, smoky fires upwind from the trees; another is to sprinkle the trees with water throughout the frosty night until after the sun rises in the morning. In the largest orchards, it may be economical to hire a helicopter to create a wind that keeps the frost from settling. In the home garden, trees can be draped with blankets or tarps. This is especially easy with small or espalier trees. Remove the covers during daytime or as soon as the temperature rises above freezing.

POLLINATION

Sometime after planting, the trees will bloom, and the subject of pollination and fertilization will become important. Both processes are essential in the production of fruit. Pollination is the transfer of pollen from the anthers of a blossom to the ripe, sticky stigma at the top of the pistil in the blossom's centre. The stigma is receptive for about a week, after which it becomes dry and brown and can no longer be pollinated. Once the pollen lands on the stigma, it germinates and extends pollen tubes down the style of the pistil to the seeds within the ovary, a process that takes about 48 hours when the temperature is between 60 and 80 degrees F (15° to 27°C), longer in cooler weather. If all goes well, the seeds are fertilized, and the fruit begins to swell. If the seeds are not fertilized, the immature fruit soon falls from the tree.

Many trees require a partner for fertilization, while some, including many plums, will do better with a partner but will bear some fruit without. The rule of thumb is that the partners should be no more than 100 feet apart. Other trees are self-fertile; they will set a full crop with pollen from their own blossoms. These include all sour cherries and some recent sweet cherries, as well as most peaches, nectarines and apricots. If a pollinator is required, it must be a compatible species and must bloom at the same time. In apples, the issue of ploidy – the number of chromosomes – arises. (See page 102.) Apples and crab apples can pollinate one another, as can Japanese plums, cherry plums, sand cherries and other native American plums.

Simply having a compatible pollinator will not guarantee fruit. Pollination is a hazardous procedure, but fortunately, only a small proportion of blossoms need to be pollinated for the tree to produce a large crop of fruit. The pollen can be damaged by rain or low temperatures, resulting in a poor fruit set. Blossom buds are more tender than the remainder of the tree, so they can be killed at higher temperatures, especially after they begin to open in spring. 'Bartlett' pear and 'Red Delicious' apple blossoms in full bloom are killed by temperatures of 29 degrees F (-2°C); cherry and apricot, 28 degrees; peaches and Italian plums, 27 degrees. Young fruits are vulnerable to temperatures a couple of degrees higher. The frost-killing of buds and young fruits often erases the harvest of early-blooming trees such as apricots and plums.

Another possible problem is the blossoms' dependence upon bees for pollination. Poisoning from insecticides is the most common cause of bee mortality in orchards. Further complications arise when cold, wet or windy weather prevents honeybee flights. Strong

In all grafting, success is achieved only if the cambium layer of the scion is held firmly in contact with the same layer of the stock, or host plant. The two pieces can be held together with special grafting tape or with various types of household tape or strips of plastic.

There is no fruit without pollination, so harvests of most northern fruits are dependent upon weather that favours bee flights and the survival of the blossoms. Bees will fly only if the weather is relatively calm and warm and even then may favour flowers other than fruit blossoms.

colonies may fly when the temperature is around 60 degrees F (15° C), but weak ones may wait until a fairly balmy 72 degrees F (22° C). Bees will not fly if winds are stronger than about 12 miles per hour. Even when the bees do fly, fruit blossoms do not have a competitive edge over flowers such as dandelions, whose nectar content is similar or higher. Mowing weeds around the trees helps. Blossoms can be hand-pollinated with a cotton swab or small paintbrush—painstaking work but possible if you have only one or two small trees. If all of the seeds within a multiple-seeded fruit such as an apple or a pear are not fertilized, the fruit will be lopsided or will not grow, because only fertilized seeds release hormones that promote growth.

GRAFTING

Most backyard orchardists will never do any grafting, but those who take the plunge often find the process so intriguing that it becomes the most enjoyable aspect of growing fruit trees. Grafting consists of uniting two parts of a tree in such a way that the cambium layer just under the bark of both parts is joined and held in place until the two grow as one. Trees have already been grafted before they are purchased—the top of the tree is grafted to the rootstock.

After the tree is planted, grafting is usually unnecessary, but the home orchardist should know the basics, because an occasional emergency situation may occur when the bark has been girdled by mice or other animals or has been injured by frost or by ice that has tightened around the trunk during winter. If this damage is discovered in early spring while the top of the tree is still alive, the tree can be saved by a process known as bridge grafting. Twigs from the tree, called scions, are inserted under the bark in union with the cambium layer above and below the damaged area so that sap can pass through the scions. Eventually, if the grafts are successful, the twigs will become incorporated into the tree.

Grafting higher up the tree is often done by growers who want more than one cultivar on a tree. This can have the practical result of positioning the pollinator next to its partner, where it will be most useful; but frequently, it is done simply so that the grower can harvest more than one cultivar of fruit from a single tree. Gardeners tend to become besotted with the procedure, and there have been cases of 40 or more varieties on a single tree. The operation is adventurous but risky. Any cultivar that becomes dominant, either because of its vigorous nature or because of its position on the tree—the higher up, the more likely it is to be dominant—will overtake the tree at the expense of less vigorous, lower cultivars. Careful maintenance pruning must be done every year.

The most ambitious use of this sort of graft-

Last of the gifts of the fruit tree is a delicious, sun-ripened harvest. The best indicators of ripeness are colour and fragrance and, for stone fruits, a slight softening. The fruit on a single tree will not necessarily all ripen simultaneously.

ing is topworking, in which every branch is replaced with a desired cultivar. This is done chiefly in areas with very cold winters; the rootstock and trunk are of a very hardy species whose fruit is not desirable, but the branches are of a cultivar that provides better-quality fruit. If the branches are killed by severe conditions, the tree will continue to survive and the branches can be grafted again.

There are several other methods of grafting, including budding, which involves placing a single dormant bud and its surrounding tissue into a T-shaped cut on the branch. Once the bud has clearly taken hold, the branch is cut off above the bud and surrounding competitive buds are removed.

In all grafting methods, the foreign element is called the scion, the host plant the stock. A twig with as many as 10 buds may be placed against the cambium of a host plant. In a type of scion grafting called cleft grafting, one or more scions are inserted into clefts in the stub of a branch that has been cut off square. Scions and buds can be held in place with grafting tape or with ordinary masking, adhesive, electrical or duct tape or strips of plastic. Masking tape has a tendency to unravel, how-ever, and strips of plastic can be difficult to secure. After the graft has joined, electrical or duct tape should be slit so that it will not impair growth.

HARVESTING

Eventually, the first wonderful crop of fruit will appear. The best indicators of ripeness are colour and fragrance and, for stone fruits, a slight softening. The best test for most types is to bite into the fruit, although some pears are best ripened off the tree. With apples and some pears and plums, frost may come before the fruit is ready to harvest. Light frosts will do little harm except to shorten the length of time fruit will keep after it is picked. A heavy frost will damage fruit, which should then be eaten as soon as possible. (See more information on harvesting in the following chapters.)

The best autumn, one that fruit growers wish for, is long, with warm, sunny days and cool nights. This is the kind of fall Andrew Marvell described in the poem at the beginning of this chapter. It is a fitting close to a season of give and take between the orchardist and the orchard.

Against the Wall

The word espalier describes a very specialized form of pruning that results in a two-dimensional tree arranged in a specific geometrical form. The tree, which might, for instance, be shaped like a fan (palmette), candelabrum (palmette verrier) or many-tiered cross (the true espalier), is grown against and supported by a wall or trellis. As such, the tree takes less space than the usual three-dimensional type and so is well suited to a small city lot. Another bonus is that trees grown against a wall are sheltered from the wind and can bask in the heat reflected off the wall. In England and western Europe, where the technique was perfected, relatively tender fruits are trained against a wall for just that reason, to ensure a crop in places where the trees might otherwise suffer. Apples, which seldom require such protection, are more frequently espaliered for decorative and space-saving purposes. The Botanical Garden at the University of British Columbia includes an impressive espalier collection, including a row of overlapping apples that resembles a kicking chorus line (called a Belgian fence) and knee-high pear trees whose foot-tall trunks culminate in two horizontal branches that extend in opposite directions along a wire. This is called a cordon, the French word for string.

Cordons can also be trained vertically. Vertical cordons are among the espalier techniques used by some commercial growers of dwarf apples to maximize their production efficiency. In another commercially popular system called the low-trellis hedgerow, trees are tied to a four-wire trellis. The wires are about 18 inches apart, and the top wire is six feet above the ground. In a home garden, this system can support a living fence along a property line.

Espalier is best suited to trees that bear their fruit on spurs, including pears, quinces and most apples. Terminal-bearing apples such as 'Rome Beauty,' 'Paulared' and 'Tydeman's Early' are not as suitable, nor are tip- or branch-bearing species such as peaches, apricots, Japanese and native plums, figs and citrus, because the severe pruning required will remove their fruiting wood and decrease the crop. If these trees are espaliered, they should be pruned in a more relaxed two-dimensional style, such as a fan or a free-form shape.

Whatever the species, the tree should be slow-growing. Vigorous trees are too unruly for the system, so gardeners need to search for dwarfing rootstocks or nonvigorous cultivars. At the University of British Columbia, where the climate is relatively warm, the rootstocks M7, M9, M26 and M27 are used for apples, and quince A is used for pears. In colder places, Ottawa 3 is a good choice for apples, and the usual seedling rootstocks should be used for pears, as quince rootstocks will be too tender in most gardens cooler than zone 6. On the prairies, where dwarfing rootstocks are not hardy but all trees grow slowly, any hardy cultivar will be suitable.

If the backdrop will be a wall, plant the trees about a foot out so that they do not suffer from drought in the rain shadow. Eyebolts secured in the wall will hold heavy-gauge, galvanized, insulated wire to which branches can be loosely tied. The tying itself can be done with insulated wire, baling twine or, most attractively, with supple strands of willow. Keep the ties loose to allow for tree growth. If the trees' backdrop will be a trellis, build it sturdily, with 4-by-4 posts set two or three feet into the ground and strung horizontally with wire or a network of wooden crosspieces.

Pruning for espalier trees begins in the first year and must be done faithfully every spring. Summer pruning, which limits growth, is also necessary if the trees are growing vigorously. Remember that in harsh areas, this should be done more than a month before fall frosts. Always have in mind the desired shape, and remember that when you head back a branch, new growth will usually appear from the first bud below the cut. Try to keep the fruit spurs clustered as close to the trunk as possible and the entire tree conforming to the desired shape. Espalier properly done is very impressive, a highly productive tribute to the finest of the orchardist's arts.

Beginning the home orchard

Some gardeners choose to grow their trees by the centuries-old pruning system known as espalier, which results in decorative, two-dimensional trees that are well suited to small lots, walls and fences.

COUNTERACTING THE RAVAGES

"It would far transcend our limits to give even a brief description of the various sorts of insects which injure gardens, cultivated fields, et cetera, and destroy the best productions of our soil. We shall, therefore, confine ourselves to stating, briefly, some of the most approved modes of counteracting the ravages and effecting the destruction of a few of those which are most injurious to the cultivator."

— THOMAS G. FESSENDEN, *The New American Gardener*, 1843

Home orchardists can protect their trees without harming the orchard environment. In summer, rabbits and rodents can be considered picturesque and innocuous, but before winter, trunks must be surrounded by plastic or metal guards to prevent damage when food is scarce and the sweet bark becomes irresistible.

27

The environmentally friendly fruit garden

In late July, Wayne Still takes another slow turn around his apple orchard looking for "coddlers," his affectionate term for fruit infected with the larvae of the codling moth. "I learned a lot about orcharding," he says, "just being among the trees all summer, picking coddlers and watching the buds develop." Still's vocation—that of growing apples organically—is one of the most difficult a commercial orchardist can choose, but here in the Similkameen Valley of southern British Columbia, Still earns a "good living," he says, from just five acres of assorted varieties, many of which will be shipped as far as Toronto. He hands me a bag of shiny, spotless 'Macs,' evidence of his success. Every year, scientists from the Agriculture Canada Research Station in nearby Summerland come to Still's orchard to try new ways to protect plants and prevent infestations without harmful chemicals. "It gives them an opportunity to work with a relatively balanced host-predator relationship," says Still.

Although Still's way of growing fruit is the exception, he and an increasing number of maverick orchardists believe that food crops are no place for dangerous chemicals. Organic growers point to a list of alarming statistics concerning conventional agriculture. For instance, in the early 1980s, the United States used about a billion pounds of pesticides annually—100 times more than 40 years earlier—but the amount of food lost to insects was

Although orchards of past centuries did not have modern pesticides, they also had fewer problems. For instance, the bacterial disease fire blight, right, began to infect West Coast and European orchards only during this century.

almost twice as great. The proportion of pesticides that actually contacted target pests was extremely small—around one-thousandth of 1 percent or even less, depending upon the pesticide and its goal. "Thus over 99 percent moves into ecosystems to contaminate the land, water and air," wrote David Pimental and Lois Levenson of Cornell University in *BioScience*, February 1986. "Many natural parasitic and predator species are reduced, resulting in outbreaks of pests that were previously not a problem."

A "pest" is simply a bug or an insect whose population has burgeoned in response to an enormous food supply. These newly created headaches are gradually able to develop resistance to the very pesticides designed to kill them. Meanwhile, pesticides may harm the plants they are meant to protect, especially if they are applied too frequently or at the wrong time.

But most important, the environment around the crop—air, water and soil—and the treated food itself are left with residues that are known toxins, sometimes mild and sometimes powerful. In an Italian experiment in which apples treated with typical chemicals were stored for several months, then washed in soapy water, the detergents removed 80 percent of one pesticide, about half of another and none of a third. Many worried buyers resort to peeling their purchased fruit, but this is no guarantee that the remaining flesh is pesticide-free. One substance that penetrates the skin, alar, or daminozide, a growth retardant used on apples to promote colouring and maintain firmness, was effectively removed from supermarket fruit and juice by a consumer boycott in 1986.

In centuries past, the situation was quite different for both growers and consumers. In *The New American Gardener*, quoted at the beginning of this chapter, Fessenden went on to write: "The preventive operations are those of the best culture, in the most extensive sense of the term, including what relates to choice of plant, soil, situation and climate. If these are carefully attended to, it will seldom happen that any species of insect will effect serious and permanent injury." His words about preventive operations are still true, but the job is more difficult today. Insects and diseases have migrated and multiplied worldwide.

For instance, until 1920, virtually no pests except aphids were found in the orchards at Summerland, British Columbia, says an Agri-

28

Integrated Pest Management strategies, which have been developed since the 1940s, have lowered the frequency of spraying in commercial orchards while maintaining fruit quality. Some of these techniques can be practised by home fruit growers.

culture Canada report, but "by 1921, the diseases powdery mildew and fire blight had become prevalent. Even more significant was the discovery of codling moths in the orchard in early autumn. Investigation revealed that a railway refrigerator car on a siding adjacent to the farm contained several empty cocoons, leaving no doubt as to the source of the infestation."

Meanwhile, shoppers have become less tolerant of blemished fruit, which was accepted as a matter of course in Fessenden's day. For commercial orchardists, the answer to the pest barrage and to mounting pressures for inexpensive, perfect fruit in abundance came in the form of pesticides, especially during and after World War II. By 1950, Ontario peaches were given seven spray treatments a year, including three of DDT. The goal was to create what Harvey Quamme of Summerland calls "a biological desert." One by one, these substances were shown to be harmful to the trees' surroundings, to wildlife and to people. The biological desert became a little too much of a reality for comfort. Quamme adds that these pesticides "created a lot of problems. What is done now is to monitor the predator and prey numbers."

What Quamme is describing is Integrated Pest Management (IPM), which has been developed in government research centres since the 1940s. IPM is not the same as organic growing. IPM growers use chemical sprays but in far smaller quantities than conventional orchardists do. Because pest populations are monitored, spraying is done only if and when it is needed. By 1971, 90 percent of Nova Scotia growers had switched to IPM methods and so applied just one or two insecticides a year. Preliminary results in Minnesota have shown that IPM trees sprayed 25 to 50 percent less than non-IPM trees yielded the same harvests.

The adoption of IPM methods in commercial orchards is good news for everyone, but the system as a whole is not particularly well adapted to the home fruit garden, as it requires close monitoring of insect populations and climatic conditions and the use of expensive insect pheromones and traps, some of which can be obtained only by professional orchardists. It also compromises benign methods with chemical sprays. Fortunately, home orchardists have some advantages. They are generally more tolerant of imperfections on the fruits of their own labours. Also, a garden with just a tree or two is less likely to have problems than an orchard of hundreds of trees. Most important, the intimacy that is at the heart of successful organic growing is easier with only a few trees.

For beginners who do not yet have trees, the first step toward success in the organic orchard is knowledge of the climatic and garden conditions and the characteristics of different fruit species and cultivars, which

Resistance to certain diseases has been bred into some trees, which gives orchardists an edge in producing healthy fruit. Apple scab, right, is one disease that can be eradicated by choosing resistant cultivars.

are described in the following chapters.

Once you have decided upon a suitable species, look for trees bred to withstand diseases troublesome in your area. Trees labelled "resistant" should not become infected with the disease at all, while those labelled "tolerant" may become infected but will not suffer as much damage as susceptible trees. A relatively new series of apples is resistant to scab, a fungus which produces scarred, misshapen fruit and can even kill trees. There are trees resistant to various other diseases, such as bacterial spot or black knot in plums or cherries. The descriptions in the following chapters point out some of these trees with inbred self-defence. Any tree, however, must be grown well to reach its potential of health and productivity. As one fruit-tree scientist says, "The way you grow a tree has more effect on the fruit than the variety does."

Healthy trees that are hardy enough to sail through the toughest winters are best able to resist ravages of all kinds. Sufficient distance from other trees, good, well-drained soil, plenty of sun exposure and good air circulation are essentials. Follow the planting directions given in the previous chapter. Fortunately, growers in cold places have fewer pests and diseases to worry about than growers in the south. For instance, winter temperatures lower than minus 25 degrees F (-32 °C) will kill any codling moth larvae not protected by snow cover. As Bart Hall-Beyer writes from Scotstown, Quebec: "Thirty or forty below is rough on a lot of pests. We should be thankful."

Once trees are planted, the most benign method of care is cleanliness. Cleanliness includes picking up dropped or withered fruit, which may harbour pests that overwinter in the ground. This helps control apple maggot and plum curculio, for instance. Leaves, which can carry fungi and bacteria, should also be raked away from under the tree. Research at the University of New Hampshire demonstrated that burning or removing fallen apple leaves can significantly lower the number of apple scab spores that survive till spring. Remove damaged parts of the tree too, and keep it properly pruned so that it will receive the greatest sun and air exposure and the top will stay within easy reach for inspecting, spraying and picking. Make cuts cleanly, leaving the circle of fleshy growth at the base of the branch to promote healing, as described on pages 18 and 19. Disinfect pruning shears between cuts by dipping them into a solution of one part household laundry bleach to nine parts water. Weeds between trees will help provide a healthy habitat for beneficial pests, but a clear circle about two feet in diameter under each tree will facilitate cleanup and help prevent rodent damage. Many pests invade the orchard from wild trees, so you may consider it worthwhile to cut down seedling apples or chokecherries near the garden.

Pest Control

It is easy to rationalize that home pesticide use is too insignificant to make a difference in the overall picture of devastation described, for instance, by Rachel Carson in *Silent Spring*. But in 1983, for example, U.S. households purchased more than 121 million pounds of pesticides, most of which were not even used but ended up polluting water systems and garbage dumps. The majority of these substances were applied in cities, where they are especially dangerous simply because of the great concentration of people.

Home gardeners do make a substantial difference in the chemical pollution of the continent. This does not mean that all sprays used on fruit trees are harmful. Even the organic gardener uses an assortment of sprays.

Benign neglect: Beyond plant choice and cleanliness, the easiest pest-control practice in the home garden is to do nothing. It is not always the most effective practice, of course, but in trees left to their own devices, a population of native pest predators, called beneficials, develops. One of the best ways to protect the natural population of beneficial insects is to avoid using pesticides, most of which kill prey and predator alike. Research has shown that in a neglected apple orchard, almost three-quarters of codling moth larvae were attacked by native parasites. Wayne Still says he learned some of his techniques from observing abandoned Okanagan orchards, where the trees nevertheless produced good fruit. These orchards had developed a host-predator insect balance that provided an acceptable level of pest control. Amalia Pucat of Agriculture Canada says, "Perhaps the biggest single factor in keeping plant-eating insects from overwhelming the world is that they themselves are eaten by other insects."

The larvae of tiny Trichogramma wasps, for instance, parasitize the larvae of various pests, some of which harm tree fruits. The wasps feed on small-flowered plants such as members of the family Umbelliferae, so planting dill or Queen Anne's lace near fruit trees will help provide a suitable habitat. In studies in Ontario, about five times as many codling moth larvae and four times as many tent caterpillar eggs were parasitized in orchards that had a rich undergrowth of flowering plants. Additional common insect predators are dragonflies, lacewings, ground beetles,

Cleanliness is important in the maintenance of healthy trees. Keep a circle under the tree clear of deep-rooted weeds to reduce disease outbreaks and the competition for soil nutrients and water.

ladybugs and flower or syrphid flies.

The importation of beneficial insects into the home orchard is not recommended. Ladybugs, which eat aphids and scale, are sold by some garden suppliers. A natural population of ladybugs will develop if there is a sufficient supply of prey, but there is no guarantee that imported insects will stay where you release them. In scientifically monitored situations, however, the introduction of natural predators has met with some notable successes, such as the importation into British Columbia of a moth that consumes woolly aphid, a pest of certain apple rootstocks. The woolly aphid is now rare in that province.

Some species of birds eat a great many insects and larvae and can be attracted to the orchard with birdhouses and feeders. English sparrows consume an average of 15 larvae per flight. At the turn of the century, downy woodpeckers and nuthatches were considered reliable predators of codling moth larvae in New England. Poultry are excellent foragers under fruit trees. In Wayne Still's orchard, a small flock of elderly hens ("I'm a vegetarian") scratches busily under the trees, looking for worms, caterpillars and insects. Pigs and chickens will eat fallen, infested fruit. A 19th-century expert recommends that to control plum curculio, "let pigs and poultry pick up all the wormy fruit that falls."

Benign neglect has its advantages, but the home fruit grower who does nothing at all will likely have pest and disease problems. Something should be done about them only when the natural situation can be improved upon. What that "something" may be can vary. The following pest-control practices are listed in decreasing order of their suitability for the environmentally friendly home orchard.

Mechanical methods: Simply shaking the tree vigorously can significantly lower populations of pests such as plum curculio, which habitually falls when alarmed. The plum curculio (pronounced "kurkoolio") is sometimes considered the toughest pest to beat organically. The adult is a long-snouted, quarter-inch-long weevil that, by laying its eggs inside the small, immature fruit—especially the genus *Prunus*—produces a characteristic half-disc-shaped scab on the surface. About a week later, the legless, quarter-inch-long larvae hatch and tunnel into the core to feed on the seeds. The larvae, which are white with a brown head, are seldom seen except in early windfalls; infected fruit usually drops. Then the larvae leave the fruit and burrow into the ground to overwinter as pupae. Fruit that drops early should be gathered every few days and disposed of away from the garden or fed to livestock.

To combat these beetles, spread a tarp under the tree just after blossom drop. One 19th-century author wrote, "Shaking the tree will not do. It must be jarred sharply, and not a day must be omitted." Another wrote, "We chose the cool of the morning for this purpose, when [the curculios] were slightly benumbed, and persevered till we had destroyed nearly 1,700." He added that because the adult curculio does not lay its eggs where the offspring may fall into water or on pavement, trees planted in such situations will be much less infested. He described a nectarine that had been planted so that it overshadowed a fishpond, "and not a curculio disturbed it."

Human beings can be natural predators of pests in other ways. Sereno Edwards Todd wrote in *The Apple Culturist* of 1871, "Entomologists may pen interesting paragraphs about the origin, hibernation, metamorphosis and habits of noxious insects and worms and suggest nostrums to repel them and check their ravages, but after all that may be said or written, if we would save our trees and fruit, in most instances, we must catch 'em and kill 'em." Hand-picking of egg masses, for instance, is quite feasible if you have only one or two trees. Tent caterpillar nests can be sprayed

with *Bacillus thuringiensis*, described on page 35, or can be burned with a torch made of newspaper. Still's practice of picking coddlers throughout the season does the double duty of accomplishing necessary thinning while sparing only the best fruit for the harvest.

Some pests are attracted to traps that, to them, resemble part of the tree. Red balls about three inches across mimic apples or cherries, attracting apple and cherry maggot flies, which are then held fast in a coating of about half an ounce of a sticky substance such as Tanglefoot or STP oil treatment. Around mid-June, hang the balls at about eye height, near the outside edge of the tree on the south side. In each tree, hang one to six traps—the greatest number for a mature standard tree—and remove twigs, fruit and foliage for about two feet around them. Clean and recoat the traps every couple of weeks, or as needed. These traps can be used for years, and their usefulness can be enhanced with scents that mimic natural plant fragrances.

Yellow panels are perceived by insects as large leaves, while white, sticky panels hung before flowering time are seen as large blossoms by pests such as tarnished plant bugs and

Some of the most destructive pests of fruit trees are moth and butterfly larvae such as tent caterpillars, which can defoliate entire branches. While hand-picking or traps are the safest way to get rid of them, there are also a number of relatively mild pesticides.

European sawflies. Hang one to six traps per tree in spring before the green leaf buds open. Clean traps and coat them afresh about every two weeks.

A sugary trap will attract fruit moths such as codling moth and Oriental fruit moth. Dissolve three tablespoons of honey, three tablespoons of molasses and a pinch of yeast in a cup of water, pour the mixture into a large can, and hang it in an apple or a peach tree.

Pests that migrate up and down tree trunks, such as the larvae of gypsy moths and codling moths, may be trapped or stopped by various barriers. One trap consists of plastic wrap coated with a sticky substance; another is a band of burlap coated with petroleum jelly. Either type of band must fit tightly around the trunk and must be replaced and renewed frequently. In studies in Pennsylvania, the barriers were most successful about three feet above the ground.

Horticultural oil: Various oils, both mineral and vegetable, have been used for at least a century to smother various pests, eggs and pupae. Oils are attractive to organic growers because their toxicity level for mammals is very low. Oil will not corrode spray equip-

ment, nor does it have a limited shelf life. Special petroleum-based oils are available in garden stores, although in some experiments, vegetable oils have proved just as effective, especially if mixed with a little dishwashing detergent or insecticidal soap.

The true dormant sprays, labelled as such in garden-supply stores, are relatively dense solutions meant to be applied before the buds open. Many researchers now recommend two oil sprays: one when trees are fully dormant in late winter and another just before the leaf buds open in spring. Summer spraying of lighter oil solutions, too, can be beneficial. Although leaf burning can occur when these sprays are used in conditions of high heat and humidity, research at the University of Maryland has shown that apples, pears and cherries sprayed four times between May and August were undamaged by the oils, provided the trees were not stressed by drought. The scientists used a 2 percent oil solution, which was very effective against aphids, scale, spider mites, leaf rollers and whiteflies. They nevertheless recommend that spraying not be done when the temperature rises above 90 degrees F (32 °C).

Tent caterpillars are sprayed by the author, right, with a solution of *Bacillus thuringiensis* in a simple hand pump. Their nests can also be physically removed from the tree or carefully burned.

An old farm pamphlet gives the following recipe for a homemade horticultural oil solution: Boil one ounce of soap in a pint of rainwater until dissolved. While still boiling hot, pour the solution into one quart of kerosene, and churn the mixture constantly until it is smooth and creamy. This stock emulsion must be mixed with nine times its volume of warm water before it is used for dormant applications.

Potash: Potash is another venerable treatment. A pound of potash dissolved in two gallons of water was recommended by D.W. Beadle in the 1870 book *The Canadian Fruit, Flower and Kitchen Gardener*: "If this be applied with a brush or swab to the bark of the trunk and larger branches before the buds burst in spring, it will make it smooth and glossy and is sure death to the bark-louse and all insects and their eggs which harbour in the crevices and under the scales of the bark." Potash should not be used, however, where soils are alkaline, such as on the prairies.

Diseases: Among the newer additions to the organic orchardist's arsenal are diseases that infect pests alone. The best known is a bacterial disease, *Bacillus thuringiensis* (Bt), sold under various brand names in garden-supply stores. One strain infects only the lepidopterous larvae—that is, the caterpillars of moths and butterflies—with which it comes in contact. Once touched by the spray, the larvae stop feeding and begin to die. Bt is not harmful to people, birds, frogs, fish or insects other than Lepidoptera and is thus an important tool for organic control. It is very effective against tent caterpillars, codling moth larvae, gypsy moths, winter moths and leaf rollers. Wayne Still considers Bt an essential part of his annual pesticide program when applied "around blossom time. That will control spanworm, fruit worms, leaf rollers and that kind of thing." Many new strains of Bt continue to be discovered and registered. Bt has a limited shelf life, as it is a live culture. Store it in the refrigerator, where it should keep for about three years if you occasionally top up the bottle with milk.

Codling moth granulosis virus (CMGV), another insect disease, has been registered in the United States for control of the worst pest of apples. It is not registered in Canada at the time of writing, but like any pesticide, small amounts (500 g or 500 mL) can be imported for personal use.

Insecticidal soap: Special insecticidal soaps or pure soaps such as Ivory dish detergent, a teaspoon to a pint of water, will kill various pests such as aphids, pear psylla, red mites, earwigs and scale. Again, the pest must come in direct contact with the soap. Insecticidal soaps can cause yellowing and dropping of leaves, as well as ringing and russetting of fruits—cosmetic damage only—but both side effects can be reduced if the tree is thoroughly rinsed by rain or a sprinkler a few minutes after spraying. As insecticidal soaps are effective only when wet, they are best sprayed during humid weather when the air is still. For small plants such as indoor citrus, dip an old toothbrush in a soapy solution and scrub off scale. Then rinse the tree with a lukewarm water spray.

Botanical insecticides: From around the world comes an assortment of compounds used by plants to protect themselves. Many of these botanical substances are just as toxic to humans as synthetic pesticides are, but they have the environmental advantage of breaking down quickly into benign by-products. One highly toxic substance, nicotine, has been used to protect plants for centuries. More readily available today in spray or powder

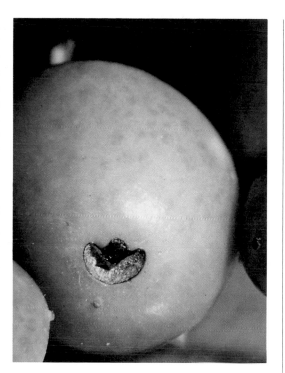

The environmentally friendly fruit garden

Distinctive evidence of the plum curculio, the worst pest of cherries, plums, peaches and other members of the genus *Prunus*, is a half-disc-shaped scab. A measure of control is gained by shaking the tree daily after blossom drop and by disposing of all fallen fruit.

form are rotenone and pyrethrum.

The first, made from the roots of certain tropical plants, is dangerous to mammals, fatal to fish and amphibians and must be applied with the same caution you would use with a synthetic pesticide. Rotenone kills a wide range of pests, such as apple maggot, codling moth, tarnished plant bug, pear psylla and European apple sawfly, as well as many beneficial insects. It can be sprayed on the tree just after petal fall to reduce plum curculio damage and will reduce apple maggot damage if sprayed on trees as soon as the red sticky traps, described on page 32, begin to attract the insects. Rotenone is said to last only a year in storage, but I have found it effective more than a year after purchase if stored in a cool, dark place.

Pyrethrum, whose active ingredients are called pyrethrins, comes from the dried flowers of certain daisies such as *Chrysanthemum coccineum*, the scarlet, or pyrethrum, daisy. It is less toxic to mammals than rotenone but nevertheless must be applied with care and can cause contact dermatitis and other allergic responses. Pyrethrum kills a wide range of pests, such as tarnished plant bugs and stinkbugs, as well as many beneficial insects. It is extremely toxic to fish and other cold-blooded organisms. Very sensitive to light, heat and moisture, this pesticide breaks down into harmless substances within hours of application but will remain active for about

10 years if properly stored in a tightly closed container in a cool, dark place. The synthetic versions, pyrethroids, which are used in many common pesticides such as Raid, do not break down as quickly after application. A mixture of rotenone, pyrethrum and ryania (a moderately toxic pesticide from a South African shrub), effective against codling moth and Oriental fruit moth and sold under the brand name Triple Plus, is recommended for use against a range of fruit-tree pests.

When applying these botanicals, wear long sleeves and long pants, rubber gloves and a mask, and make sure that any breeze is at your back. Wash your clothes after spraying.

New botanicals are constantly being discovered and tried. Neem, mint, goldenrod, pawpaw bark, garlic, petunias and citrus oil have all been found effective against certain pests, but most are not commercially available because the registration process for pesticides is long, complicated and expensive. Home gardeners have often been successful with homemade concoctions including garlic, chili pepper and the like.

Pheromones: Pheromone traps rely on synthetic insect hormones to regulate growth or to attract or confuse males of species such as the Oriental fruit moth so that they will be less likely to mate. Timing is critical with such procedures, and components are expensive and seldom easily available to home gardeners. If not used properly, the pheromone can

actually increase problems by attracting pests from surrounding areas. These are not generally recommended for home fruit growers, but if you want to try them, check in garden stores and catalogues that specialize in ecological pest control, as new devices become available every year.

ANIMALS AND BIRDS

Since people began to cultivate fruit trees, they have devised a number of means, some practical, some fanciful, for keeping four- and two-legged pests away. In *The Expert Gardener* of 1640, "sundry Dutch and French authors" recommended that to keep deer away, "Take the pisse of a Deere and anoint the Tree therewith," and against rabbits, "Spit in thy hand, and anoint the sprouts therewith, and no Hare will hurt them."

Such fantasies aside, rodents, including mice, rats and rabbits, are among the most destructive pests of fruit trees, whose bark they find irresistible winter food. Rodents can girdle and kill an entire orchard before spring. Physical barriers are the first line of defence: tree guards, foil or quarter-inch wire screening set in place before the ground freezes in fall, as described in the previous chapter. Deer, goats and cattle can cause even more damage. Deer and goats will browse on the tender branches, while cattle will rub against the trunks, destroying the bark.

High or electric fences should be used to keep large herbivores away from fruit trees. Small bars of perfumed soap hung in trees as soon as they are planted will help discourage deer; hanging the bars after the deer have had a taste, however, may have no effect. Deer are also repelled by a monthly winter spray of two raw eggs blended in a cup of water, then diluted in two gallons of water. Cats can also be very destructive if they habitually sharpen their claws on the trunks. Trees close to the house often become scratching posts. Keep young trees surrounded by guards until the bark is thick enough to resist claw damage. Watch, too, for dogs that include your fruit trees on their habitual urination paths. Trees at building corners and gateways are especially vulnerable to slow death by the excessive nitrogen content of urine. Against fruit-stealing birds, the most effective barrier is netting, but individual, almost ripe peaches or clusters of cherries can be protected by paper bags secured around the branch with a twist tie.

Birds are among the most welcome visitors to fruit trees until the fruit is almost ripe, when netting of trees, hanging of scare devices or bagging of cherry clusters may become necessary.

Aphids are soft-bodied, sap-sucking insects whose production of honeydew encourages fungal diseases and discolours fruit. They can be washed off with a hard spray of water or killed with a solution of insecticidal soap.

DISEASE CONTROL

Diseases are often more devastating than pests, because many attack the tree from within and may prove fatal within a few years. They are especially common when summer humidity is high, when trees grow in wet ground or shade or when they have been weakened by harsh winters. But sometimes, disease strikes even under optimal growing conditions. Diseases may be difficult to diagnose, as some display symptoms that mimic those of nutrient disorders or pest damage, especially to the untrained eye. If you need advice about identification, ask a nearby commercial grower or a government specialist. Also, there are government pamphlets available that include photographs and descriptions of various disorders.

Diseases are of four main types: viral, mycoplasmic, bacterial and fungal.

Viral: Viral diseases are incurable but not unavoidable. One way to make sure viruses do not attack, at least at the outset, is to buy plants and rootstocks that are certified virus-free or come from a disease-free nursery, because infection can easily occur during the propagation process. Virus-free stock is particularly important with plums, cherries and their relatives (*Prunus* spp) in the eastern part of the continent. It is also important with clonal rootstocks—the type propagated vege-

tatively. Rootstocks propagated from seed do not carry viruses. Because of virus problems with the Merton-Malling (M or MM) series of apple rootstocks, the EM (East Malling) and EMLA (East Malling Long Ashton) virus-free stocks were developed. In the garden, even virus-free plants can eventually be infected by carriers such as aphids or pollen, but the disease will take a while to cause harm. Viruses produce a variety of symptoms and will eventually affect yields and lead to gradual or quick decline of the trees. The only way to cure viral problems is to cut down the trees and remove or burn them. Do not replant the same species in that spot.

Mycoplasmic: Mycoplasmic diseases, similar in cause and effect to viral ones, have only recently been defined. The ailment known as X-disease (because its cause was unknown for some time) affects stone fruits such as peaches and cherries. Trees gradually weaken, becoming susceptible to winterkill. The diseases may be spread by leafhoppers from wild chokecherries to cultivated trees, so one of the best control measures is the eradication of nearby chokecherries. Trees infected with mycoplasmic diseases must be cut down.

Bacterial: Like people, trees can be attacked by bacteria, and like people, trees may respond to injections of antibiotics; but this sort of drastic resort is feasible only for commercial growers. For the rest of us, bacterial diseases are best avoided by keeping trees healthy and

37

The gypsy moth larva is one of several defoliating caterpillars that migrate up and down tree trunks. Their population can be lowered with sticky material painted on the trunk or bands of coated fabric tied tightly around the trunk about three feet above the ground.

vigorous and by pruning carefully, sterilizing equipment between cuts.

Fire blight, which is such a common and deadly disease of pears that it eradicated the northeastern pear industry earlier in this century, is probably the best-known bacterial disease. Apples, crab apples and many ornamentals such as mountain ash are also vulnerable to it. Fire blight's characteristic symptom, which gives the disease its name, is a blackening of twigs that spreads gradually to larger branches. As soon as an infected area is spotted, prune off the blighted wood at least six inches below the infection, preferably at the branch base. Burn diseased wood and foliage as soon as possible, and sterilize pruning equipment. Some cultivars are more resistant to fire blight than others, so read catalogue descriptions before buying. Bacterial diseases can sometimes be treated or prevented with the substances described below for fungal diseases.

Fungal: Fungal diseases are rampant among fruit trees. They include various leaf spots, rusts, cankers and mildews, as well as the common scab of apples and their relatives and the black knot of plums and cherries. As with bacterial diseases, infected portions of the

tree may have to be removed down to healthy tissue. Brown rot in cherries can be countered by removing all mummified fruit and cankered twigs from the previous year before bud break. Clean pruning shears in disinfectant after each cut. Fortunately, the greatest progress in breeding for disease resistance involves fungal ailments. Seek out cultivars resistant to such diseases as scab, cedar-apple rust, powdery mildew and leaf spot.

Most ecologically acceptable fungicides and bactericides contain sulphur and/or copper as active ingredients. Sulphur has been used to protect plants for centuries. In 1982, almost 60 million pounds of sulphur and copper-sulphate fungicides were used in the United States. Effective against fungal diseases such as powdery mildew and rust and against some insects and mites, sulphur compounds can also harm beneficial insects and may cause plant injury if applied when the humidity is high or when temperatures are over 82 degrees F (28°C). Overapplication can lead to soil acidification, and sulphur may increase russetting on some fruits. An Arkansas grower recommends that sulphur be applied to the leaves in fall just before they drop. At that

stand overnight to dissolve. The next day, stir four ounces of washing soda into a gallon of cold water, pour this mixture into the copper-sulphate solution, and spray to help prevent scab on apples and pears. Copper, like sulphur, can cause damage and should be sprayed once only before leaves grow.

A solution of one teaspoon household baking soda (sodium bicarbonate) to a quart of water, with the addition of a small amount of insecticidal soap, has been found effective against the fungal diseases black spot and powdery mildew on roses. This solution might be tried on fruit trees to guard against mildew and other fungi.

Bacteria and fungi are most active just before or during bloom. Their spread is aided by rain, so try to spray just prior to or within 12 hours of the beginning of a period of rain. If the rain lasts more than 12 hours, spray again directly afterward. Surgery is, unfortunately, the means the grower may need to adopt if an infection has taken hold.

Sprays

Many substances are applied as sprays. If you are dealing with only one or two trees, it is most practical to use a hand pump sprayer, the thumb-operated type shown on page 34. This is tiring work that will produce hefty hand muscles, but you will not have to do it often. Where there are more trees or if the trees are too tall to reach easily with a hand sprayer, the backyard orchardist may want to invest in a sprayer operated by a small electric or gasoline motor. Power sprayers with a capacity of 10 to 30 gallons can be used in larger orchards. Some seed companies and farm-supply stores sell them. Never use a sprayer that has been used previously for herbicides.

Use rainwater or distilled water, if possible, when formulating sprays, as hard water can lessen the effectiveness of the other ingredients. Concentrate on spraying the upper half of the tree, and the lower half will receive the drift. Most important, apply when there is little or no wind, and be sure that any breeze is at your back.

Most essential in the control of both diseases and pests is vigilance. Watch for changes in the trees and their habitat. Problems spotted quickly can often be remedied before they become serious. In the organic orchard, the familiar phrase needs reworking: the best offence is a good defence.

time, there is no need to worry about leaf or fruit damage.

Bordeaux mixture, which has two active ingredients, lime and copper sulphate, was formulated in France more than a century ago for the protection of grapevines. It is now considered useful against both bacterial and fungal diseases and in preventing egg laying by apple maggots. To make it, add six tablespoons of spray lime and two tablespoons of copper sulphate to a gallon of water for a weak mixture, eight tablespoons of both for a strong mixture. Dissolve the copper sulphate completely in a cup of water, then slowly add the lime, continuously shaking, and shake the mixture while spraying. On apples and pears, apply the strong mixture, combined with dormant oil, when the green tips of the leaf buds appear, and spray the weak mixture during bloom. Spray the weak mixture on dormant peaches and nectarines to help prevent leaf curl.

Burgundy mixture also has copper sulphate as the active ingredient but replaces lime with washing soda (sodium carbonate). Stir three ounces of copper sulphate into a gallon of hot water in a plastic bucket. Let the mixture

LOVELIEST OF TREES

"Loveliest of trees, the cherry now
Is hung with bloom along the bough,
And stands about the woodland ride
Wearing white for Eastertide."

– A.E. HOUSMAN, *Loveliest of Trees, The Cherry Now,* 1896

Magnificent in bloom, cherries also provide beautiful wood and very variable fruit, from the tiny berries of some shrubby species hardy on the northern prairies to the large, delectable sweet cherries, which thrive in only the warmest corners of Canada and the northern United States.

Loveliest and largest of fruit trees, producing the first tree fruit of the season in July, the sweet cherry is beloved not only of poets but also of birds, a matter of some consternation to ecologically aware growers who love birds and cherries alike. Even the species name of the sweet cherry, *Prunus avium*, means "for the birds," a name which detracts not at all, of course, from the beauty and grandeur of a tree that may grow more than 100 feet tall in European woodlands, draped in white blossoms in spring and in hundreds of pounds of delicious fruit and fat robins in summer. The name simply reminds the home orchardist of one of this species' two great weaknesses. The other is tenderness. Sweet cherries can be damaged by winter temperatures below minus 10 degrees F (-23°C), so they thrive only in the parts of North America most like Housman's England. Sweet cherries are slightly hardier than peaches but less hardy than apples.

Small comfort, perhaps, for gardeners in cooler places is that they can grow pie, or sour, cherries (*Prunus cerasus*), which are too tart for most people to enjoy fresh off the tree—even the birds like them less—but make the best pies and preserves. Pie cherries will survive winter lows of at least minus 25 degrees F (-32°C). For gardeners beyond even these limits, there are North American and Siberian cherries, some of which yield fruit, smaller than a pie cherry but similar in flavour, on bushes hardy to minus 40 degrees. Compact,

productive and tough, these bushy cherries deserve to be better known and more widely grown in the north. They, too, have a faithful following of birds.

Cherries are technically known as drupes, fruits that have an outer skin, a fleshy layer and, in the centre, a hard stone protecting the true seed inside. In legend, the stone within the cherry, like the thorn on its cousin the rose, has been portrayed as a blot on botanical perfection, a symbol of the balance of good and evil. "I gave my love a cherry that had no stone," goes a folk song that promises pure affection. The cherry's Achilles' heel, its attractiveness to birds, can be seen in somewhat the same fashion as the stone within the flesh. The flesh itself, varying from white to red to black, from sweet to sour, is always appealing, even when it is best suited to wines and jellies, as is the lip-puckering fruit of the chokecherry.

There are cherries native to almost all areas of the temperate northern hemisphere. Sweet and pie cherries were raised to their current state of perfection in the area around the Caspian and Black seas and so require warm summers, relatively mild winters and well-drained soils similar to those of the Caspian shores. They will suffer winter damage, disease and death if forced to endure the indignity of wet feet. When these trees stop bearing, they yield some of the most valuable timber in the orchard.

All cherries, like the other common northern tree fruits, are members of the rose family, Rosaceae, and so have lovely five-petalled blossoms. There are many ornamental types, beloved signs of spring in Japan.

Sweet Cherries

An enormous 'Bing' in the backyard of the Vancouver house where I spent my childhood had a certain matronly beauty, although almost all of its fruit was beyond reach, even from the house roof, and was harvested by an assortment of birds. Still, there was so much fruit that plenty was left for us. For gardeners who can grow these trees—climatic zone 6 or warmer—sweet cherries are long-lived, prolific trees that begin to produce fruit four or five years after planting and can bear about 50 pounds at 10 years of age and as much as 200 pounds at 20 years. At that rate, one does not begrudge the birds their share.

There are two types of sweet cherries. The first type, by far the most common in home

Cherries are among the first tree fruits to harvest. The sweet types, right, come to market in early July, the shrub and pie types following shortly after.

Some species such as
Japanese cherries are
beloved signs of spring and
beautiful shade trees in
summer, but their fruit is
better appreciated by birds
than by people.

gardens, is the dark, or black, sweet cherry typified by such names as 'Bing,' 'Hedelfingen' and 'Stella.' These cherries are the best type for fresh eating, the kind that appear in farmers' markets and in supermarkets in early summer. They are also delicious canned; the best canning types produce purple juice. The second type of sweet cherries, which includes such cultivars as 'Emperor Francis,' 'Vega,' 'Rainier' and the centuries-old 'Napoleon,' or 'Royal Ann,' has white or yellow flesh. They are grown mostly for processing, especially for the production of maraschino cherries, a name that comes from a bitter cordial made from marasca cherries in Italy centuries ago. Now, maraschino cherries are made by bleaching and pitting cherries before soaking them in a syrupy solution of colouring, flavouring and sugar.

The blossoms of sweet cherries have, until recently, required cross-pollination in order to set fruit, a situation complicated by the fact that cherries are choosy: there are several closely related groups whose members cannot be counted upon to pollinate one another. For instance, 'Bing,' 'Napoleon,' 'Lambert' and 'Vernon' belong to one group; 'Van,' 'Sodus,' 'Windsor' and 'Venus' belong to another; and 'Black Tartarian' and 'Early Rivers' belong to yet another. Even if the correct match is made, pollination will occur only when conditions are optimal: warm, fairly dry weather without strong winds that would hamper bee flights. In much of the north, this type of weather in early spring is discouragingly rare. Normally, only a few of the blossoms will set fruit, and the remaining unfertilized fruit will fall, in a phenomenon known as June-drop. Although this seeming loss of most of the crop causes consternation in many a beginning orchardist, the result is bigger, better fruit and sufficient energy to develop next year's supply of blossoms. Cherry fruit buds begin to develop around late June of the year before they bloom. The fruit buds develop on the bases of year-old shoots and from spurs on the sides of two- and three-year-old branches, producing a whorl of buds that open into one to three flowers apiece.

The sweet-cherry pollination scene has recently been revolutionized by the development of self-pollinating, or self-compatible, cultivars that will gradually change the old rule ("Plant two if you want fruit") into a histor-

Certain cultivars of sweet cherry are resistant to cracking, which can occur after the onset of heavy rains when fruit is almost ripe. Perfect fruit indicates not only a suitable cultivar choice and just the right amount of rain but also a mild winter and no frost after late April.

ical footnote. The first of the self-fertile sweet cherries, 'Stella,' came from the work of K.O. Lapins at the Agriculture Canada Research Station in Summerland, British Columbia. Many new types are now being tested at Summerland as well as at Vineland, Ontario, and Cornell, New York. All Vineland cultivars, incidentally, have names that begin with the letter V. Not only do the new self-pollinating cherries need no partner in order to produce fruit, but they can fertilize all other varieties. These trees, such as 'Stella,' 'Lapins,' 'Sunburst' and 'Starkrimson,' should be the first choice of the backyard orchardists who can grow sweet cherries.

For planting and pruning directions, see pages 15 to 20. Sweet cherries tend to grow tall and upright, like woodland trees, so the tops should be pruned back every spring. Do this only after severe winter weather has passed; the best time is in April or early May.

Sweet-cherry roots are more tender than the trunks, so they must be mulched with snow, straw or leaves to overwinter in marginal areas. In such places, the trees are prone to winter damage followed by bacterial canker. Bark splitting and other trunk injuries are common in trees with a southwestern exposure. Paint the trees as directed on page 22. The flower buds are somewhat more frost-sensitive than those of other stone fruits just before and while opening. The trees usually bloom around late April, and if frost occurs then or thereafter, the subsequent crop will be harmed and perhaps lost entirely. A frost of only a couple of degrees can cause considerable injury.

Other than frost damage, the most common physiological problem of sweet cherries is fruit cracking, which occurs when it rains; water is absorbed through the skin, causing the flesh to swell and, eventually, split the skin. Split cherries must be harvested quickly, before they rot. Cultivars vary in their resistance to cracking.

One of the most troublesome diseases is leaf spot, a fungal disease that produces small reddish purple spots on the leaves and may lead to defoliation and weakening of the tree. Brown rot is caused by a fungus that makes small, circular brown spots which spread rapidly on the fruit. Black knot is described on page 77. Bacterial canker attacks most parts of sweet-cherry trees. Gum oozes from

the dark, sunken cankers that appear on twigs and limbs. The disease appears on foliage as dark purple spots surrounded by a ring of light green.

The worst problem is birds, although the plum curculio, a beetle pest of all stone fruits (described on page 32), can also destroy the crop. Black-cherry aphids, which may appear as soon as the buds swell, are best combated with sprays of insecticidal soap. John Josselyn, author of a 17th-century journal, had a more imaginative approach when he wrote of cherry trees: "The best way to cure them when they are lowsie is to bore a hole in the main root with an auger, and pour in a quantity of Brandie or Rhum and then stop it up with a pin made of the same tree."

SOUR CHERRIES

The sour, or pie, cherry (*Prunus cerasus*) is as close as most northern orchardists can get to sweet cherries, in terms of fruit and tree size, although the tree is only about half as big—around 15 feet—and the fruit distinctly less sweet. The smaller tree size is better for most home-garden situations, however, as is the fact that all pie cherries are self-fertile; you need plant only one. Sour cherries start to bear three to five years after planting and are long-lived. A 10-year-old tree should bear 50 to 100 pounds of fruit.

Most important for northerners, the pie cherry blooms about a week later than the sweet cherry and is hardier all around, although still not as tough as most apples. In midwinter, when the buds are fully dormant, sour cherries have survived temperatures below minus 25 degrees F (-32 °C), but in spring, a couple of degrees of frost can damage them. 'Meteor,' 'Northstar' and 'Morellenfeuer' are more cold-resistant when flowering than are 'Montmorency' and 'Stockton Morello.'

There are two types of sour cherries, amarelle and morello. The amarelle varieties, which produce clear juice, are the best known. Grandmother of the sour cherries is the amarelle 'Montmorency,' a French cultivar some four centuries old and still the most important processing cherry in North America. The morello types, such as the excellent home-garden cultivar 'Northstar,' produce dark red juice.

The first year after planting, prune sour cherries in the modified central leader system described on pages 17 to 19. Because the branches tend to grow upright, train them into a more horizontal position with clothes pins or round wooden toothpicks wedged into branch crotches. Sour cherries are vulnerable to the same pests and diseases as are sweet cherries, but they are less prone to splitting.

Midway in quality between the diploid sweet cherries and triploid sour cherries are hybrids of the two species, the tetraploid Duke cherries (*Prunus gonduini*), whose fruit varies from sweet to somewhat sour. The trees are smaller than sweet-cherry trees.

ROOTSTOCKS

Most sour and sweet cherries are propagated on the roots of a *Prunus mahaleb* or *P. avium* (mazzard cherry) seedling, both of which produce large trees. Mahaleb rootstocks give trees a vertical orientation. These trees fare best in sandy soils; if the soil is heavy, their susceptibility to soilborne diseases often kills them. Mazzard trees are more spreading and better suited to clay but still require well-drained soil. To find out whether you have mahaleb or mazzard, cut a few small pieces of slender root when you are planting the tree. Scrape off the bark, and leave the pieces of root in a little

All cherries are likely to be harvested by the birds just as they approach perfection. The surest defence is netting, but it is most practical on a small tree or a shrub.

clean water for about half an hour. If the water remains clear, the root is malaheb; if it turns pink or orange, it is mazzard.

BUSH CHERRIES

The remarkable toughness of the bush cherries is attributable to their origins. Some are native to North America, while the best, in terms of fruit quality, come from Manchuria or Siberia. When possible, look for named selections rather than the unimproved species, which are quite variable. Many of the cultivars are carried by northern nurseries.

One of the best of the bush cherries, hardy to about minus 40 degrees, is the Manchu, Nanking or Hansen's bush cherry (*Prunus tomentosa*), a native of central and western Asia whose cultivation is widespread in China, Korea and Manchuria. It was introduced to North America and popularized by Neils Hansen of the South Dakota Agricultural Experiment Station, in Brookings. Hansen was responsible for introducing several other cold-hardy fruits, such as sand cherry-plum hybrids, the ornamental purple-leaf plum (*P. cistena*) and the rosybloom crab. In late July or mid-August, *P. tomentosa* ripens its half-inch fruit, which has white to bright red skin and creamy to pink flesh. The fruit has a pleasant acid flavour and is rated fair for jelly, juice, jam and pies. The bush, which is resistant to black knot, usually grows about six feet

high but may form a small tree as tall as nine feet. It is used as a windbreak and hedge on the prairies. Some of the plants are self-fertile, but most fruit dependably only if at least two plants are grown. Expect 10 to 20 pounds of fruit per plant, although the occasional star has yielded more than twice as much. Campbell Davidson of Morden, Manitoba, Bob Osborne of Petitcodiac, New Brunswick, and Irene Wallace of Beaverlodge, Alberta, include *P. tomentosa* on their lists of suggested fruit for northerners, and Paul Olsen of Thunder Bay, Ontario, reports, "Fruit is sweeter than *P. fruticosa* or *P. japonica*."

Also recommended by Davidson, Olsen and Wallace is *Prunus fruticosa*, the Mongolian cherry, or European dwarf cherry, which is so hardy that it can survive in the most northerly limits of outdoor gardening in zone 2. The three-to-five-foot bush produces many suckers and an abundant crop of quarter-to-half-inch dark red berries in mid- to late July. John Davidson of the Agriculture Canada station in Beaverlodge, Alberta, says that the fruit is "too sour to eat fresh, although one or two selections come close for people who really like tart things. Cooked, they have exactly the same texture as a sweet cherry but with a distinctive tang that survives cooking. They make a lovely dessert wine." Like *P. tomentosa*, this is a useful shrub for northern hedges. Set plants four to six feet apart. The Mongolian cherry requires cross-pollination, but since plants are genetically variable, any two plants will suffice.

Several additional edible species are available from some northern nurseries. These include the pin cherry (*Prunus pennsylvanica*), an ornamental North American tree or tall shrub whose tiny fruit, which ripens in late summer, makes an excellent jelly. Campbell Davidson includes this species on his recommendation list.

Davidson also suggests that northerners try the chokecherry (*Prunus virginiana*), which blooms in mid-May and ripens at the end of July. In the 19th century, Canadian pioneer Catharine Parr Traill described the fresh fruit as "not unpalatable, but so very astringent that it causes a painful contraction of the throat if many berries are eaten at one time." It makes an excellent syrup, jelly or juice, however. The bush grows 8 to 10 feet tall. The closely related black cherry (*P. serotina*) bears edible but slightly bitter fruit on a tall tree.

The western sand cherry (*Prunus besseyi*), a

Although chokecherries are considered acrid when fresh, the plants are very hardy, and the tiny fruit can be sweetened to make excellent syrups, juices, jellies and wines.

five-foot shrub native to the North American plains, produces three-quarter-inch berries with dark purple skin and yellowish green flesh that make a delicious jelly. Only the selection 'Mando' is rated acceptable for fresh eating. Paul Olsen writes that the cultivars 'Fritz' and 'Hans' are "fairly sweet." Another native sand cherry is P. pumila, which comes from the shores of the Great Lakes. The pea-sized purple-black fruit was described by Traill: "In flavour, it partakes more of the nature of the damson or plum." The fruit is very variable, however, with some shrubs bearing cherries that are bitter.

Some hybridization has been done with cherry species such as Prunus besseyi and P. tomentosa. As one would expect, these hybrids exhibit characteristics of both parents. Prunus besseyi is also one of the parents of the cherry plum, described on page 76. Hybrids of the Japanese bush cherry (P. japonica) and the Himalayan cherry (P. jacquemontii) have resulted in the cultivars 'Jan' and 'Joy,' which were developed by Elwyn Meader, an outstanding New Hampshire breeder of hardy plants. These shrubs grow about four feet tall and will survive minus 30 degrees F (-35°C) yet are capable of producing fruit that is similar to the standard sour cherry.

FOR THE BIRDS

Meader developed these hybrids partly because he could not protect his large sour cherries from birds. 'Jan' and 'Joy' can be easily draped with netting, the most secure defence against avian predation. More than a century ago, Traill bemoaned the fact that the birds were so fond of the native sand cherry: "It is difficult to obtain any quantity even in its most favoured localities."

Unfortunately, this depredation affects home gardeners more than it does commercial orchardists, because fewer trees mean that more fruit, proportionately, is taken. Nearby woods increase the bird population and the disappearance of fruit, especially the dark, sweet cherries. Hanging aluminum pans and installing hawk kites, plastic owls or balloons decorated with bright target designs may help, but netting the tree and bagging clusters of almost ripe fruit are the only sure cures. Alternatively, develop a love of birds that exceeds your love of cherries.

Because there are so many cultivars, I asked a group of North American fanciers to recommend their favourite trees, ones they would choose for a small dream orchard in their own climatic area. As you read through the list, take note of the climatic zone and geographic area of the cherry's sponsor and compare it with your own, as you will likely have the greatest success with cherries that have been found superlative in your own growing conditions. Recommendations about the hardy species cherries are given on pages 46 and 47.

SWEET CHERRIES

'Bing': Although it may be phased out by new cultivars that are self-pollinating or crack-resistant, 'Bing,' a West Coast antique selected from 'Napoleon' seedlings in Oregon more than a century ago (a sister, chosen at the same time, is the still popular 'Lambert'), has long been the top choice for flavour. On the West Coast, its big, firm, dark fruit, which ripens in mid-July, is still the most common type sold fresh on the market. The tree is vigorous, upright and spreading. On the negative side, 'Bing' is one of the most cold-sensitive sweet cherries. The blossoms are often injured by cool weather in winter and spring, even on the West Coast. It is susceptible to bacterial canker, and the fruit cracks readily in rain. Layne and Quamme both recommend 'Bing' for its top-quality fruit. Pollinators include 'Van,' 'Sam' and 'Stella.'

'Compact Lambert': From Summerland in 1973 came this radiation-induced, pint-sized mutant of the classic 'Lambert.' 'Compact Lambert' is only one-fifth to one-sixth the size of a standard cherry. Also in its favour are late blossoming, an early first crop and heavy crops thereafter. The tree requires excellent soil, irrigation and the best care, or it will be stunted and the fruit small. Fruit cracking is slight. It is one of the last sweet cherries to ripen, near the end of July on the West Coast, and is recommended by Benowitz.

'Compact Stella': This half-sized, radiation-induced mutant has the same self-pollinating feature as its parent 'Stella,' the world's first commercially introduced self-fertile sweet cherry, which came out of the Summerland station in 1968. 'Compact Stella,' too, can be used to pollinate all other sweet cherries. While young, it begins to bear large crops of

Most sweet cherries are dark red, often described as black, while a few are medium red or orange. The few termed white are actually yellowish or pinkish.

'Rainier,' left, a relatively new white cultivar developed in Washington, is considered tastier than the better-known white heritage variety 'Royal Ann,' or 'Napoleon.'

black fruit whose flavour and quality are considered good to fair. It is reported susceptible to bacterial canker in the Maritimes. Benowitz, Quamme and Sherk recommend it.

'Hedelfingen': Important commercially in the east, this German heirloom is valued for early-bearing, productive trees, although they are very cold-tender. The oval fruit, which has a sweet-sour taste, is somewhat resistant to cracking. It colours before it is fully mature but is soft, so it must be picked as soon as it is ripe—a few days after 'Bing,' the last week of July around the southern Great Lakes. The tree is spreading, with slightly drooping branches. Craig and Layne both recommend it, and Lord notes, "Excellent quality," although he cautions that sweet cherries are not generally advised for New Hampshire.

'Lapins': The offspring of 'Van' and 'Stella' and released in 1984 from Summerland, 'Lapins' is another of the new self-compatible cultivars. The large, dark, firm fruit ripens late, about two days after 'Lambert,' and has excellent flavour and texture. The tree grows upright. It is one of the cherries recommended by Quamme, who writes: "It is more resistant to rain-splitting than 'Bing.' "

'Rainier': This Washington-bred 'Bing' x 'Van' seedling, introduced in 1960, is unusual in that its large fruit is of the type described as white—in reality, pale yellow with a pink blush. 'Rainier' is of better quality than the standard white cultivar, 'Royal Ann' ('Na-

poleon'), a European heritage variety with which it will cross-pollinate. Quamme recommends 'Rainier' as "a white-fleshed cherry with good taste."

'Sam': The large, black fruit of this 1953 Summerland selection is resistant to rain-splitting. The upright, spreading tree comes into bearing relatively slowly and blooms late, making it one of the most frost-resistant of sweet cherries. The fruit, which ripens in early July, has a coarse texture and a fair flavour when eaten fresh and is highly crack-resistant. It is very suitable for canning, producing a dark syrup. Craig recommends 'Sam,' as does Lord, who calls the fruit "large and flavourful."

'Summit': This 1973 Summerland selection produces moderate to heavy crops of sweet, good-flavoured fruit that is large to very large. It is very cold-sensitive, like 'Bing,' and ripens around the second week of July on the West Coast. Quamme recommends it as "more split-resistant than 'Bing.' "

'Sunburst': A fraternal twin of 'Lapins,' 'Sunburst' has the same advantage of self-fertility. The very large, dark, soft midseason fruit is more resistant to splitting than most commercial types. This is the most productive and largest-fruited cultivar tested at Summerland. Its consistent, high yields make it a good choice in marginal sweet-cherry areas, where the fruit set may be low. Quamme recommends it.

'Valera': Introduced at Vineland, Ontario,

49

Considered by many experts to be the best of the pie cherries, 'Meteor,' right, blooms a little later than its famous parent, 'Montmorency,' and thus is slightly more frost-tolerant. It also has some disease resistance and is a natural semidwarf.

in 1968, 'Valera' is a 'Hedelfingen' x 'Windsor' hybrid that begins to bear early and is vigorous, consistent and productive. The fruit, which matures early, is medium-sized, firm, dark and richly flavoured, although it is susceptible to severe cracking. Both buds and trees are cold-tender. Layne and Sherk recommend it.

'Van': A "V" cherry that does not come from Vineland, 'Van' has become the second most popular cultivar on the West Coast (after 'Bing') since its 1944 release from Summerland. It also has a large following in Europe.

The fruit, which has an unusually short stem and lustrous skin, cracks less than 'Bing', and both blossoms and tree are hardier (it survived a fall freeze in the state of Washington in 1955). The firm, almost black fruit ripens in mid- to late July, one of the last sweet cherries of summer. It is considered very fine in flavour and quality, although the fruit bruises easily and the tree is susceptible to brown rot and bacterial canker. Craig, Layne and Lord recommend it, although Lord does so cautiously because of climate.

'Venus': This 'Hedelfingen' x 'Windsor' hybrid, introduced at Vineland in 1958, produces big, high-quality, shiny black cherries with fairly light-coloured flesh. Fruit is produced early, but the tree is cold-tender. Fruit cracking is moderate. It tends to overset if conditions favour pollination, resulting in smaller fruit and lower quality. It is recommended by Layne.

SOUR CHERRIES

'Evans': A morello type that is a heavy producer—five-year-old, seven-foot trees have produced 10 gallons of inch-wide fruit—'Evans' has the decided advantage of great cold resistance. It was discovered producing bumper crops of large fruit near Edmonton, Alberta. Vick writes, "It will not be commercially available for a year or two."

'Meteor': The 1952 St. Paul, Minnesota, offspring of 'Montmorency,' 'Meteor' blooms two to four days later than its famous parent and thus is a little more resistant to spring frosts. The tree, which is resistant to the fungal disease leaf spot, is smallish, but St. Lawrence Nurseries finds it more vigorous than 'Northstar' and recommends it, as do Osborne and Lord. The latter comments: "Semidwarf growth habit. Good quality."

'Montmorency': This antique French variety from the Montmorency Valley, which has been grown for at least four centuries, is still judged "the best tart cherry" by Lord and is the cultivar of choice for most commercial growers. The tree is globe-shaped, with attractive, shiny leaves. Craig, Osborne and Sherk also recommend it. But it has its drawbacks. It blooms early and thus is susceptible to frost damage, and the tree is larger than 'Meteor' or 'Northstar.' Obtain virus-free stock, as some strains are infected with virus diseases. Olsen writes, "This cultivar can be grown successfully in Thunder Bay, but there is often considerable winter damage to the fruit buds."

'Northstar': Relatively hardy and semidwarf in size, this morello cultivar, developed in St. Paul, Minnesota, in 1950, is often recommended for home gardens and city lots. The branches tend to droop, creating an attractive shape. The reddish black fruit, with good flavour and texture, ripens in late July. A New York State bulletin notes, "The longer the harvest is delayed, the more sugars accumulate. For best quality, fruit should be left on the tree until a deep colour develops." Craig, Osborne and Sherk favour it.

Harvest Dates
Cherries

The range of dates refers to the approximate beginning of the harvest in the most popular fruit-bearing areas of the north.

Venus	June 30-July 15
Valera	July 1-15
Sam	July 1-15
Summit	July 1-15
Rainier	July 1-15
Bing	July 5-20
Compact Stella	July 5-20
Van	July 5-20
Hedelfingen	July 10-30
Compact Lambert	July 15-30
Northstar	July 15-30
Montmorency	July 20-30
Meteor	July 25-Aug. 5

The experts who were asked to recommend cultivars for their own area:

Sam Benowitz, owner, Raintree Nursery, Morton, Washington (USDA climatic zone 8).

William E. Craig, tree-fruit specialist, Agriculture Canada Research Station, Kentville, Nova Scotia (Agriculture Canada climatic zone 6a; USDA zone 6a).

Dr. Richard C. Layne, head, Horticultural Science Section, Agriculture Canada Research Station, Harrow, Ontario (Agriculture Canada climatic zone 7a; USDA zone 6a).

William G. Lord, extension specialist (fruit), University of New Hampshire, Durham, New Hampshire (USDA climatic zone 5b).

Paul Olsen, owner, Roseberry Gardens, Thunder Bay, Ontario (Agriculture Canada climatic zone 3a; USDA zone 4a).

Bob Osborne, owner, Corn Hill Nursery, Petitcodiac, New Brunswick (Agriculture Canada climatic zone 4b; USDA zone 4b).

Dr. Harvey Quamme, research scientist, Agriculture Canada Research Station, Summerland, British Columbia (Agriculture Canada climatic zone 6; USDA zone 6a).

Lawrence C. Sherk, formerly with Agriculture Canada, now chief horticulturist of Sheridan Nurseries, Georgetown, Ontario (Agriculture Canada climatic zone 6a; USDA zone 5b).

Roger Vick, curator, Devonian Botanic Garden, Edmonton, Alberta. Vick submitted the preferences of Sprout Farms, a family-owned business specializing in fruit trees in Bon Accord, Alberta (Agriculture Canada climatic zone 3a; USDA zone 3a).

HANDSOME AND DELICIOUS FRUIT

"This very handsome and delicious fruit can be grown in the open air only in the most favoured parts of the province, and even there, the fruit is very liable to be destroyed by late-spring frosts, on account of the habit of the tree in putting forth its blossoms at the first approach of spring."

—D.W. BEADLE, *The Canadian Fruit, Flower and Kitchen Gardener*, 1870

The apricot resembles a small peach or a fuzzy yellow plum, but this Asian native is actually most closely related to the almond, which shares the apricot's love of warm summers and its tendency to bloom early. Some cultivars of apricot have sweet pits that are edible and taste like almonds.

Apricots bloom the earliest of all northern fruits, a week or two before peaches. When Beadle wrote *The Canadian Fruit, Flower and Kitchen Gardener* in 1870, only the tender European apricots were known in North America. A half-century later, far hardier Siberian and Manchurian species would arrive, but even these burst into bloom with discouraging eagerness. Gardeners in very mild areas can grow European apricots, and gardeners in quite cold places can grow the Asians; it is gardeners in between who have trouble with this fruit's habit of blossoming at the first breath of spring.

Because apricot trees require only a short period of dormancy, their pink or white blossoms may appear during an unusually warm spell in March or April. Like other members of the rose family, apricot flowers are dependent upon insects for pollination. The beautiful blossoms may attract a cloud of honeybees — little other forage is available when they bloom — but if the weather is windy or wet, the bees may not fly. Even if the blossoms are pollinated, subsequent frosts can kill the flowers or the tiny fruits. No wonder many a northern gardener considers the apricot solely an ornamental, a role this tree, like the cherry, has gracefully performed in Oriental gardens for centuries. But anyone who wants fruit is likely to become discouraged with a show of blossoms that signals not the beginning but the end of the tree's generosity for the season.

Apricots are not recommended for commercial growing in areas cooler than climatic zone 7. The Persian name for the fruit, which means "seeds of the sun," is apt.

Apricot growing and fruiting is not out of bounds for everyone in climatic zone 6 or cooler, however. The Asian types can be grown in protected places in gardens as cool as climatic zone 3. Paul Olsen, who owns the zone-3 nursery Roseberry Gardens, in Thunder Bay, Ontario, says: "In cold climates, plant the trees as ornamentals. If the tree does produce fruit, consider it a bonus." Even some European cultivars can be considered possibilities for city or suburban gardens, which may have the sort of sheltered but sunny situations the trees require. A plus is that most European apricots are self-fertile, so you need only one.

EUROPEANS

All apricots originated in Asia, but the common orchard type, *Prunus armeniaca*, has undergone centuries of selection, especially in Europe, where it arrived via Armenia — hence the species name. It is, then, suited to a more or less Mediterranean climate, both in hardiness and disease resistance. The European apricot has done well in California, where it was introduced by Spanish missionaries. Its fruit has yellow, orange or reddish skin and flesh that is usually freestone, sweet, meaty and somewhat dry. The European apricot can be grown

Called "seeds of the sun" in Persian, apricots blossom earlier in spring than any other northern tree fruit and so are very vulnerable to late frosts.

wherever peaches and sweet cherries grow, and some cultivars are considerably more cold-hardy than peaches. It is the fruit of this tree that is sold fresh in supermarkets and in cans and jars. It is a much less hardy tree than the Manchurian and Siberian species, but the fruit is of better quality and flavour.

Apricot fruit, which is technically known as a drupe, is a little like a small peach or a yellow, slightly fuzzy plum, which it was thought to be until this century. "The apricot is essentially a plum without a downy covering, as the nectarine is a peach with the covering off," wrote E. Davenport in *Domesticated Animals and Plants* in 1910. However, a mutant plum tree producing apricots has never been found. The apricot is more closely allied to the almond, which blooms earlier and is even more tender. The fruits of some almonds resemble small apricots, and some European apricots have sweet pits that resemble and taste like almonds, an added harvest for growers of so-called alpricots such as 'Harcot,' 'Vivagold' and 'Moorpark.'

If *Prunus armeniaca* trees do set fruit, it will be ready for harvesting in July or early August, after the sweet cherries and before most peaches. Commercial growers consider *P. armeniaca* to fall into three groups: those best for canning (relatively small, firm and good-tasting); those best for fresh market (the largest and often the softest, also good-tasting); and those best for processing into jams, nectars and such (productive and of good colour but not necessarily the best-tasting). For home gardeners, qualities such as disease resistance, hardiness and vigour are more important. Among the hardiest of the *P. armeniaca* apricots are 'Alfred' and 'Harlayne.' For vigour and disease resistance, check the list at the end of this chapter, and read the fine print in plant-nursery catalogues.

MANCHURIANS AND SIBERIANS

The introduction of Manchurian and Siberian seedlings to the Agriculture Canada Research Station in Morden, Manitoba, in the 1930s brought to North America apricots that are genetically able to withstand relatively cold but consistent winters. Both the Manchurian apricot (*Prunus armeniaca mandschurica*), which hails from Manchuria and Korea, and the Siberian apricot (*P. armeniaca sibirica*) from eastern Asia can survive winter temperatures of minus 30 degrees F (-35 °C) or colder.

The Manchurian grows into a bush about 12 feet high and, depending upon seedling, produces one-to-two-inch fruit that varies from sweet to sour. It has spawned the most successful selections, including 'Sungold' and 'Moongold' from the University of Minnesota and the Canadians 'Brookcot' and 'M-604.' 'Scout,' released from Morden in 1937, was the first Manchurian seedling to gain popularity in the prairies. The best-quality, although also earliest-blooming, of the prairie apricots, 'Westcot,' released from Morden in 1982, has as its parents 'Scout' and 'McClure' (which has some European genes). Siberian seedlings have been less noteworthy, but a few are offered by prairie nurseries.

Be wary of apricots without cultivar names, as their quality is so variable that the fruit may be unpalatable. They are lower in price, however, and can be used as pollinators for other Asians for more dependable crops. Nanking cherries will also suffice as pollinators. The close relationship of some cherries, plums and apricots is also manifest in the crosses of Asian apricots with later-blooming *Prunus* species, such as sand cherries and Japanese plums. Selections of the latter, known as plumcots, such as 'Kahinta' and 'LaCrescent,' are described on page 75.

In common with other apricots, both of the Asian species blossom early—the first of all *Prunus* species, according to records kept in Manitoba, where they bloom in late April—and thus seldom produce a crop of fruit where May frosts are common. At Morden, there is no apricot crop about five years out of six. Irene Wallace writes from the more severe climate of Beaverlodge, Alberta, that "no apricots have been found consistently dependable." But the Asian apricots are nevertheless worth a try in sheltered areas in southern prairie and midwestern gardens, where a long,

Apricot trees should be pruned soon after they bloom, because earlier pruning can induce premature bloom. The beautiful spring blossoms may be the tree's only contribution if frost follows.

steadily cold winter will keep them safely dormant as late as possible and where frost protection can be given in May. When frost threatens, cover the bush with blankets overnight.

APRICOTS AT HOME

The secret of apricot selection, then, is to buy trees bred for conditions similar to your own. Keep prairie types in places where winters are cold and steady. In more favoured places or where winter temperatures are variable, the tough little Siberians and Manchurians do not fare well, because early warm spells coax them into bloom more easily than their European cousins. Also, they are more susceptible to the fungal diseases troublesome in warmer, wetter places. By the same token, it is best to choose eastern types of *Prunus armeniaca* for the east and western for the west. Attempts to grow British Columbia apricots in Ontario or Washington successes in New York have met with frequent failure because of disease and dormancy problems.

Shop through the catalogues, and look for what is newest and most improved. Compared with other tree fruits, apricots have received relatively little breeding attention. The negative characteristics of their wild forebears — early blossoming leading to small fruit that drops as soon as it is ripe — may show up in heirloom trees. Active programs in many northern places such as Vineland, Ontario (whose cultivar names start with the letter V), Harrow, Ontario (whose cultivar names start with the syllable Har), and Summerland, British Columbia, are producing apricots that are the best bets for northern gardeners. The smallest trees can be grown in pots, as described on pages 118 to 122.

Unless it is small enough for a pot, allow plenty of space for any European apricot tree. A 'Harcot' I bought as an unpromising, foot-long whip 10 years ago is now about 30 feet tall and almost as wide (and although it blooms, I have picked no fruit; 'Harcot' is an especially early bloomer). Allow at least 20 feet from other trees, 10 feet from walls and fences. Siberians and Manchurians need about half as much space. Like peaches and sweet cherries, all apricots must have soil that drains well, preferably sandy or coarse. Soil in which water collects will leave trees much more vulnerable to disease and winter damage. A slight slope is best. Surprisingly, a northern orientation is recommended, as this cooler position will delay blossoming. Allow the tree some shelter from prevailing winds — consider a position near the house — and avoid low spots, where cold air will gather.

There are no recommended dwarfing rootstocks suitable for apricots grown outdoors in the north, but there are several genetically smaller cultivars, including 'Goldcot,' 'Puget Gold' and 'Harglow,' that grow 15 to 18 feet tall. Dwarfs such as 'Garden Annie' and 'Stark Goldenglo' should be grown in containers and wintered indoors. The longest-lived, most vigorous apricots are grafted onto apricot seedling rootstocks such as 'Haggith,' 'Morden 604,' 'Goldcot,' 'Veecot' and Manchurian. Some nurseries use peach, plum, *Prunus tomentosa* or *P. besseyi* rootstocks, which do produce smaller trees but at the expense of productivity and longevity. If you really want a dwarf, hardy apricot, choose one of the Asians, which are genetically smaller than the Europeans, about 6 to 15 feet high at maturity.

European apricots should be pruned to the modified central leader system, described on pages 17 to 19. Keep the main leader headed back to encourage the growth of side branches and to keep the tree growing slowly. It is important to permit penetration of light to the tree so that new wood will grow in the lower part and the tree will not grow too high, producing all its fruit on top. When you head back the central leader, always cut it back to a lateral branch. Apricot branches tend to grow vertically and may need weighting or pushing into a more horizontal position. Spring-type clothespins can be clipped to the trunk about half an inch above the branch base so that the shoot is forced to form a wide angle. Trees should be pruned soon after they blossom, as earlier pruning can induce an early bloom. Many Asian apricots are shrub-like in form, so pruning consists largely of thinning overcrowded branches and keeping the shrub open to the sun and air.

PROBLEM SOLVING

Watering is essential for apricots growing on the well-drained land they need. When rain does not fall, water deeply every week from full bloom until harvest.

Apricots will drop most excess fruit on their own, but if fruits touch, hand-thinning should be done for several reasons: it will help keep the fruits disease-free; it will allow them to ripen fully and grow to full size; and it will help discourage the tree from settling into a pattern of biennial bearing—bumper crops of small fruit one year and no fruit the next. Heavy cropping leaves the tree and buds more vulnerable to winter damage. About a month after full bloom, remove the smallest fruits and any which have the crescent-shaped, quarter-inch scars that denote plum curculio egg laying. The remaining fruits should be at least two inches apart.

Fortunately, the apricot suffers little from pests or diseases in most northern gardens. See page 32 for defences against plum curculio, the tree's worst pest, and pages 21 and 22 for ways to avoid southwest injury, another common problem. As apricots are vulnerable to verticillium wilt, a fungal disease that also affects tomatoes, peppers, potatoes, raspberries and strawberries, do not plant apricots where those crops have grown within the past four years. Phil Matthewson, who grows 35 varieties of apricots organically in southern Ontario, wards off perennial canker with a Bordeaux mixture (see page 39) applied during late summer and fall. Brown rot, which causes infected fruit to rot within, then wither and drop, is most troublesome on susceptible cultivars during hot, damp summers. European cultivars, bred in relatively damp conditions, are more resistant to the disease than are the Asians. To guard against it, thin the fruits so that no two touch, and remove some leaves to permit greater air circulation. If signs of rot

appear, spray with wettable sulphur, repeating every 10 to 12 days if the weather is wet and allowing at least 10 days between the last spray and the harvest. Cultivars resistant to another disease, bacterial spot, are 'Alfred,' 'Harcot,' 'Hargrand' and 'Harlayne.' The last three are also resistant to brown rot and perennial canker.

If you have been lucky with frosts, European apricots should begin to bear four or five years after planting, Asians sooner, with most fruit on a tree ripening within about 10 days. Check trees daily, because the fruit on most cultivars will drop as soon as it is ripe, a tendency of the wild species which breeders have not yet altered. A standard European tree in good health should produce three to four bushels, with Manchurians and Siberians producing proportionately less; quantities are variable, however, as they are so dependent upon the spring weather.

Pick fruit when it is fully ripe and all the green has disappeared. Apricots are prone to bruising, so handle them with care. They will keep for several weeks in the refrigerator. Apricots have more vitamin C than other tree fruits and far more vitamin A, perhaps the reason the ancient Chinese thought that they conferred prophetic powers. They make an excellent juice that blends well with apple, and they are easy to can or to dry, according to the directions on pages 131 to 133.

Apricot growing is surely risky business, but anyone really determined to have this "handsome and delicious fruit" should choose the cultivar carefully and should grow the tree in as sheltered a place as possible, perhaps even keeping it in a container and wintering it indoors. Even if a crop comes only one year in six, as is the case in some prairie gardens, the tree is ornamental in the meantime, and the harvest will be worth the wait.

Because there are so many cultivars, I asked a group of North American fanciers to recommend their favourite trees, ones they would choose for a small dream orchard in their own climatic area. As you read through the list, take note of the climatic zone and geographic area of each apricot's sponsor and compare it with your own, as you will likely have the greatest success with apricots that have been found superlative in growing conditions similar to your own.

EUROPEAN APRICOTS

'Goldcot': A hardy, genetic semidwarf that grows about 18 feet tall, 'Goldcot' was released from South Haven, Michigan, in 1967. It is valued for productivity and dependability. The midseason fruit is rather dry, medium-sized and slightly soft, with fair colour and quality. It is susceptible to brown rot and bacterial spot. Lord recommends 'Goldcot,' although he cautions that apricots are generally not advised for New Hampshire.

'Harcot': Early to bloom and among the first of all European apricots to bear (about July 25 near the southern Great Lakes), this 1977 Harrow, Ontario, introduction has medium-sized, orange, somewhat clingstone fruit with very good flavour and texture. The trees are hardy, vigorous and productive, with tolerance to bacterial spot, brown rot and perennial canker. The kernels are sweet and edible. It is considered good for fresh eating but not canning. Craig and Layne recommend it, and Sherk suggests it as an early companion to 'Harlayne.'

'Harglow': A genetic semidwarf that grows about 18 feet tall, this 1982 Harrow selection is late-blooming and ripens in midseason. The bright orange, freestone fruit is medium-sized, with a light blush. Sweet and juicy, with a smooth texture and rich flavour, it is considered suitable for fresh eating and home canning. The tree is somewhat susceptible to brown rot but very resistant to bacterial spot and perennial canker. Craig and Layne recommend it.

'Hargrand': Freestone orange fruits as big as ripe peaches distinguish this self-fertile, hardy variety released from Harrow in 1980. The flesh is orange, juicy and firm, recommended for fresh eating. The tree is resistant to perennial canker, brown rot, fungal canker and bacterial spot. It blooms relatively late, and the harvest is also late, a few days before 'Harlayne.' Craig and Layne both recommend it.

'Harlayne': Released in 1980, this is one of the hardiest Harrow selections, slightly hardier than 'Goldcot.' Nevertheless, it is productive and tolerant of perennial canker, bacterial spot and brown rot. The freestone fruit, which is orange with a red blush, may be smallish but has good quality for fresh eating. Layne recommends 'Harlayne,' and Sherk

Apricots should be thinned to hang a couple of inches apart. This practice discourages disease, encourages annual bearing and allows the remaining fruits to attain full size.

Apricots are classified as clingstone or freestone. The latter is the type whose pit is separate from the flesh and thus is easiest to prepare for drying or processing.

suggests it as a late-fruiting companion for 'Harcot.' It is the latest-ripening of the Europeans on this list, around the end of the first week of August near the southern Great Lakes.

'Harogem': This mid-to-late-season apricot, which ripens a couple of days before 'Harlayne' and 'Hargrand,' is exceptional for its keeping quality. The smallish freestone fruit, which is firm and juicy with a glossy red blush, will keep for a week at room temperature and several weeks in the refrigerator. Released from Harrow in 1979, it is hardy and productive, with good tolerance to perennial canker and brown rot but susceptibility to bacterial spot. Craig and Layne recommend it.

'Harval': Released from Harrow in 1989, 'Harval,' which has 'Veecot' as one parent, is relatively cold-hardy, consistently productive and resistant to bacterial spot, perennial canker, brown rot and cracking. The fruit is large and very attractive, with a red blush on a bright orange background. The firm, melting flesh is completely freestone. It ripens late, about a day before 'Harlayne.' Layne recommends it.

'Perfection': The advantage of this seedling discovered in Washington in 1937 is very large, attractive fruit, but its shortcomings include a need for cross-pollination and fruit buds that are very cold-tender in late winter. Pick this when fully ripe for best flavour. It is recommended by Lord, although he cautions that any apricots are risky in New Hampshire.

'Puget Gold': Introduced by Washington State University, this westerner sets fruit in cool spring weather when all others fail on the coast. Prolific crops of delicious oval fruit ripen in early August. The tree is a natural semidwarf that can be maintained at 15 feet tall. It is recommended by Denowitz.

'Skaha': This selection from Summerland, British Columbia, named in 1973, produces large freestone apricots whose texture and flavour are fair to good for both fresh eating and preserving. The tree is vigorous, wide-spreading and productive, begins to bear early and is relatively hardy in both tree and bud. It is not self-fertile but can be pollinated by most other apricots. Quamme recommends it: "A large-fruited apricot that is firm and bright orange. It should be allowed to reach full orange colour before picking." The fruit is ready to pick in late July at Summerland.

'Sundrop': Named in 1975, this Summer-

Some cultivars of both European and Asian apricots have an attractive red blush, but regardless of appearance, all contain more of the vitamins C and A than other tree fruits, perhaps the reason the ancient Chinese thought that apricots conferred prophetic powers.

land selection is very productive and moderately hardy in wood and buds. The fruit is firm and bright orange, with fair texture and flavour. Taste this fruit before you harvest, as it becomes orange before it is fully ripe and the flavour is not yet developed. It ripens around the same time as 'Skaha.' Quamme recommends it: "Blossoms are more cold-hardy than other apricots such as 'Blenheim.'"

'**Veecot**': A 1964 release from Vineland, Ontario, this is the favourite commercial apricot in Ontario, where it ripens in early August. The round, freestone, medium-sized fruit

has a bright orange blush. The flesh, which is firm, very smooth and slightly juicy, is excellent for canning. Do not pick until a dark orange background colour develops. The trees are productive but susceptible to bacterial leaf spot. It is recommended by Craig.

MANCHURIAN AND SIBERIAN APRICOTS

'**Brookcot**': This Manchurian selection, released from Brooks, Alberta, in 1979, produces 1½-inch fruit that is bright yellow or orange with a red cheek. It is juicy, has good flavour and is slightly clingstone. The tree is tall, upright and branches poorly. It is recommended by Alberta Agriculture and submitted by Roger Vick.

'M-604': A cross between 'Scout' and 'McClure' released from Morden, Manitoba, in 1946 but never named, this hardy tree was embraced by prairie gardeners because its fruit, when cooked, is rated the finest that can be grown on the prairies. The fruit is golden yellow, very tasty, sweet and almost two inches wide. The tree is tall and upright and blooms a little later than 'Scout.' Davidson and Osborne recommend it.

Manchurian: Seedling trees vary in size and hardiness, and the fruit varies in flavour, size and colour. "Think of them as a horticultural lottery ticket," writes Hall-Beyer. They are recommended as hardy apricot pollinators by Alberta Agriculture, as submitted by Roger Vick. You may be lucky with the fruit.

'Scout': The first Manchurian seedling to gain acceptance on the prairies, 'Scout,' released from Morden in 1937, survives only in protected sites. The dryish, freestone, bronze-gold, thin-skinned fruit is large, sometimes wider than two inches. It ripens in late July or early August on trees up to 12 feet tall and is best for processing. Campbell Davidson recommends it, as does Roger Vick.

'Sunrise': A hybrid of the Siberian apricot and 'McClure' released in 1980 from Lakeshore Tree Farms in Saskatchewan, this prairie-hardy apricot produces medium-sized, sweet, golden, freestone fruit on a bushy, compact tree. The blossoms are light pink. It is submitted by Vick.

'Westcot': This hybrid of a Manchurian apricot and 'McClure,' released from Morden in 1982, is the most highly recommended of all the prairie apricots by our roster of experts. 'Westcot' offers better bud hardiness than many others, although it tends to bloom very early—before April 20 in Morden. The fruit, almost two inches wide, is yellow to orange with a light reddish blush. The juicy, freestone flesh is orange, with fine texture and a mild, sweet flavour. Davidson, Osborne and Vick recommend it. Olsen says, "Best quality of all apricots hardy to zone 3."

The experts who were asked to recommend cultivars for their own area:

Sam Benowitz, owner, Raintree Nursery, Morton, Washington (USDA climatic zone 8).

Harvest Dates
Apricots

The range of dates refers to the approximate beginning of the harvest in the most popular fruit-bearing areas of the north.

Harcot	July 10-30
Sundrop	July 20-30
Skaha	July 20-30
Goldcot	July 25-Aug. 5
Harglow	July 25-Aug. 5
Veecot	July 25-Aug. 10
Hargrand	July 25-Aug. 10
Harogem	July 25-Aug. 10
Harlayne	July 30-Aug. 15

William E. Craig, tree-fruit specialist, Agriculture Canada Research Station, Kentville, Nova Scotia (Agriculture Canada climatic zone 6a; USDA zone 6a).

Dr. Campbell Davidson, research scientist, Agriculture Canada Research Station, Morden, Manitoba (Agriculture Canada climatic zone 3b; USDA zone 3b).

Bart Hall-Beyer, owner, Sursum Corda, Scotstown, Quebec (Agriculture Canada climatic zone 4a; USDA zone 4a).

Dr. Richard C. Layne, head, Horticultural Science Section, Agriculture Canada Research Station, Harrow, Ontario (Agriculture Canada climatic zone 7a; USDA zone 6a).

William G. Lord, extension specialist (fruit), University of New Hampshire, Durham, New Hampshire (USDA climatic zone 5b).

Paul Olsen, owner, Roseberry Gardens, Thunder Bay, Ontario (Agriculture Canada climatic zone 3a; USDA zone 4a).

Bob Osborne, owner, Corn Hill Nursery, Petitcodiac, New Brunswick (Agriculture Canada climatic zone 4b; USDA zone 4b).

Dr. Harvey Quamme, research scientist, Agriculture Canada Research Station, Summerland, British Columbia (Agriculture Canada climatic zone 6; USDA zone 6a).

Lawrence C. Sherk, formerly with Agriculture Canada, now chief horticulturist of Sheridan Nurseries, Georgetown, Ontario (Agriculture Canada climatic zone 6a; USDA zone 5b).

Roger Vick, curator, Devonian Botanic Garden, Edmonton, Alberta. Vick submitted the preferences of Sprout Farms, a family-owned business specializing in fruit trees in Bon Accord, Alberta (Agriculture Canada climatic zone 3a; USDA zone 3a).

ELSE THE PEACH WILL NOT THRIVE

*"The soil must be warm, dry and
porous, else the peach will not
thrive. This delicious fruit can be
grown in the open ground only in the
warmer parts of the province of Ontario, and then only in warm and
dry gravelly or sandy soils and in
sheltered aspects not subject to late-
spring frosts. Trained against the
wall, it does well in Nova Scotia
and in other sections where the fruit
buds are not killed
by the winter's cold."*

–D.W. BEADLE, *The Canadian Fruit, Flower
and Kitchen Gardener,* 1870

Anyone with a garden in a
favoured climatic area
should try growing a peach
or nectarine, as the trees are
decorative and the fruits,
fresh-picked and fully ripe,
are among the most
exquisite treats of summer.
'Elberta' peach, left, is a
popular canning variety
whose seedlings are used
for rootstocks.

Peaches and nectarines

Peaches are tender creatures. They thrive only in a few favoured parts of the north and, even there, only with luck and the cooperation of nature. Slender, tenuous bands of peach country exist around bodies of water: the southern Great Lakes, Okanagan lakes, Finger Lakes, Hudson River and sheltered bays on the Atlantic and the Pacific. Now and then, a winter comes along that kills buds, twigs, branches or even entire trees to the snow line. Even in British Columbia's otherwise amenable Okanagan Valley, a winter tough enough to erase the peach harvest happens about once every seven years. Northern peach growers are consequently a philosophical lot. It is no climatic accident that the bulk of North America's peaches comes from California, Arkansas, Texas and Georgia, places that are not only warm but also fairly dry in summer.

Those who can grow peaches and their fuzzless sisters the nectarines are fortunate. Both are excellent home-garden fruits: self-fruitful, decorative and little troubled by diseases in the north. Trees begin to bear soon after they are planted, grow quickly and respond well to pruning. They are good candidates for the more relaxed styles of espalier (described on page 25), and the smallest cultivars can be grown in pots. The delectable fruit ripens after cherries and apricots but before most plums, pears and apples. If you have space, it is possible to pick fresh fruit from several trees with varying ripening dates, so the harvest can extend from the end of July until mid-September. Peaches and nectarines are best fresh right off the tree, of course, but they can also be frozen, canned and made into preserves and juices.

Peaches and nectarines (*Prunus persica*) are natives of China, where they have been cultivated for thousands of years. Centuries ago, however, the fruit was tough, bitter and nothing to celebrate. The trees the Chinese loved, which probably resembled today's so-called flowering peaches, were valued most for their beautiful, fragrant flowers and the shape of their branches and, eventually, for their excellent firewood. As the trees moved westward with various migrations, selection resulted in improved fruit that came to be known as Persian apples (hence the botanical name). Like apricots, there are no native North American species, although the fruit, brought to Mexico by the Spanish in the late 1500s, was quickly adopted by the indigenous peoples and transported as far north as it would grow. William Penn found peach trees in native gardens in New England in 1682: "There are very good peaches in Pennsylvania; not an Indian plantation is without them." Now, peaches are the third most important fruit crop in the United States, behind oranges and apples.

There are two major classes: freestone and clingstone, describing the attachment of the flesh to the pit. Those in between are called semiclingstone or semifreestone. The yellow, melting-flesh freestones are the most common type for the fresh market and home garden. The most popular of these are the 'Haven' series, including 'Redhaven,' which were released from the South Haven Experimental Station in Michigan between 1924 and 1963. A number of important northern cultivars, some with greater cold hardiness, have since been released from Vineland and Harrow in Ontario and from New Hampshire, North Carolina, Michigan and New York. There are also white, tender-fleshed types that are not commonly grown now, although a half-century ago, they were the first choice in Italy, still the world's top peach producer (followed by the United States). The cling peaches, valued for canning and baby foods, are unattractively dubbed "rubber-fleshed"—to differentiate them from their melting-flesh relatives—because of their firmness even when ripe, a quality that helps them hold their shape when canned. Most notable in the north is the

The beautiful, fragrant flowers of the peach appear two or three weeks before those of apples and so are frequently harmed by late frosts. Gardeners in marginal areas should choose late-blooming cultivars.

In botanical terms, the nectarine is simply a peach without fuzz, although it does have other differences. In general, nectarines prefer warmer conditions than peaches, and the fruits tend to be smaller, tastier and later to ripen.

'Babygold' series, developed in New Jersey.

Nectarines are simply peaches without fuzz, naturally occurring mutations that appear occasionally on peach trees and that were celebrated by the Chinese several centuries before the time of Christ. Nectarine culture is the same as that for peaches, and nectarines can be grown anywhere peaches will grow. Nectarine trees tend to be less productive than peach trees, however, and the fruit is usually smaller, tastier and later to ripen, overlapping the end of peach season from late August until mid-September. Nectarines are more susceptible to some fungal diseases such as brown rot and mildew, because the fruit lacks the protective skin fuzz. Again, there are clingstone, freestone and intermediate types. Some of the hardiest nectarines are 'Stark Earliblaze,' 'Earliscarlet,' 'Harblaze,' 'Harko,' 'Hardired,' 'Lexington' and 'Mericrest.'

The earliest-ripening peaches and nectarines generally bear the smallest fruit. 'Harbinger,' earliest of the good peaches grown at Geneva, New York, where it ripens around July 18, bears fruit about 2¼ inches wide, while the two largest peaches grown there, both wider than three inches, are 'Topaz,' which ripens August 26, and 'J.H. Hale,' which ripens September 12. Midseason and late peaches are often sweeter than early ones, with tender flesh that is well coloured. Within all seasons, however, there is a great deal of variability in quality, size, hardiness and productivity, and what does well in one place may fail in another. Harvey Quamme writes from Summerland, British Columbia: "It is hard to discriminate among peach cultivars. Most recently introduced red-skinned peaches, such as 'Vivid,' 'Harbrite,' 'Redhaven,' 'Harbelle' and 'Vanity,' are all good if picked tree-ripe. Home growers should grow more than one cultivar to spread the harvest date. The 'Peentoo' from China is a high-quality peach with a very flat shape. It could be of interest to home growers as a novelty. The Chinese emperors were said to eat them, as the juice did not run down their faces."

The choice of a cultivar for a home garden is based largely on hardiness. After that, other characteristics, such as disease resistance and fruit size and quality, can be considered. Bud injury is the main limitation to peach growing. The flower buds of most peaches will die if winter temperatures of minus 13 degrees F (-25°C) persist for three consecutive nights. Every hard freeze between December and early March kills a number of fruit buds. Although peaches bloom later than apricots, their beautiful pink blossoms may appear two or three weeks before those of apples. Just a couple of degrees of frost during blossoming can wipe out almost the entire crop of even the hardiest cultivar. Immediately after blooming, peaches begin to produce their new crop of fruit buds. These dormant buds can be damaged when a mild fall is followed by a very

Peaches and nectarines

The gnarled foliage that distinguishes leaf curl, a fungal disease that commonly strikes peaches, is most likely to appear after a period of cold, wet weather. Combat the disease with lime-sulphur sprays on dormant trees.

cold winter or when a winter thaw is followed by a cold snap.

The trees themselves will die at minus 25 to minus 30 degrees F (-32° to -35°C). Even if the temperature does not fall this far, cold weather in early winter or fluctuating winter temperatures are destructive. Injured tissue is vulnerable to invasion by peach canker. In marginal areas, the trees will suffer some dieback each winter and will compensate by growing vigorously in spring until a really cold winter finally kills them. The hardiest peaches can be grown in protected places in zone 5b, but all grow best where temperatures do not drop below minus 10 degrees F (-23°C).

After the 1984 test winter in West Virginia, when temperatures dropped to minus 18 degrees F (-28°C), scientists at the university experimental farm rated peach and nectarine trees for vegetative injury, spring bloom and subsequent harvest. Those which survived the winter best included the peaches 'Cando,' 'Cresthaven,' 'Emery,' 'Glohaven,' 'Madison,' 'Redglobe,' 'Redhaven,' 'Troy,' 'Whynot' and 'Winblo' and the nectarines 'Earliblaze,' 'Lexington' and 'Redbud.'

Trees that are healthy and vigorous will be better able to withstand any kind of adversity. This means, initially, planting the trees in a sunny place that is sheltered from the wind, has deep, well-drained soil and is preferably on a slight slope. Wet feet will almost certainly lead to winter damage, fungal diseases and eventual death. On the other hand, consistent, deep watering during drought will help keep trees growing well. Mulching the soil around the trunk with a foot of straw or fallen leaves and extending the mulch out as far as the reach of the branch tips will help protect the roots. Two peach lovers in Minnesota manage to pick peaches every year but only by mulching their entire trees with either snow or straw for the winter and by protecting them from early frosts.

For greatest hardiness, avoid any rootstock that promises to dwarf the tree. An exception is the Harrow rootstock Siberian C, an exceptionally hardy stock that dwarfs trees by about a third. Nanking cherry (*Prunus tomentosa*) rootstocks produce trees only about seven feet tall, but there are incompatibility problems with some cultivars. There is usually little advantage to dwarfs, as peaches can be kept at medium height by pruning, and winterkill may do more pruning for you. Peaches are generally grafted onto seedling peach roots, grown from cannery pits, of varieties such as 'Elberta' or 'Halford.'

Peaches and nectarines produce fruit on new wood, not on spurs, so a good harvest depends upon plenty of new growth. If trees are not pruned annually, the fruiting wood will grow farther from the trunk and the ground every year, until the fruit is difficult to pick and the branches become so long that they can be broken easily by the wind or a heavy fruit load.

Prune peaches and
nectarines after they
bloom, because dormant
pruning can encourage early
flowering. The later the
trees flower, the better
the chances of a full
crop of fruit.

Except for the first year of planting, peaches in most of the north should be pruned in June. Early-spring pruning tends to encourage early blooming. Do not do any pruning, fertilizing or cultivating around the trees after June, as it can result in late, tender growth. (On the West Coast, peaches can be pruned after leaf drop in autumn.) Peaches are easy to prune using the modified central leader technique described on pages 17 to 19. Head the tree back every year so that it does not grow more than 14 feet tall.

Select a cultivar that is resistant to diseases troublesome in your area. Peach leaf curl, the most common disease in home gardens, is caused by a fungus that thrives in cold, wet weather. It distorts, discolours and thickens leaves in early spring. Symptoms may disappear in summer, but repeated attacks will gradually wear down the tree, making it more susceptible to winter injury. Lime-sulphur sprays on dormant trees will help prevent it. Powdery mildew, a fungus that produces a white growth over the young twigs, leaves and fruit, should be combated with two sprays of lime sulphur or wettable sulphur two weeks apart at blossom time. Brown rot, a fungal

disease of all stone fruits, causes infected blossoms to shrivel and die under a blanket of greyish mould. Infected fruit has small, circular brown spots that increase rapidly in size. Peach, or perennial, canker, which also infects apricots, produces gummy sores after it enters wounds caused by pruning or winter damage. To help avoid perennial canker, remove all deadwood from the tree and cease pruning by the end of June to allow maturation of the wood before winter. Do not overfertilize. Remove brown, discoloured bark and any cankers that form. A fall spray of lime sulphur, after the leaves have fallen and when the air is dry and temperatures in the shade are above freezing, will help protect the trees from fungal diseases.

The worst pest is the plum curculio, whose control is described on page 32. The peach twig borer, whose half-inch larvae are reddish brown with black heads, burrows into the tips of new shoots, causing them to wilt and die back. The larvae of the second generation enter the fruit and burrow to the pit. To combat the problem, spray a lime-sulphur solution at blossom time. Earwigs may become pests of cultivars whose pits split. The best defence is

Most of the flesh of the peach fills out during the last month before harvesting, provided there is sufficient water. Before that, the seed and pit grow to full size, and the pit hardens.

a split-resistant cultivar. The grey-winged Oriental fruit moth emerges in late May or early June and lays its eggs on leaves and twigs. They hatch in about a week, and the larvae rapidly enter the shoots or fruits. Spray daily with Bt for two weeks after the moths appear. One organic pest-control method has been shown to increase hardiness in peaches as well. During experimental trials at Utah State University, a late-winter and early-spring spray with horticultural oil enhanced bud hardiness by as much as 10 Fahrenheit degrees (6 Celsius degrees) and delayed blooming by as many as four days.

If left unattended, peach trees grown in optimal conditions will produce a big crop of smallish fruit. The tree will shed some of the excess fruit during June drop but not enough. Ideally, peach and nectarine fruits should hang six to eight inches apart, which will require hand-thinning soon after June drop. The fruit goes through three growth stages. Within the first month or so after bloom, the stone and the seed within it attain nearly full size. During the next month, the pit hardens and the fruit increases slightly in size. In the third stage, which continues until harvest, the volume of flesh increases greatly. Now, watering becomes very important, since fruit is composed largely of water. The size of the fruit may increase by almost 50 percent in the month before harvest. During ripening, the skin colour changes from green to yellow as the flesh softens and becomes sweeter and tastier.

The first peaches to ripen, such as 'Earlired,' are smallish and of the clingstone or semifreestone type. The larger freestones ripen in August or September. Peaches and nectarines do not ripen all at once, so they must be picked every three to five days. Commercial growers pick peaches slightly underripe, because the fruit handles better then and will continue to ripen somewhat when stored at room temperature out of sunlight; but peaches taste best if they are allowed to ripen fully on the tree. An advantage in the home garden is that the fruit can be left on the tree as long as possible. The red-skinned cultivars, such as 'Redhaven,' may look ready to pick before they are fully ripe. Sample the fruit to be sure. Pick it carefully, as when it is ripe, it is very easily bruised. Ripe fruit can be stored in the refrigerator for about two weeks. Do not wash peaches and nectarines until just before eating. The cultivars described below under "Experts' Choice" as nonbrowning are slow to oxidize and thus can be frozen or sliced for desserts or salads without the use of ascorbic acid or some other antioxidant.

Peaches and nectarines are available fresh on the market in summer, of course, and for many northerners, this relatively local fruit comes as close as possible to homegrown. For the daring who do not live too far from peach country, however, there is little to be lost in cultivating one of these Oriental beauties.

Because there are so many cultivars, I asked a group of North American fanciers to recommend their favourite trees, ones they would choose for a small dream orchard in their own climatic area. As you read through these, take note of the climatic zone and geographic area of each sponsor and compare it with your own, as you will likely have the greatest success with peaches and nectarines that have been found superlative in growing conditions similar to your own.

PEACHES

'Early Redhaven': This is one of three approved strains of an early-ripening sport of 'Redhaven' from Michigan. The other two are 'Garnet Beauty' and 'Earlyglow.' 'Early Redhaven,' recommended by Quamme, ripens from early to mid-August, depending upon location. The red-skinned fruit is medium-sized and semiclingstone, with yellow flesh that may be tinted red. It ripens about three days after 'Garnet Beauty.' The trees are fairly hardy, similar to 'Redhaven.'

'Garnet Beauty': This early-ripening, vigorous sport of 'Redhaven,' discovered in the Garnet Bruner orchard in Ontario, is ready to pick the first week of August near the southern Great Lakes. It is less freestone than 'Early Redhaven' and not quite as hardy. The nonbrowning fruit is of medium size with few split pits. It is recommended by Craig.

'Golden Monarch': "This is my personal favourite," says Lord. "The flesh is flavourful, juicy and firm. It is freestone when fully ripe. The fruit size is very uniform, and fruits colour beautifully. This cultivar is hardier than 'Redhaven' at Durham, New Hampshire."

'Harbelle': Released from Harrow, Ontario, in 1968, this cold-tender tree is moderately productive, compact, spreading and tolerant of bacterial spot and brown rot. The fruit, which ripens the first week of August around the southern Great Lakes, is about 2½ inches across and smooth, with a red blush on a bright yellow background. The semiclingstone flesh is rich, bright yellow, juicy and slow to brown when cut. It is considered suitable for home freezing. Sherk and Quamme recommend it.

'Harbinger': This cold-tender peach, which ripens about a month before 'Redhaven,' was released from Harrow in 1971. It produces attractive, somewhat small clingstone fruits with a red blush. The yellow flesh has good flavour

for an early peach. Split pits are common. Sherk recommends it, noting, "Very early."

'Harbrite': This 1969 Harrow cross of 'Redskin' and 'Sunhaven' is a very productive, somewhat hardy tree whose attractive, medium-sized fruit ripens in mid-August near the southern Great Lakes. The fruit is freestone, roundish and nearly smooth, with a bright red blush on a yellow background. The yellow flesh is slow to brown when cut and has a pleasant flavour and texture. It is rated good for home canning and freezing. Tolerant of bacterial spot and brown rot, this cultivar has been grown experimentally on Grand Manan Island, New Brunswick. Quamme recommends it for late-season areas.

'Harcrest': Introduced from Harrow in 1983, this tree, which is similar to 'Cresthaven' but hardier, is open, spreading, vigorous and productive. The fruit is medium to large in size, with a red blush. It ripens late – mid-September near the southern Great Lakes. The yellow freestone flesh, light red around the pit cavity, is very firm and fine-textured and is good both fresh and processed. Trees are somewhat resistant to perennial canker, brown rot and bacterial spot. It is recommended by Layne.

'Harken': This 'Redskin' x 'Sunhaven' hybrid, introduced from Harrow in 1970, ripens with 'Harbrite' and is similar to it, although the fruit quality is somewhat higher and the tree less hardy, with good tolerance to bac-

The skin of the Vineland cultivar 'Vivid,' photographed while still green at the end of June, will become bright red when the fruit is ripe in mid- to late August. The peaches on this tree have been properly thinned to hang no closer than six inches apart.

terial spot and brown rot. The medium-to-large fruit is yellow with a red blush. The bright yellow freestone flesh is nonbrowning, firm, sweet and juicy with very good flavour. 'Harken' is rated very good for home canning and freezing. Layne recommends it, as does Benowitz, who writes, "Best-flavoured peach in our climate. It is very sweet."

'Harrow Beauty': Introduced from Harrow in 1983, 'Harrow Beauty' produces a big crop of large, high-quality, freestone fruit in late August or early September. The fruit, which has a red blush on a yellow background, does not drop readily even when fully ripe, and the pits seldom split. The delicious yellow flesh, tinted red at the pit, is firm and nonbrowning, with a smooth texture. The trees are open, spreading, very productive and somewhat cold-hardy. They have moderate resistance to perennial canker, brown rot and bacterial spot. It is recommended by Layne.

'Harrow Diamond': A cold-hardy cross of 'Redskin' and 'Harbinger' released from Harrow in 1986, this tree is resistant to bacterial spot and brown rot and is moderately tolerant of perennial canker. The medium-sized fruit ripens very early, about July 26 at Harrow. The smooth skin is bright yellow with a red blush. The flesh is clear yellow and juicy, with flavour that is fair to good, "fully satisfactory for the season." The flesh is nonbrowning and does not adhere to the pit when fully ripe. There are a few split pits. It is recom-

mended by Layne.

'Harson': Released from Harrow in 1982, this attractive, yellow-fleshed peach ripens around mid-August. The fruit is medium to large, with a red blush on a yellow background. The flesh is slow to brown, firm, smooth, sweet and juicy. It is suitable for canning and freezing. The very productive trees have medium hardiness and are resistant to bacterial spot and brown rot. It is recommended by Layne.

'Loring': This Missouri introduction has tender buds and blooms very early, but the large, freestone fruit, yellow with a bright red blush, is of high quality. 'Loring' is less cold-hardy than 'Redhaven,' not recommended for marginal places. The flesh browns easily. It ripens about 15 days after 'Redhaven.' Sherk notes: "Early September, the best. I bought some the size of grapefruit last September."

'Q 1-8': Benowitz's second choice, this unnamed, leaf curl-resistant release from the experiment station at Mount Vernon, Washington, has sweet flesh that is white and semifreestone. The fruit ripens in early August on the West Coast. Crops are moderate but dependable. Benowitz writes, "Great for fresh eating."

'Redhaven': The standard early-midseason peach in North America, this Michigan cultivar ripens August 17 in Geneva, New York, and Vineland, Ontario; August 20 in Massachusetts; September 1 in the Maritimes. The red-skinned fruit is large and freestone; the flesh is yellow, firm, juicy and nonbrowning. The trees are hardy and productive. The crop ripens unevenly and must be picked several times. Quamme recommends it for midseason. Craig writes: " 'Redhaven' is the only peach that I make a point of obtaining. It is one of the hardier cultivars, good for freezing, has fewer split pits and thus fewer earwig problems."

'Reliance': Developed at the University of New Hampshire, this peach has unusual bud hardiness and has cropped after winter temperatures of minus 25 degrees F (-32 °C). The trees are very productive, generally requiring heavy thinning. The fruit is medium-sized, with greenish yellow skin and juicy, freestone flesh that browns when cut and is not as tasty as the 'Redhaven' types. The fruit ripens just before 'Redhaven.' Craig writes: "Tends to bear fruit when other cultivars are winter-injured." Quamme and Sherk also recommend it for cold areas.

'Veteran': Even hardier than 'Reliance,' this very productive cultivar, released from Vineland, Ontario, in 1928, produces large, medium-quality, yellow-skinned fruit that ripens about three weeks after 'Reliance.' The yellow, soft, freestone flesh browns when cut. An important variety in the British Columbia interior, it is recommended by Quamme only for places where other types will not thrive.

'Vivid': Released from Vineland in 1974, 'Vivid' has bright red, very attractive, high-quality fruit. The productive, vigorous trees, with average hardiness, yield large, almost three-inch, medium-to-dark red fruits about five days after 'Redhaven.' The freestone flesh is nonbrowning and is considered fair to good for canning and good for freezing. Quamme recommends it for late season.

NECTARINES

'Earliblaze': A cultivar of Stark Bros. Nurseries in Missouri, sometimes called 'Stark Earliblaze,' this medium-hardy tree is rated not very productive in Geneva, New York, but productive in protected parts of the Maritimes. The medium-sized red fruit is oval, with good-quality, semiclingstone, yellow flesh that is nonbrowning and has a sweet, mild flavour. Quamme recommends it.

'Fantasia': A late-season California nectarine that produces attractive fruit, bright red over a vivid yellow undercolour. The fruit is of high quality, freestone, medium to large, with large pits. Hardiness is average, and the tree is susceptible to bacterial leaf spot. Quamme recommends it.

'Hardired': Released from Harrow in 1974, this nectarine ripens about five days after 'Redhaven' peach. It is the hardiest of all nectarines tested at Harrow, although not as hardy as 'Cherokee' in tests at Geneva. The buds are about as hardy as those of 'Reliance' peach. The medium-sized trees are very productive, so fruit must be thinned to size properly. Fruit is smallish but attractive and red, with good-quality, freestone flesh that is yellow and firm. The tree is tolerant of bacterial spot and brown rot. Quamme and Craig recommend it.

'Harko': Released from Harrow in 1974, this hardy nectarine, recommended by Craig, ripens just after 'Redhaven' peach. The smallish, good-quality, red-skinned fruit is semiclingstone, with yellow, nonbrowning flesh. The tree is medium-sized, spreading and productive. Flower buds are slightly hardier than those of 'Redhaven' peach. It is tolerant of bacterial spot and brown rot. The crop requires careful thinning to attain full size. It is recommended by Craig and by Benowitz, who notes: "The best nectarine choice for our area."

The experts who were asked to recommend cultivars for their own area:

Sam Benowitz, owner, Raintree Nursery, Morton, Washington (USDA climatic zone 8).

William E. Craig, tree-fruit specialist, Agriculture Canada Research Station, Kentville, Nova Scotia (Agriculture Canada climatic zone 6a; USDA zone 6a).

Dr. Richard C. Layne, head, Horticultural Science Section, Agriculture Canada Research Station, Harrow, Ontario (Agriculture Canada climatic zone 7a; USDA zone 6a).

William G. Lord, extension specialist (fruit), University of New Hampshire, Durham, New Hampshire (USDA climatic zone 5b).

Dr. Harvey Quamme, research scientist, Agriculture Canada Research Station, Summerland, British Columbia (Agriculture Canada climatic zone 6; USDA zone 6a).

Lawrence C. Sherk, formerly with Agriculture Canada, now chief horticulturist of Sheridan Nurseries, Georgetown, Ontario (Agriculture Canada climatic zone 6a; USDA zone 5b).

Harvest Dates
Peaches and Nectarines

The range of dates refers to the approximate beginning of the harvest in the most popular fruit-bearing areas of the north.

Harbinger	July 15-25
Harrow Diamond	July 25-Aug. 5
Garnet Beauty	July 30-Aug. 10
Early Redhaven	July 30-Aug. 10
Harbelle	July 30-Aug. 10
Earliblaze nect.	Aug. 5-20
Reliance	Aug. 10-15
Redhaven	Aug. 10-25
Harken	Aug. 15-25
Harbrite	Aug. 15-25
Harson	Aug. 15-25
Vivid	Aug. 15-25
Harko nect.	Aug. 15-30
Hardired nect.	Aug. 15-30
Harrow Beauty	Aug. 25-Sept. 5
Loring	Aug. 25-Sept. 5
Veteran	Sept. 1-10
Harcrest	Sept. 5-20
Fantasia nect.	Sept. 5-20

FRUIT SO DESIRABLE

*"This tree is so hardy in all parts
of the country, and the fruit is so
desirable for the table and for
preserving, that we might expect its
general cultivation."*

— W.C. STRONG, *Fruit Culture*, 1885

The magic of sun and time
will turn a glorious crop of
plum blossoms into fruits
that may be large, small,
sweet or sour, depending
upon species and cultivar.
Plums come in a greater
variety of sizes, shapes and
colours than any other fruit.

Plums, prunes and cherry plums

A plum is very much like a cherry, except that a plum tends to be bigger and its pit is flat. Those small differences are worth stating at the outset of this chapter, because members of the genus *Prunus* are a friendly lot and certain plums and cherries are apt to commingle. Another notable fact about plums is that there are probably more species native to North America than to all the rest of the world. This does not mean that native plums dominate our gardens and orchards. That role falls to species whose forebears were selected and bred in Europe. What it does mean is that some plums are naturally adapted to the rigours of the north and that plums are so variable, one species from another, they might as well be different fruits, like plums and cherries. In short, as W.C. Strong said a century ago, there are plums for everyone.

The European plums (*Prunus domestica*), which derive from species native to Eurasia, include the common oval blue or purple prune plums that ripen after 'McIntosh' apples in September and October. There are also a few other types highly regarded in Europe but relative rarities in North America: the so-called damsons (*P. insititia*), small, tart purple plums that make delectable preserves, and the small yellow greengages, described as "celestial" by British gardener Hugh Johnson (their name comes from Sir William Gage, who brought that fruit to England from France, where they are called Reine Claude plums). 'Mirabelles,' too, are small, round and sweet. As a group, the Europeans have less juicy flesh than other plums. The prune plums are not only meaty but also so sweet that they will dry successfully even with their pits intact, a quality which endeared them to early civilizations with limited means of food preservation.

Because of their good quality, flavour and sweetness, European plums are still the varieties of choice in North American orchards, especially on the West Coast. Harvey Quamme of the Agriculture Canada Research Station in Summerland, British Columbia, says: "I prefer the European plum. It is good fresh if it is tree-ripe and is better for preserves and in cooking than the Japanese plum." Fortunately, some are also fairly hardy, compared with other stone fruits. I grow a 'Fellenberg' and a 'Mount Royal' in my climatic-zone-5 garden. The fruit buds of Europeans may, however, be injured at temperatures of minus 15 to minus 20 degrees F (-26° to -29°C).

A bonus for city gardeners is that some

types of European plums are self-pollinating, such as 'Mount Royal,' 'Oneida,' 'Damson' and 'Stanley.' Others will set adequate fruit on their own, but cross-fertilization will result in larger, more consistent crops. The European plum is hexaploid, so it will not cross-pollinate with the diploid Japanese plum.

The Japanese plum (*Prunus salicina*), actually a native of China, is a more recent arrival in North America, having been brought to California a little over a century ago. These plums are best known for their roundish shape and soft, watery red or yellow flesh that is sweet near the skin but often sour at the pit. The fruits are usually clingstone and two or three inches across, with yellow, gold, red or black skin. The usual large-fruited selections and hybrids bloom earlier than the Europeans, so they are more vulnerable to frost damage. They are also somewhat more tender, being best suited to climatic zone 6 or warmer. Fruit buds may be injured at temperatures of minus 10 to minus 15 degrees F (-23° to -26°C). Another drawback for home gardeners is that the species requires cross-pollination, but this can be accomplished not only by other Japanese types or hybrids but also by American natives.

Plums, prunes and cherry plums

The Japanese plum is best known for its roundish shape and soft, watery red or yellow flesh that is sweet near the skin but often sour at the pit. The fruits are usually clingstone and two or three inches across, with yellow, gold, red or black skin. Most bloom earlier than the European plums.

Most Japanese plums ripen before 'McIntosh' apples, from July until mid-September.

Prunus simonii, a Chinese hybrid of *P. salicina* and apricot, is a short-lived tree known as a plumcot. It has been used in a few North American breeding programs to produce small, hardy fruits, such as 'Kahinta' and 'LaCrescent,' with a definite apricot flavour.

The third relatively distinct group of plums consists of the North Americans, including the only two species native to Canada: Canada plum (*Prunus nigra*) and American plum (*P. americana*), a thick-skinned type. The fruits of North American natives tend to be smaller than the others and watery like the Japanese plums, but many are delicious. They were valued by the indigenous people from coast to coast long before the Europeans arrived. The plums Jacques Cartier recorded seeing in native canoes on his first voyage up the St. Lawrence River in 1534 were undoubtedly *P. nigra.* Another species, the beach plum (*P. maritima*), is sold by some nurseries. Hardy to zone 4, it bears small, deep purple fruit on thorny shrubs. Like other wild fruits, seedling plums are variable in size, fruit quality and such, but cultivated varieties have been devel-

oped, especially from *P. nigra,* and these, of course, have the advantage of predictability. In 1920, E.O. Wilson, noted Harvard botanist and plant explorer, wrote, "A century hence, these American plums will probably be in the first rank among stone fruits of this country."

In fact, a limited number of breeding programs, mostly in difficult climatic areas such as South Dakota and Manitoba, have focused on native plums. Cultivars hardy enough for the prairies are the result of either selections from native species—*Prunus nigra* selections include 'Bounty' and 'Norther'—or selections from hardy, small-fruited strains of *P. salicina,* such as the 'Ptitsin' series and 'Ivanovka,' brought from Manchuria during this century. In areas with very cold winters, these plums are worth a try. After severe winters, they will die back to the ground but will rebound vigorously in spring. Then there is always the possibility that their blossoms will be injured by late-spring frosts. John Davidson of the Agriculture Canada Research Station in Beaverlodge, Alberta, says, "In this part of the world, plum growing is strictly for fun."

Somewhat less hardy than the native selections but nevertheless tougher than the Jap-

Plums, prunes and cherry plums

The beach plum (*Prunus maritima*) is a North American native shrub that is hardy to zone 4 and bears small, deep purple fruits that vary in sweetness from plant to plant.

anese or Europeans are Japanese-American hybrids, sometimes called simply hybrid plums in catalogues. The species hybridize readily, the Japanese parent contributing larger fruit size and the American offering greater hardiness and disease resistance. Breeding at Ottawa to produce new hardy hybrids has involved crosses of Japanese plums with both Canada and American plums. These hybrids often retain the Japanese habit of needing only a short rest period, so they are apt to bloom at the first hint of warm spring weather and thus will not produce full crops in places with fluctuating winter temperatures. None are self-fruitful—crosses between different species generally produce poor pollen—so a Japanese or American cultivar must be planted nearby to ensure pollination. 'Toka' is sometimes recommended as a pollinator for all of the hybrids. For late-blooming types, such as 'Brookred' and 'Pembina,' sand cherries can be used as pollinators.

An interesting group of hardy plums consists of sand cherry x Japanese plum hybrids, known as cherry plums, which bear fruit about an inch wide but with the quality of a plum. The flesh may be green ('Opata,' 'Compass'), yellow ('Convoy,' 'Minnesota 40,' 'Claude Bugnet') or red ('Dura,' 'Manor,' 'Sapa,' 'Sapalta'). The trees tend to be smallish, even shrublike, usually less than 10 feet tall and therefore ideal for small gardens, especially as they are also decorative in bloom and

may be somewhat self-fertile. Cherry plums will pollinate one another if planted no more than eight feet apart, or pollination can be ensured by planting sand cherries close by. Like Japanese-American hybrids, these shrubs are best suited to climatic areas where winters may be relatively cold but are consistent until a slow, steady thaw in spring. They are resistant to drought and are hardier than most other cultivated plums, although less hardy than sand cherries and some of the American plum selections. Like all fruits, they fare best in sheltered places. Irene Wallace, manager of Beaverlodge Nurseries, northwest of Edmonton, Alberta (climatic zone 2), says that although cherry plums produce only sporadically for her, "some more favoured locations with lighter soils, such as along the major river valleys, have fair success with 'Opata' and 'Manor' cherry plums and with 'Ptitsin' and 'Dandy' plums." She adds: "Plums and cherry plums are very unpredictable in this area. Often, they set fruit and make good growth until late August, when they are just beginning to ripen; then our nights get cooler and longer, and they just sit there and do not progress any further." In places warmer than zone 2, however, these hardy plums do have time to ripen before frost.

Hardiness is the first quality to consider when choosing a plum: the toughest American selections for the coldest places, cherry plums and American hybrids for those a little less severe, then the Europeans and, in the warmest places, the large-fruited Japanese. The Japanese are the most tolerant of heat, but no plums thrive in tropical conditions.

Unlike other members of the genus *Prunus*, plums will tolerate rich, even heavy soil, as long as it is well drained. The site should be sunny or mostly sunny, preferably slightly sloping and protected from prevailing winds. The European types may require some thinning, especially of suckers and water sprouts, but other than that, little pruning should be done after the first couple of years, because the fruit is produced on vigorous spurs at least two years old, not on new shoots. Japanese types fruit on year-old shoots and older spurs. These and the Americans and hybrids need heavier pruning than the Europeans. Plums and cherry plums tend to send up suckers, which should be cut off at the base. (See pages 15 to 20 for planting and pruning directions.)

Plums grow into pleasant smallish-to-middle-sized trees, even shrubs in the case of the

American natives. The standard rootstock for European trees is the myrobalan plum (*Prunus cerasifera*), a small-fruited native of the Caucasus and Turkestan areas used by Balkan peasants to make a rough plum brandy called slibowitz. The tree's rootstock produces a full-sized, hardy tree. St. Julien, a *P. insititia* plum whose roots produce a semidwarf tree, can be used for European and Japanese trees, as can a St. Julien strain, 'Pixy,' which produces half-sized trees that are very susceptible to drought and, in the north, are best suited to containers only. A hardy rootstock for American hybrids is *P. americana. Prunus besseyi* produces dwarf American hybrids that require staking, and seedlings of Nanking cherry (*P. tomentosa*) can also be used by home gardeners wishing to experiment. Agriculture Canada recommends that for the prairies, seedlings of hardy plums such as 'Norther' or 'Bounty' and seedlings of Nanking cherry be used. Prairie trees should be planted with the graft union several inches below the soil surface to anchor the root system securely.

The most severe disease of plums, especially Europeans, is black knot, which produces large black tumours that girdle branches and kill the wood beyond them. The best time to control black knot is while the trees are dormant in winter, when a sulphur spray can be used (see pages 38 and 39); but if the infection has taken hold, prune several inches below any knots on branches or an inch into healthy tissue around knots on the trunk. These knots are the source of spores that spread the infection. If other plums are growing in the area, you may choose to cut down the infected tree as a control measure. Also, wild plums and cherries within 600 feet of cultivated trees should be cut down or at least closely watched for knots, as they are carriers of the disease.

Brown rot, which is most troublesome on Japanese plums and their hybrids, is a fungal disease that quickly rots ripe fruit. Damp weather helps it spread. Prune to encourage air circulation through the tree, thin the fruit, and remove and destroy any diseased fruit as soon as you spot it. Clean away all fallen fruit and leaves from around the tree throughout the season.

The worst pest is the plum curculio, a dark brown, quarter-inch beetle that makes crescent-shaped incisions in which it lays one egg per fruit. When the egg hatches, the larva bores to the pit. The best way to combat the curculio is by shaking the branches when the

Plums, prunes and cherry plums

Cherry plums such as 'Opata,' left, are hybrids of Japanese plums and sand cherries that are worthy of notice because they are very hardy and their fruits are sweet and prolific, although only about an inch wide.

beetles are first sighted and continuing daily until no more appear on a blanket spread underneath the tree.

Curculio damage contributes to the falling of some fruit during late spring, a process known as June drop. Further hand-thinning may be required so that fruits hang about four to six inches apart. Otherwise, heavy harvests leave trees vulnerable to fungal diseases and winter damage and lower the likelihood of a good crop the following year.

If tended properly, plums should begin to bear fruit in three to five years. A standard European tree might yield five bushels of fruit, a hardy bush-sized species one. Harvest plums when they are fully ripe, at which time they will fall into your hand when slightly twisted. For cooking, the European types are best, while the Japanese and native plums are best eaten fresh. Pit before canning, because the pits can release cyanic acid.

Plums are not likely to overtake apples as the favourite fruit of northern gardeners, so closely attached are we to that other hardy and generous tree. But there are so many kinds with so many useful and attractive qualities that plums deserve a place in almost every orchard.

Because there are so many cultivars, I asked a group of North American fanciers to recommend their favourite trees, ones they would choose for a small dream orchard in their own climatic area. As you read through the list, take note of the climatic zone and geographic area of each sponsor and compare it with your own, as you will likely have the greatest success with plums, prunes and cherry plums that have been found superlative in your own growing conditions.

EUROPEAN

'Bluefré': Vigorous trees of this Missouri variety produce an abundance of large blue, freestone prune plums of fair quality in September. The fruit hangs well on the tree after ripening, although many split pits are produced. Thinning is usually required. Craig recommends it.

'Fellenberg,' or 'Italian Prune': This European heirloom, perhaps two centuries old, has long been valued for fresh eating and for drying. The oval, dusky purple fruit has firm freestone flesh that is sweet, juicy and delicious, although it oxidizes quickly when cut. It is best allowed to mature on the tree and will hang for about two weeks in good condition after it ripens in September. The trees are self-fruitful and grow best in zones 5 to 7. It is recommended by Sherk and Benowitz.

'Iroquois': 'Fellenberg' is one of the parents of this freestone prune plum released from Geneva, New York, in 1966. It ripens about a week before 'Stanley' on a medium-sized tree that is self-fruitful and very productive. The fruit is considered just fair for fresh eating but good for canning. Recommended by Sherk.

'Mount Royal': A mysterious tree discovered thriving in Montreal, Quebec, it is described by Olsen as "the hardiest prune plum, even possible for trial in zone 3b. It has produced fruit in Thunder Bay." The fruit, which is blue with yellow clingstone flesh, will hang on the tree about two weeks when ripe without much deterioration. Hall-Beyer recommends it for zone 5.

'Seneca': One of the parents of this 1972 Geneva cultivar is 'Fellenberg,' which 'Seneca' beats to the harvest by about two weeks. It bears large, reddish blue, freestone fruit on a vigorous, upright tree. The fruit is resistant to cracking. Benowitz recommends it, noting, "It has proved one of the best European plums in the Mount Vernon [Washington] tests."

'Stanley': The most popular prune plum in the northeast, this 1926 release from Geneva bears large blue fruit that is inferior to 'Fellenberg' in sweetness and quality, but the flesh does not oxidize quickly, and the trees are superior in crop consistency and size. In fact, crops benefit from thinning. Trees are self-fertile, vigorous and bear around early September. 'Stanley' is very susceptible to black knot. Craig, Layne, Sherk and Quamme recommend it, the last noting, "Old standard. Good quality."

'Valor': This purple prune plum, released from Vineland, Ontario, in 1967, has larger fruit and bigger crops and comes into bearing earlier than 'Fellenberg.' The semicling fruits have greenish flesh and are of excellent quality. The variety is not self-fruitful but can be pollinated by 'Fellenberg,' 'Stanley' or 'Verity.' It is very susceptible to black knot. Layne recommends it, and Hall-Beyer suggests it for zone 5. Quamme notes: "Medium-large blue European plum; quality excellent."

'Verity': This good-quality freestone plum, released from Vineland in 1967, has dark purple, orange-fleshed fruit that ripens at the same time as 'Fellenberg' but is more plentiful. The tree is not self-fruitful but can be pollinated by 'Iroquois,' 'Fellenberg,' 'Stanley' or 'Valor.' Layne recommends it, as does Quamme, who writes: "Medium-sized plum of good quality. Productive."

JAPANESE AND HYBRIDS

'Brookgold': This is a *Prunus salicina* but much hardier than the usual Japanese plum, because it originated from a parent seedling collected in Manchuria. 'Brookgold,' released from Brooks, Alberta, in 1980, bears golden, freestone, blushed fruit that resembles 'La-Crescent,' but yields are better. The tree is medium-sized and moderately vigorous. It blooms early, and fruit ripens in mid-August. Submitted by Vick, it is recommended for zone 3 by Hall-Beyer. Olsen writes: "Medium-sized, only fair-quality fruit, but the tree is very hardy. This is the best yellow plum for zone 2."

'Brookred': Another hardy *P. salicina*, this one is a seedling of the variety 'Ivanovka' released from Brooks in 1962. The tree is large, upright, spreading and a moderate producer of fruit which ripens in late August. It is good fresh and excellent for jam. Olsen notes: "Medium-sized, good-quality red fruit with red flesh. The tree is very hardy."

European or prune plums have flesh that is very sweet and somewhat dry but is well suited to fresh eating as well as to canning or drying. 'Stanley,' left, is a New York release that is the most popular plum in the northeast. It is self-fertile, and its crops are consistently large.

'Burbank': Introduced by the U.S. Department of Agriculture in 1893 in honour of Luther Burbank, this clingstone has maintained its popularity because of its large crops of attractive, dark red fruit with good flavour for fresh eating or canning. 'Burbank' ripens unevenly, beginning around late August or early September. The crop may need thinning. The trees are low-growing, flat-topped and somewhat drooping, prolific and hardy to zone 5. It can be pollinated by 'Early Golden.' Craig recommends it.

'Early Golden': This Canadian seedling of 'Shiro' or 'Burbank' was first marketed in Ontario in 1946 and is still highly regarded, especially for the earliness of its fruit. In Vineland, it ripens around July 31, the first of all plums, about two weeks earlier than 'Shiro,' although its freestone fruit, yellow with a red blush, is somewhat smaller. The trees are very vigorous, with a biennial habit that may be discouraged by careful thinning. It requires several pickings and is a good pollinator for 'Burbank.' Layne and Sherk recommend it.

'Elite': This 1960 *P. salicina* x *P. nigra* hybrid from the University of Saskatchewan is very hardy, worth a try in sheltered corners of zone 2. Its dark red, juicy fruit, almost two inches wide, has excellent flavour. Hall-Beyer recommends it for zone 3.

'Ember': Best for zones 3 and 4, 'Ember' produces moderate yields of cling fruit that ripen around early September. Olsen says, "Large yellow fruit with orange flesh (hence the name) and very good flavour."

'Kaga,' 'Kahinta': Released from South Dakota around the turn of the century, these *P. americana* x *P. simonii* hybrids produce large crops of small plumcots with crimson skin and golden clingstone flesh that is firm with a sweet, aromatic flavour. " 'Kahinta' takes forever to begin to bear," cautions Hall-Beyer, who nevertheless recommends it for zone 4. Olsen says: "*Prunus simonii* in their parentage gives these cultivars a delicious flavour not present in most plums."

'LaCrescent': Released from the University of Minnesota in 1923, this plumcot, a hybrid of 'Shiro' and 'Howard Yellow,' is hardy to zone 3. The fruit, which ripens in late August, resembles an inch-wide apricot in appearance and flavour. The tree is very vigorous but slow to begin bearing, and yields are modest. Davidson and Osborne recommend it.

'Santa Rosa,' right, is a century-old heritage variety that is still popular because of its large crops of red fruit in mid-August. An added attraction is self-fertility, which is relatively uncommon among Japanese varieties.

'**Ozark Premier**': This very large, bright red, excellent-quality clingstone was released from Missouri in 1946. The fruit ripens unevenly and about the same time as 'Burbank.' Craig and Layne recommend it, as does Hall-Beyer, who suggests it for zone 5. Lord says, "Produces a beautiful, large, flavourful plum in southern New Hampshire." Quamme notes: "Good-quality Japanese plum. Not self-fruitful."

'**Patterson's Pride**': Released from the University of Saskatchewan in 1960, this *P. nigra* x *P. salicina* hybrid is hardy to zone 2. The red fruit has excellent quality and "keeps till December," says Hall-Beyer. The dwarf, very productive trees have an attractive weeping habit. Osborne recommends the cultivar, noting in his catalogue: "Stake for the first two years to get a good central stem established. A favourite with us." Olsen writes: "A good selection for limited space. Good-quality fruit."

'**Pembina**': The oldest variety still recommended by Saskatchewan Agriculture, this hybrid of *P. nigra* and *P. salicina* was released from Brookings, South Dakota, in 1917. The deep red fruit with bright yellow flesh, which ripens in late August, is good fresh and fair for canning. Davidson recommends it, and Quamme observes: "Noteworthy quality for the Prairies."

'**Perfection**': Released from the University of Saskatchewan in 1960, this hybrid of *P. nigra* and *P. salicina* is hardy to zone 2. It has good-quality fruits more than an inch wide with dark red skin and yellow flesh. Submitted by Vick and recommended by Olsen, who notes: "Large red fruit; very good flavour."

'**Plum Parfait**': A plumcot with apricot-sized fruit that has pinkish skin and amber, freestone flesh. The semidwarf tree is self-fruitful. It is recommended by Lord, who says: "Not a reliable cropper under New Hampshire

conditions, but the few fruits that develop are superb. They are firm, extremely flavourful and hold their quality for several weeks. They ripen September 15 in southern New Hampshire. Early bloom and frost damage are the primary problems."

'**Ptitsin #5**,' '**Ptitsin #9**': Released from Morden, Manitoba, in 1939, these are selections from a *P. salicina* seedling of Manchurian origin. '#5' has light green flesh that is good for jam and green skin which turns yellow when fully ripe. It is somewhat less hardy than 'Ptitsin #9,' which has inch-wide fruit with red-orange skin and yellow flesh that is sweet and juicy, good for jam. Osborne recommends '#5,' and Hall-Beyer recommends '#9' for zone 3.

'**Santa Rosa**': One of Luther Burbank's cultivars, this century-old plum is still popular because of prolific crops of large red fruit that surpass 'Burbank' in quality. Trees begin to bear early, blossoms are relatively hardy, and fruit matures in mid-August. An added attraction is self-fertility, although the tree sets more fruit in the company of other Japanese or hybrid plums. Quamme notes: "Attractive, with good fruit size."

'**Shiro**': A chance seedling introduced by Luther Burbank in 1898, this round, yellow, 1½-inch plum with a pink blush has clingstone, sweet, very juicy flesh described as "exquisitely flavourful" by Hall-Beyer, who recommends it for zone 5. It ripens around mid-August. Craig and Benowitz also recommend it. Benowitz writes: "The most reliable of the Japanese plums and among our favourites. It is ridiculously juicy. Be sure to bend over when eating one, or wear a bib."

'**Superb**': Released from the University of Saskatchewan in 1960, this *P. nigra* x *P. salicina* hybrid bears medium-sized, good-quality fruit with yellow to red skin and light yellow flesh. It is worth a try in zone 2, although Hall-Beyer recommends it for zone 3, noting, "Keeps several months."

'**Tecumseh**': This 1918 hybrid of 'Shiro' and 'Surprise' from Brookings, South Dakota, is notable for the relatively large size of its bright red fruit and its good flavour when eaten fresh. It ripens in mid-August. Davidson and Osborne recommend it, as does Hall-Beyer, who suggests it for zone 3.

NORTH AMERICAN

'**Bounty**': So hardy that it is rated to zone 1, this *P. nigra* 'Assiniboine' selection, released from Morden, Manitoba, in 1936, ripens its dark red fruit in late August. The skin is slightly bitter, but the orange-yellow flesh is fair when fresh and good for canning. Davidson recommends it.

'Norther': A slightly less hardy sister of 'Bounty' released from Morden in 1943, 'Norther' ripens in early August. Bushes bear heavy annual crops of bright red fruit a little over an inch wide. It is hardy to zone 2. Submitted by Vick.

CHERRY PLUMS

'Manor': A larger-fruited version of 'Sapa' selected in Morden in 1945, with dark purple-red fruit a little wider than an inch, rated excellent for canning. Submitted by Vick and recommended by Olsen.

'Opata': A 1908 release from Brookings, this *P. besseyi* x 'Gold' hybrid has purple skin and yellowish green flesh rated good both for fresh eating and in preserves. The bushy tree, which will bear in its second year, is hardy in sheltered corners of zone 2b, although Irene Wallace writes from Beaverlodge, Alberta: "Against the south side of our house, we have one tree of 'Opata' that produced a good crop last year, but it does so only sporadically." Submitted by Vick and recommended by Davidson.

'Sapa': Also from South Dakota in 1908, this *P. besseyi* x *P. salicina* hybrid has dark purple fruit slightly smaller than that of 'Manor.' The greenish semiclingstone flesh is rated just fair for fresh eating but is considered excellent for canning and jam, "even better than 'Damson,' " note the authors of *Fruit Tree Cultivars in British Columbia*. 'Sapa' is recommended by Davidson and Olsen.

'Sapalta': A 1941 *P. besseyi* x *P. salicina* hybrid from Brooks, Alberta, 'Sapalta' has inch-wide, nearly freestone fruit with glossy, dark purple skin and sweet, juicy purple flesh. Self-fruitful bushes often bear the first year after planting and are dependable producers in zones 5 to 8. Olsen recommends it.

The experts who were asked to recommend cultivars for their own area:

Sam Benowitz, owner, Raintree Nursery, Morton, Washington (USDA climatic zone 8).

William E. Craig, tree-fruit specialist, Agriculture Canada Research Station, Kentville, Nova Scotia (Agriculture Canada climatic zone 6a; USDA zone 6a).

Harvest Dates
plums

The range of dates refers to the approximate beginning of the harvest in the most popular fruit-bearing areas of the north.

Early Golden	July 25-Aug. 5
Shiro	Aug. 5-15
Santa Rosa	Aug. 10-20
Ozark Premier	Aug. 25-Sept. 5
Burbank	Aug. 25-Sept. 5
Mount Royal	Aug. 25-Sept. 5
Stanley	Sept. 10-25
Bluefre	Sept. 10-25
Fellenberg	Sept. 10-30
Valor	Sept. 10-30
Verity	Sept. 10-30

Dr. Campbell Davidson, research scientist, Agriculture Canada Research Station, Morden, Manitoba (Agriculture Canada climatic zone 3b; USDA zone 3b).

Bart Hall-Beyer, owner, Sursum Corda, Scotstown, Quebec (Agriculture Canada climatic zone 4a; USDA zone 4a).

Dr. Richard C. Layne, head, Horticultural Science Section, Agriculture Canada Research Station, Harrow, Ontario (Agriculture Canada climatic zone 7a; USDA zone 6a).

William G. Lord, extension specialist (fruit), University of New Hampshire, Durham, New Hampshire (USDA climatic zone 5b).

Paul Olsen, owner, Roseberry Gardens, Thunder Bay, Ontario (Agriculture Canada climatic zone 3a; USDA zone 4a).

Bob Osborne, owner, Corn Hill Nursery, Petitcodiac, New Brunswick (Agriculture Canada zone 4b; USDA zone 4b).

Dr. Harvey Quamme, research scientist, Agriculture Canada Research Station, Summerland, British Columbia (Agriculture Canada climatic zone 6; USDA zone 6a).

Lawrence C. Sherk, formerly with Agriculture Canada, now chief horticulturist of Sheridan Nurseries, Georgetown, Ontario (Agriculture Canada climatic zone 6a; USDA zone 5b).

Roger Vick, curator, Devonian Botanic Garden, Edmonton, Alberta. Vick submitted the preferences of Sprout Farms, a family-owned business specializing in fruit trees in Bon Accord, Alberta (Agriculture Canada climatic zone 3a; USDA zone 3a).

Irene Wallace, owner, Beaverlodge Nurseries, Beaverlodge, Alberta (Agriculture Canada climatic zone 2; USDA zone 2).

PERFUMED FLAVOURS

*"On several accounts, the pear pos-
sesses advantages over other fruits.
The first is its delicious quality, as
found in the finest varieties—its buttery or melting texture, and its delicious and perfumed flavour. In this
respect, it greatly excels the apple and
keeps nearly as well. Even the peach
is scarcely superior, while it lasts only
two or three days."*

—J.J. THOMAS, *The Illustrated Annual Register
of Rural Affairs,* 1859

Standard pears are large
trees, about 25 feet wide
and at least as tall. Related
to the apple and almost as
hardy, pears are less
frequently grown than
apples in North America
only because of their
susceptibility to one fatal
disease, fire blight.

It sounds, from Thomas's description, as though the pear is the perfect fruit. Anyone who has tasted a ripe 'Bartlett' with a chaser of a wedge of Camembert will agree. The elegant "buttery texture" and "perfumed flavour" of ripe pears have been beloved in western Europe for generations. But Thomas goes on to admit that "the pear, like everything highly desirable and valuable, cannot be had without attention, labour and skill." In fact, no other fruit is so limited by its susceptibility to just one disease. Seldom do orchardists speak of pears in the north without talking in the same breath about a bacterial disease called fire blight.

This does not mean that pears are impossible to grow. Pears are the second most popular tree crop in the world. This statistic is bolstered by an enormous production in China of what North Americans call Oriental, Asian, apple or sand pears. Nashi is the Japanese name for them. The Asian pears have been cultivated in China for thousands of years. Egg-shaped or flattened like apples, they have greenish to orange, golden or bronze skin and flesh that is firm, juicy and gritty. This "sand" consists of stone cells, which are short, squarish and thick-walled—a detriment, some think, but the Asians have a great advantage in their resistance to fire blight. Asian pears are probably all derived from the species *Pyrus serotina*, which has been crossed with the European pear to produce cultivars such as 'Kieffer' and 'LeConte.'

Like all pears, the Asian pears are pome fruits. Most botanists divide the rose family, Rosaceae, into four subfamilies, two of which contain all of the popular northern tree fruits. The subfamily Pyroideae, or Pomoideae, includes apples, pears and quinces, all of which are pomes (fruits that have cores). The fleshy, edible part of a pome is the floral cup that expands after the blossom is fertilized. The thin, papery layer around the core, enclosing the seeds, is the ovary wall. The subfamily Prunoideae produces fruits called drupes, such as cherries, plums, apricots and peaches.

The European pear (*Pyrus communis*) boasts the familiar pear shape, known as pyriform, and a texture usually described as melting or buttery, as J.J. Thomas notes in this chapter's opening quotation. There are far fewer stone cells in the flesh of the best of these pears. In fact, many of the heirlooms, such as 'Anjou' and 'Bosc,' originally had the French word *beurre* (butter) as part of their name: 'Beurre Bosc,' 'Beurre d'Anjou.'

These pears are the result of the selection and hybridization of some five different species native to Europe and western Asia; the species name *communis* means "common" or "general." Many of the best cultivars of European pears, some of them still highly esteemed, originated in France and Belgium; however, until a century ago, the British valued the pear not for fresh fruit but for its mellow version

Most European pears have the familiar shape technically known as pyriform and a texture usually described as melting or buttery, in contrast to the more crisp and watery texture of Asian species.

The petals of pear blossoms will fall away after pollination, but if all goes well, the floral cup, or receptacle, will swell into edible flesh, leaving the calyx still visible on the bottom end of the fruit.

of cider, called perry. The tree was much admired as an ornamental as well, since it, like the apple, produces its fruit on spurs and so is amenable to being pruned to resemble a fan, a candelabrum or any of a number of two-dimensional shapes. Western Europeans found that if they grafted their pears to dwarfing rootstocks and trained them to grow against south-facing walls, the trees took up little space in small gardens while making the best use of the northern sunshine. (The espalier technique is described on page 25.)

Hardiness

European and Asian pears are most comfortable in commercial apple-orchard country, where temperatures do not fall much below minus 20 degrees F (-29°C). Lower temperatures may damage fruit buds and wood. The trees, which are thus best suited to climatic zones 6 through about 9 and perhaps sheltered spots in zone 4 or 5, may be injured even by warmer winters if the temperature drops suddenly or if the trees are not fully dormant at the time of the freeze.

That stated, it is essential to keep in mind that some European pears are hardier than others; 'Flemish Beauty,' once a leading commercial variety, is one of the hardiest, rated at zone 4 or 4b by Canadian fruit-tree nurseries. Cold hardiness is the most important priority for any northern gardener considering growing a pear. The list at the end of this chapter gives an indication of the relative hardiness of some favourite varieties. As is the case with apples, the rootstock has considerable bearing on hardiness. For suitable rootstocks, patronize nurseries in a climatic zone similar to your own. For gardens colder than those where *Pyrus communis* and *P. serotina* will thrive, there are new pears bred from hardy Asian species.

During this century, selections and hybrids have appeared that make use of the stone, Siberian, Ussurian or white pear (*Pyrus ussuriensis*), which is native to Manchuria and northern Korea, where winter temperatures below minus 35 degrees F (-37°C) are not uncommon. Not only can these pears survive winters on the prairies, but they have the added attraction of fire blight resistance. These selections would be perfect for the north if only the fruit were better. Described as "hardy and horrible" by one scientist, the fruit from most cultivars is best used for preserves or perry rather than for fresh eating.

In late July, I was standing under a huge Ussurian pear tree at the Agriculture Canada Experiment Station in Morden, Manitoba, when the station's director, Campbell Davidson, handed me a small green fruit and said, "I like to take my students out for pear tasting. They can't believe how awful they are. Feel this." I could not pierce the skin with a fingernail. "When they're ripe," he said, "they don't

Although somewhat like a pear, the related quince is not as commonly grown because it is less cold-hardy and is a tart fruit that tastes best when cooked and sweetened.

get much softer." Recently, however, the far better 'Ure,' whose *Pyrus communis* ancestry is evident, emerged from Morden. Davidson promises that it will soon be followed by an even more appealing hardy pear.

QUINCE

At the opposite end of the hardiness scale is a close relative of the pear, the quince (*Cydonia oblonga*), which can tolerate temperatures of only about minus 15 degrees F (-26°C). This pome fruit resembles a knobbly pear that turns yellow when ripe. The flesh has more stone cells than do European pears, and there are more seeds in the core. Like damson plums, quinces retain a devoted European following earned during an era before refrigerators, when cooking and sweetening was a reliable method of preservation. Cooked with sugar, the tough, sour flesh of the quince turns soft, pink and delicious and makes an excellent jam or jelly. The Greeks and Romans associated the quince with love, happiness and fruitfulness and dedicated it to Venus. More important for those northerners who might not pick fruit, the tree is very attractive, with

crooked branches. Although it tends to produce suckers from the trunk, it can be kept quite easily to a reasonable height of just 10 to 20 feet. Where it is hardy, it is one of the first trees to bloom in spring, producing its solitary pink flowers at the tips of new shoots. It is self-fruitful. The flowering quince (*Chaenomeles japonica*) produces small greenish fruit that also makes excellent jelly. Because of the lack of cold hardiness—most northern nurseries do not sell it—the quince will be given no further space here, although sources are listed at the end of this book.

FIRE BLIGHT

Quinces and European pears, and to a lesser extent other pears, are susceptible to fire blight, a North American disease that reached the British Isles and northern Europe just 40 years ago. "After hardiness, the greatest problem with pears is fire blight," says Campbell Davidson. A bacterial disease that also infects apples and a host of ornamentals, including mountain ash and hawthorn, fire blight is worst where the weather is wet and less troublesome in places too cold for pears to grow particularly well in any case. It is also less of a problem where the climate is dry, which is one reason most North American commercial pear orchards are in the arid valleys of the western states.

The bacteria that cause fire blight enter through blossoms, wounds or pruning cuts during the damp days of spring and work their way down through twigs and branches. Flowers and leaves near the tips suddenly wilt, turn brown or black and appear to have been scorched by fire—hence the name. Blackened new growth is often curled at the tip, a phenomenon known as shepherd's crook. As soon as blighted twigs are noticed, prune them at least 10 inches below the infected area, and burn the diseased growth. After each cut, sterilize the pruning tools in a solution of 10 percent bleach or 70 percent ethyl alcohol or denatured alcohol. To remove cankers on the trunk and branches—easiest to spot on sunny winter days as dark patches, to which blackened leaves may adhere—cut into healthy bark about four inches around the canker while the tree is dormant in midwinter. Disinfect the wound with household bleach.

There are various defences against fire blight, some of which are described on pages 38 and 39. Plant pears away from potential sources of infection, such as hawthorn and mountain ash. Fire blight, like scab, infects wet plants, so trickle-irrigate or water the ground under the trees instead of spraying the treetops. Keep cover crops mowed to reduce humidity and insect populations around the trees. Also, do not prune just prior to or during flowering, when the disease is most active; the bacteria can enter through pruning wounds. Trees that have been excessively pruned or heavily watered or fertilized are most susceptible. J.J. Thomas advises that if all else fails, "whenever one tree dies, plant out two more."

The summer I was in Morden came on the heels of just the sort of hard winter and wet spring that guarantees fire blight infections. In his office at the agricultural station, Campbell Davidson told a worried grower over the phone: "There's no good solution to fire blight. If you're going to prune it off, disinfect between each cut. If it's too severe an infection, it will just run its course." Davidson told me that there have been many attempts to develop fire blight resistance in European pears. "Every time you think you've got a resistant variety, you'll find a plant with fire blight."

R.C. Lamb of Geneva, New York, admits:

Some cultivars of pear can survive and bear fruit in places where winters are severe. The gardener beyond commercial pear country must choose cultivars carefully.

"We all know that fire blight is everywhere." His request for samples of resistant trees brought many replies, but all proved disappointingly susceptible in greenhouse experiments. In recent studies involving the U.S. Department of Agriculture pear-cultivar collection in Beltsville, Maryland, a paltry 9 of 522 cultivars remained disease-free after artificial and natural inoculation with the bacteria. Among those judged "highly susceptible" were many favourite varieties, such as 'Anjou,' 'Clapp's Favourite,' 'Bartlett' and even a sport called 'Blight Resistant Bartlett.' The most resistant varieties were virtual unknowns because of poor fruit quality, but the most blight-free of the better-known pears turned out to be 'Magness,' 'Ayers' and 'Moonglow.' Many of the newer pears, although not entirely free of blight, are more resistant than their forebears. Pear breeders consider the production of a blight-resistant tree a high priority. Asian pears are more resistant, the cultivars 'Shinko,' 'Va Li' and 'Shin Li' having excelled in experiments in Alabama.

POLLINATION

The next consideration for gardeners contemplating trying their hand at pears is that, like apples, most are not reliably self-pollinating. Among the Europeans, 'Seckel' is a notable exception. Almost any pear will pollinate almost any other, provided the two bloom at the same time. The late-blooming Asians will

Various pears
and quinces

Asian pears have juicier, crunchier flesh than European pears and are more resistant to fire blight. They are such an important fruit in the Orient that pears are the second largest tree crop in the world.

cross-pollinate with the early-blooming Europeans. If the spring weather is ideal, almost any tree may self-pollinate, but ideal springs are the exception in the north. It is better to grow two compatible pears, as the bees will choose almost any flower in preference to pear blossoms, whose nectar is low in sugar. The closer the trees are planted, to about 20 feet apart, the better the chances of adequate pollination and thus good fruit set. A few Asian cultivars are somewhat self-fertile.

European pears blossom around the same time as sour cherries — in late March or early April on the West Coast, as late as May in colder places. Asian pears bloom even earlier; the latest of these, such as 'Yakumo,' overlap with the earliest Europeans, such as 'Bartlett.' If frost follows, the crop may be diminished or destroyed. Although pear blossoms are less susceptible to frost damage than cherries and peaches, they will not produce dependable crops in places where the last spring frost comes after May 10. Unfortunately, the hardiest prairie pears bloom very early, so the farther north they grow, the more likely it is that they will suffer from spring frosts. John Davidson reports that in his northern Alberta

outpost at Beaverlodge, pears "don't usually have a crop, because they bloom three weeks earlier than apples and get hit by frost." In the nearby Beaverlodge Nurseries, owner Irene Wallace grows Ussurian pears as ornamentals only — a role for which, with their white blossoms and red fall leaves, they are well suited.

PESTS

The most serious pest of both pear and quince is the pear psylla, a small, aphidlike, sap-feeding insect that was accidentally introduced to the United States around 1832 and appeared in Canada by the turn of the century. Its feeding produces honeydew, a sticky substance that usually becomes mouldy, ruining the fruit. Also, the psylla weakens trees and spreads the mycoplasmic disease pear decline, which is a severe problem on the West Coast. Combat this pest by applying horticultural oil when the tree is dormant, watering only moderately and fertilizing little or not at all. Remove water sprouts and suckers, which attract the pests, and encourage ladybugs, which are natural predators. Several caterpillars can also be a nuisance to pears, but they can be kept under control with Bt, described on page 35. Russetted areas that develop where young fruit has been damaged are perfectly edible, as are the dark green to black spots caused by pear scab. They appear on susceptible varieties about 15 days after wet weather from May to August.

ROOTSTOCK

Another consideration in pear choice is rootstock. If you buy from a reputable nursery in your own climatic zone, the choice of rootstock will probably have been made for you, although some nurseries offer the buyer a selection. European seedlings, such as 'Bartlett,' are the most common rootstocks for orchards, resulting in trees that are vigorous and relatively hardy. For home growers, there are several additional possibilities. Corn Hill grafts their trees onto seedlings of *Pyrus ussuriensis*, as these roots are vigorous, resistant to fire blight and hardy, although they are very susceptible to pear decline. 'Old Home' x 'Farmingdale' hybrid rootstocks, which have the designation OHXF, provide predictable vigour and tree size. Quince is used frequently as a pear rootstock in areas that are not too cold, because it produces a dwarf tree which begins to bear three or four years after planting, as opposed to seven years or more on standard rootstocks. Trees on quince roots must be staked or otherwise supported. Quince roots are not compatible with many pear cultivars, such as 'Bartlett,' and in these cases, an interstem of another cultivar must be used.

When grafted to Asian pears, quince roots produce tiny trees, only about 5 percent the size of standard trees. Asian pears are more frequently grafted to the usual pear stocks or to other species such as *Pyrus calleryana*, a small-fruited central Chinese pear popular in North America as an ornamental.

Pears require deep, well-drained soil, preferably sandy loam. Plant and prune according to the directions on pages 14 to 19. Give the trees about an inch of water a week during dry weather in spring and summer. Paul Olsen of Thunder Bay, Ontario, writes that many prairie pears tend to be small in size "because the tree lacks water. If the tree is watered regularly, 'John' fruit can attain the size of 'Bartlett.' "

Standard European pears are large trees, about 25 feet wide and at least as tall. Asians are usually the same, although some cultivars may reach 40 feet. Pear trees tend to have an

upright structure, so branches will benefit from being trained downward. But they should not be bent more than 45 degrees from vertical, not only because the wood is brittle and can break easily but also because water sprouts may emerge from an exaggerated bend. Do not head back limbs, as that can make them grow more stiffly and more upright, resulting in branches which are not flexible enough to be weighted down by the crop. As pruning delays bearing, which is late in pears in any case, confine it to what is absolutely necessary. Another drawback of heavy pruning is that it encourages the tree to produce succulent growth, which is both susceptible to fire blight and attractive to the pear psylla. Prune lightly every year to keep the fruit spurs and fruiting wood in a healthy, vigorous condition.

Old, neglected pear trees may produce only very small fruit, because they suffer from being spur-bound; the tree becomes a mass of very slow-growing, dense, shady spurs. Such trees can be invigorated if some of the older spurs are removed. Also head back branches, and apply a little fertilizer in spring.

HARVEST

Pears ripen from August until October, depending upon climate and cultivar. A gardener may wait as long as 10 years to pick fruit from a standard-sized pear tree on roots other than quince; but once a healthy tree starts

Many of the most popular European pears are antique varieties that have been grown for at least a century. One is 'Bosc,' right, formerly called 'Beurre Bosc,' a late-ripening pear that is recommended by more of this book's experts than any other variety.

bearing, it is capable of continuing for decades. A standard-sized tree in good health can deliver about 15 bushels of fruit a year. When fruit does set, hand-thin the crop if it is heavy, because large crops encourage pears to settle into a pattern of biennial bearing. If cold weather arrives during the last month of ripening, premature ripening, called pink end, affects the fruit of some varieties, especially 'Bartlett.' The symptoms are early yellowing of fruit at the bottom (the calyx end) and accelerated softening. The fruit must be harvested and eaten at once, or it will quickly spoil.

Asian pears will ripen satisfactorily on the tree, but unlike other fruits, most varieties of European pears are best picked slightly green and allowed to ripen indoors. D.W. Beadle writes in *The Canadian Fruit, Flower and Kitchen Gardener* of 1875: "The best time for taking the fruit from the trees is usually indicated by a slight change in the colour of the pears and by the stalk parting readily from the tree when the fruit is gently lifted. After the fruit has been gathered, it should be placed in a box or keg and stored in a cool room to ripen. If kept in a body together, where there is sufficient quantity, or kept from too rapid

evaporation by being wrapped in paper, their flavour and plumpness are fully preserved, and in due time, the fruit will acquire its full colour and perfect maturity. Many sorts, if allowed to remain too long on the tree, rot at the core, while others become dry, mealy and flavourless." Store pears in a dark, cool room near freezing but not more than a degree or two below. Be careful not to store them near green vegetables such as cabbage and lettuce or root vegetables such as carrots and potatoes, which will impart off-flavours to the fruit.

Early pears may need just a few days of storage for the flavour and texture to become acceptable, but late pears, such as 'Anjou,' 'Winter Nelis,' 'Packham's Triumph' and 'Hardy,' taste better after a month or so of storage. Pears do not ripen fully in storage, so they should be ripened at room temperature for a day or two before they are wanted. If fruit is kept too long in storage, the cores will break down. This brown, watery collapse of tissue beginning near the core of the fruit is a natural occurrence in ageing pears. Properly stored, however, late pears will keep for months. Fresh pears at Christmas are among the most elegant treats of the home fruit garden.

Because there are so many cultivars, I asked a group of North American fanciers to recommend their favourite trees, ones they would choose for a small dream orchard in their own climatic area. As you read through the list, take note of the climatic zone and geographic region of the pear's sponsor and compare it with your own, as you will likely have the greatest success with pears that have been found superlative in growing conditions similar to your own.

EUROPEAN

'**Anjou**': This heirloom grew in France almost two centuries ago and is still a top cultivar. A bright green pear that reaches its highest quality as a dessert fruit around November, 'Anjou' will keep from one to three months longer in refrigeration. The vigorous, spreading tree is an inconsistent producer but is hardier than 'Bartlett' and more resistant to fire blight. The fruit ripens about five weeks after 'Bartlett,' in late September or early October. It is recommended by Layne and, for zone 5, by Hall-Beyer. 'Bartlett' is pollinated by 'Anjou.'

'**Aurora**': This 1964 release from Geneva, New York, ripens just before 'Bartlett,' one of its parents. The large, bright yellow, russetted fruit keeps better than 'Bartlett' in refrigeration, although neither is a good keeper. The flesh is smooth, melting and juicy, the flavour sweet and aromatic. The tree is vigorous and spreading but susceptible to fire blight. It is recommended by Layne and by Quamme, who calls it "an exceptionally high-quality fruit." 'Aurora' will pollinate most cultivars.

'**Bartlett**': Discovered in England around 1770 by Mr. Williams—Europeans know it as 'Williams' Bon Chretien'—'Bartlett,' named for the Bostonian who popularized it in North America, still sets the standard by which other pears are measured. It is the chief canning variety worldwide because, as Quamme writes, "it is high in esters that are heat-stable and are responsible for the fine flavour after processing." This is a midseason pear, ripening in late August on the West Coast, early to mid-September around the southern Great Lakes and on the East Coast. The skin is green when picked but turns yellow with brown freckles when ripe. The tree is upright in habit, fast-growing and requires careful training. It is fairly sensitive to cold and fire blight. Craig and Layne recommend it, and Sherk writes, "My favourite." Hall-Beyer recommends it for zone 5. Quamme says, "Red sports such as 'Maxred' lack vigour and are not as productive as the standard." It will pollinate 'Anjou.'

'**Bosc**': This venerable dessert pear, recommended by more of our experts than any other cultivar, originated in Belgium in 1807. Unfortunately, it is fairly cold-tender, although Hall-Beyer suggests it for zone 5. Also, it ripens about three weeks after 'Bartlett' and so requires a long growing season. The delicious fruit, which has an unusually long, slender shape and is borne singly on the tree rather than in clusters, has rich yellow skin russetted cinnamon and soft, buttery flesh. It keeps three or four months at temperatures just above freezing. Quamme recommends 'Bosc' as a late-season storage pear but cautions: "The tree tends to develop a sprawling form, which makes it difficult to train. It is susceptible to fire blight. Buyers should obtain virus-free nursery stock, as stony pit virus can be a problem with the cultivar." Craig, Layne, Sherk and Tukey also recommend it, the last saying: "An excellent pear when ripened off the tree, much better than 'Bartlett,' 'Anjou' and 'Comice' in my area. I suggest a quince rootstock to give a medium-sized tree (10 to 12 feet) that can be trained on a trellis."

'Clapp's Favourite': Thadeus Clapp of Dorchester, Massachusetts, developed this early pear around 1800. It ripens in mid-August on the West Coast and late August around the southern Great Lakes. A large, well-coloured pear, with sweet, juicy flesh and pale yellow skin, lightly marbled red in the sun, it is good fresh and for canning but does not store well. The tree, upright and spreading, is quite cold-hardy but very susceptible to fire blight. It is recommended as an early variety by Craig, Osborne and Sherk. Hall-Beyer notes that it can be grown in zone 4.

'Comice': An heirloom developed around 1849 in France, where it is also known as 'Doyenne du Comice,' this large, yellow pear has sweet, juicy, melting flesh that is unusually smooth-textured. It is very late, ripening five or six weeks after 'Bartlett.' It is recommended by Benowitz, who writes: "Many think it provides the flavour standard by which to measure all others." Quamme cautions, " 'Comice' is susceptible to fire blight and does not mature properly in most climates in Canada."

'Earlibrite': Released from Kentville, Nova Scotia, in 1989, this medium-sized pear is a good keeper with outstanding quality considering its early ripening—mid- to late August in Kentville. 'Earlibrite' has greenish yellow skin with a bright orange-red blush. The tree is moderately vigorous, and its growth is upright and spreading. It is recommended by Craig.

'Flemish Beauty': This hardiest of the high-quality pears was developed before 1800 in Belgium, where it is called 'Belle de Flanders.' It was a leading commercial variety not long

ago but lost its position because it is highly susceptible to fire blight and scab. The fruit—clear yellow with a red blush on the sunny side—is good fresh and for canning. It ripens in September. The tree is productive and vigorous and is a good pollinator for other varieties. It is recommended by Craig, who cautions, "Very susceptible to pear scab."

'Gourmet': Released by South Dakota State University in 1988 and therefore hardy enough to survive conditions immediately beyond those where pears are commercially grown, this dessert pear combines features of Asian and European species. The fruit is two to three inches wide, with greenish yellow to yellow skin, coarse but tender flesh and a rich, sweet flavour. The trees are moderately productive and have some tolerance to fire blight. Hall-Beyer recommends it for zone 5.

'Harrow Delight': Released from Harrow, Ontario, in 1982, it surpasses its parent, 'Bartlett,' in several ways. 'Harrow Delight' is fire blight-resistant and ripens two weeks earlier, about the same time as 'Clapp's.' The quality of the yellow, red-blushed fruit is similar to that of 'Bartlett,' with juicy, melting flesh—much better than 'Clapp's.' Layne and

The heirloom variety 'Seckel,' photographed soon after the fruit began to swell, has lost popularity during this century because of its small size, but its self-fruitfulness, hardiness and disease resistance and a distinctive spicy flavour recommend it to marginal-area gardeners who want a European pear.

Quamme recommend this variety, which the latter named. Quamme writes: "It has attractive, spicy-flavoured fruit as large as 'Bartlett.' The tree is small and begins to fruit early."

'Highland': A 'Bartlett' x 'Comice' hybrid released from Geneva in 1974, 'Highland' is a high-quality dessert pear ready to pick about four weeks after 'Bartlett.' The large, yellow, lightly russetted fruit develops better quality if stored about a month before ripening and will keep in refrigerated storage until January. The flesh is juicy and nearly smooth in texture, with a sweet, rich flavour. The tree is moderately vigorous and productive but susceptible to fire blight. It is recommended by Benowitz, who says, "The highest-quality keeper pear for our region."

'Luscious': Released from South Dakota, 'Luscious' has proved itself hardy in many northern states and in Canada. The rather small fruit has yellowish green skin and is very juicy, sweet and firm yet melting, with a flavour similar to 'Bartlett' but more intense. It is ready to pick in September or early October, ripens in storage about a week after harvest and then remains in good condition for about two weeks. The tree is resistant to fire blight.

It is recommended by Osborne.

'Rescue': Found growing near Vancouver, British Columbia, rescued after its owner's death by a nursery (hence the name) and recently released by Washington State University, this is a reliable annual bearer of early, orange-blushed fruit, sometimes six inches long, that is ready to harvest in late August to early September on the West Coast. The fruit will store until December. The trees are upright, vigorous and productive. This is Benowitz's first choice, and he calls it "a showstopper."

'Seckel': Named for the man who grew it in Philadelphia about 1820, 'Seckel' was very popular around the turn of the century because of its delicious fruit, but now, larger pears have taken its place. Ready to pick in September, it has yellow-brown, russetted skin and "an exceedingly rich, spicy flavour and very pleasant perfume," according to a 19th-century author. The tree is hardy, compact and self-fruitful and, although slow to come into bearing, is a consistent bearer thereafter. The fruit is somewhat susceptible to scab, but the tree is resistant to fire blight. Quamme recommends this late pear: "Very

Fire blight-resistant and hardy to nearly minus 50 degrees F (-45°C), 'Summer Crisp' is recommended by several experts who live beyond commercial pear-growing country. The fruit, more than two inches long, has fairly good flavour and crisp flesh.

high quality but small. It is used for pickling." It will not pollinate 'Bartlett.'

'Spartlett': A seedling of 'Bartlett' discovered in 1963 by a farmer in Michigan, this similar pear, which ripens about 12 days after its parent, is renowned for its huge fruit size. After storage, when the skin turns from green to yellow and the fruit is ready to eat, the flesh is somewhat grainy and slightly fibrous. Lord recommends it as a "good-quality traditional pear with a mild, pleasant pear flavour. The fruit size is exceptional, but it is not a heavy producer under New Hampshire conditions."

ASIAN

'20th Century': Currently among the four leading Asian pears in North America, this variety produces round, medium-sized fruit with clear yellow skin and the typical crunchy, sweet white flesh of the species. It ripens in early September in southern New Hampshire, where it is recommended by Lord, who writes: "Extremely precocious and fruitful. The fruits are crisp, juicy and have a mild, pleasant flavour. Another positive note: this cultivar is not affected by the pear psylla."

USSURIAN

'Golden Spice': This pear, about two inches long, was released from the University of Minnesota in 1949, although its parentage is unknown. The skin is medium yellow, lightly blushed with dull red, and the flesh is deemed fair for fresh eating but very good for sauce. Ripening from early to mid-October near the Great Lakes, it will not keep well. The vigorous tree is a good pollinator and somewhat fire blight-resistant. Submitted by Vick, it is recommended by Hall-Beyer for zone 3 and by Davidson.

'John': Released from the University of Saskatchewan in 1960, this is generally considered the best of the university's Apostle series. It ripens in late September but is best harvested immature and ripened off the tree. The fruit is unusually large for a prairie pear, at about three inches long. It has greenish yellow skin blushed red and cream-coloured flesh that is juicy, aromatic and rated fair for cooking. Most stone cells occur near the core, with the remaining flesh mellow and juicy. The flavour is especially strong when the tree is grown on dry soil. It is recommended by Hall-Beyer and by Olsen, who writes, "Fruit is not edible fresh from the tree, but it is considered good for canning."

'Patten': This pear ripens around mid-September in the Great Lakes region but should be picked about a week earlier and allowed to ripen off the tree. The fruit is large and resembles 'Bartlett.' It is fire blight-tolerant but not as hardy as some, best for zone 4. Osborne recommends it as a "good-quality keeping pear and also the best for canning. It is very hardy."

'Summer Crisp': Of unknown parentage, released from the University of Minnesota in 1986, this is a very early hardy pear that ripens in mid-August in Minnesota and has survived winter temperatures of nearly minus 50 degrees F (-45°C). The fruit, more than two inches long, is yellowish green with a red blush. It has fairly good flavour and crisp flesh like that of Asian pears. Pick it while the flesh is still firm and before any yellow colour develops. The fruit will keep for six weeks if refrigerated immediately after harvest. If allowed to ripen on the tree, the fruit develops stone cells and a strong aroma, and the flesh browns around the seeds. The trees, which grow 18 to 25 feet tall, are fire blight-resistant. Osborne and Hall-Beyer recommend 'Summer Crisp,' which is Davidson's third choice after 'Ure' and 'Golden Spice.'

'Ure': Released from Morden, Manitoba, in 1978 and named for a plant breeder there, this pear, which has 'Bartlett' in its ancestry, has the best-quality fresh fruit of the hardy selections. The fruit, about two inches wide with greenish yellow skin, is very sweet and juicy, good for fresh eating and canning. It will keep for six weeks in refrigerated storage. The tree is a natural semidwarf that is resistant to fire blight. It is recommended by Davidson and Hall-Beyer and by Olsen, who writes: "Small fruit but best flavour." Another improved cultivar is promised from Morden.

The experts who were asked to recommend cultivars for their own area:

Sam Benowitz, owner, Raintree Nursery, Morton, Washington (USDA climatic zone 8).

William E. Craig, tree-fruit specialist, Agriculture Canada Research Station, Kentville, Nova Scotia (Agriculture Canada climatic zone 6a; USDA zone 6a).

Dr. Campbell Davidson, research scientist, Agriculture Canada Research Station, Morden, Manitoba (Agriculture Canada climatic zone 3b; USDA zone 3b).

Bart Hall-Beyer, owner, Sursum Corda, Scotstown, Quebec (Agriculture Canada climatic zone 4a; USDA zone 4a).

Dr. Richard C. Layne, head, Horticultural Science Section, Agriculture Canada Research Station, Harrow, Ontario (Agriculture Canada climatic zone 7a; USDA zone 6a).

William G. Lord, extension specialist (fruit), University of New Hampshire, Durham, New Hampshire (USDA climatic zone 5b).

Paul Olsen, owner, Roseberry Gardens, Thunder Bay, Ontario (Agriculture Canada climatic zone 3a; USDA zone 4a).

Bob Osborne, owner, Corn Hill Nursery, Petitcodiac, New Brunswick (Agriculture Canada climatic zone 4b; USDA zone 4b).

Dr. Harvey Quamme, research scientist, Agriculture Canada Research Station, Summerland, British Columbia (Agriculture Canada climatic zone 6; USDA zone 6a).

Lawrence C. Sherk, formerly with Agriculture Canada, now chief horticulturist of Sheridan Nurseries, Georgetown, Ontario (Agriculture Canada climatic zone 6a; USDA zone 5b).

Dr. Loren D. Tukey, professor of pomology, Pennsylvania State University, University Park, Pennsylvania (USDA climatic zone 5b).

Roger Vick, curator, Devonian Botanic Garden, Edmonton, Alberta. Vick submitted the preferences of Sprout Farms, a family-owned business specializing in fruit trees in Bon Accord, Alberta (Agriculture Canada climatic zone 3a; USDA zone 3a).

Harvest Dates
Pears

The range of dates refers to the approximate beginning of the harvest in the most popular fruit-bearing areas of the north.

Harrow Delight	Aug. 10-30
Clapp's Favourite	Aug. 10-30
Aurora	Aug. 20-Sept. 10
Bartlett	Aug. 20-Sept. 10
Flemish Beauty	Sept. 1-25
Seckel	Sept. 5-25
Spartlett	Sept. 10-30
Bosc	Sept. 10-Oct. 10
Highland	Sept. 20-Oct. 10
Comice	Sept. 20-Oct. 15
Luscious	Sept. 25-Oct. 10
Anjou	Sept. 25-Oct. 15
Golden Spice	Oct. 1-15

ABUNDANT FRUIT

*"Beyond question, this is the most
important fruit of our latitude. The
abundance, cheapness and certainty
with which the apple can be raised
are important points in its favour."*

— W. C. STRONG, *Fruit Culture*, 1885

Hardy, adaptable and
varied, apples grow almost
everywhere in the tem-
perate world. 'McIntosh,'
left, is the standard-bearer
of the sweet, red-skinned,
full-sized types. It is still
popular more than a
century after its discovery
in an Ontario orchard.

97

Apples and crab apples

Abundant is the right word for apples. Apples grow everywhere in the temperate world, naturalized in the wild by seeds that have taken root with adventurous tenacity. Generations of gardeners have selected the best of these seedlings, so there are now more than 6,500 cultivars, a prodigious number that bulges the fences around heirloom apple collections and continues to rise as scientists rein in the apple's wild ways by making their own crosses. As if in response to all this fecundity, apples are preyed upon by more diseases and pests than any other northern tree fruit. Nevertheless, the crops are also big, about 30 bushels a year from a standard tree in good health. Add the fact that the best-quality apples come from relatively cool places, and it is easy to understand why the apple accounts for more than half of the world's entire production of tree fruit.

Apples have been reserved for the last chapter of this part of the book, not because they are unimportant but because they are often the last fruit of the season, continuing to ripen even as the snow falls in October and November. Indeed, this book could have been about apples and nothing else. There are extremely hardy apples, apples for warmer places, trees 30 feet tall and trees small enough to fit into the corner between the garage and the neighbour's fence. Unless a gardener truly dislikes the fruit or cannot offer a tree anything but shade and bog, everyone should consider adopting at least one apple tree.

My own first two apples, a 'McIntosh' and a 'Cortland,' were selected from only about four varieties sold around 15 years ago by a local nursery. They were popular varieties, so I chose them without a second thought, but both are disease-susceptible—an important consideration for an organic gardener like me—and neither is a particularly good keeper. If I had invested some time visiting nearby orchards, tasting apples and considering disease resistance, my choices would have been different; but I am stuck with them for as long as I live in this house. I do pick apples from these trees and am grateful every time I do, but they could be better apples, and there could be more of them.

In 1892, L.H. Bailey of Cornell University compiled an inventory of all the apples sold in North American nurseries and came up with 878 varieties. By 1922, the number had dwindled to 100. Thanks to just a few eclectic nurseries, this number has held relatively steady, but they cater mainly to home gardeners and small orchardists. Large orchards are dominated by 'Red Delicious' and 'McIntosh,' the former representing almost half of the entire 1989 crop in the United States.

The largest proportion of the 100 or so cultivars offered consists of apples called heirlooms or antiques that date from before the turn of the century. A few—'McIntosh,' 'Golden Delicious,' 'Granny Smith' and 'Cox's

Considered essential attributes of pioneer farms, apple trees promised fresh fruit from fall till spring as well as a supply of delicious baked goods and refreshing cider.

Orange Pippin'—are still among the most popular apples worldwide. Names that include the word pippin refer to a seedling apple. The North American pioneers usually grew pippins because seeds were the easiest form in which to transport apple trees. No pioneer was more zealous than professional arborist and missionary John Chapman, who started nurseries of apple trees in Ohio and Indiana with seeds he collected from cider mills, thus becoming known as Johnny Appleseed. When seedling trees began to bear fruit, the pioneers could select the best to save, while the fruit from the worst went to the pigs. Hundreds more varieties have been developed in this century, including some considered the best-tasting of all by reviewers not beguiled by nostalgia. Luther Burbank, famed American plant breeder of the last century, once wrote, "There are 8,000 named varieties of the apple, but who shall estimate the uncounted opportunities for further apple improvement?" Many of the new apples carry a bonus of greater disease resistance than their forebears had. The apples sold today are not propagated by seed, a kind of genetic lottery, but by grafting the desired variety onto a rootstock.

Among all of these choices, old and new, there are apples that ripen in July and others that ripen in October, some that are best for fresh eating, others best for cider, others for sauce and slices, some that should be eaten within a few days and some that will keep in a cool basement until the following spring. Skins may be red, yellow, orange, green or brown, the flesh pinkish, greenish, cream or white. Taste, of course, is a purely subjective matter, but there are apples that are sugary sweet, bland, tart or spicy in flavour, with textures varying from crunchy to mealy. The best cooking apples are tart, with flesh that does not fall apart when heated. The best apples for eating fresh are sweeter and juicier. "Why do we need so many kinds of apples?" writes L.H. Bailey in *The Apple Tree* of 1922. "Because there are so many folks. A person has a right to gratify his legitimate tastes. If he wants 20 or 40 kinds of apples for his personal use, running from 'Early Harvest' to 'Roxbury Russet,' he should be accorded the privilege. There is merit in variety itself. It provides more points of contact with life and leads away from uniformity and monotony."

The domestic apple (*Malus domestica*), best known of the pome fruits—those with cores—originated in western Asia. Inch-wide apples

Apples and crab apples

Crab apples are best known for their showy blossoms, but they also mean edible fruit on trees that may be hardier than those of the larger-fruited apples.

were eaten by the lake dwellers of Europe around 3000 to 2000 B.C., and the fruit had already spread to the Atlantic by prehistoric times. Various apples are native to eastern Asia and North America too, but these species, which tend to grow into smallish trees with small green fruit, probably came from western Asia and across the Bering Sea with the first human inhabitants of the continent. Commercial apples are all based on species that are natives of the Old World.

CRAB APPLES

Suitable for the coldest places are hybrids and selections of the Siberian crab apple *Malus baccata*. Many are tolerant of temperatures as low as minus 40 degrees, and 'Rescue,' possibly the hardiest decent apple, has survived minus 55 degrees F (-48°C). When is an apple a crab apple? John Davidson, director of the Agriculture Canada Research Station in Beaverlodge, Alberta, says that the definition depends on size and flavour, not necessarily on species: "Edible crab apples are those too tart for dessert or for fresh eating but suitable for canning whole, making applesauce, et cetera. All are under 1½ inches." If the fruit is too tart to be eaten fresh, it is nevertheless excellent for juice, wine, cider and jelly, where its high pectin content ensures success even when it is blended with other fruits. Hybrids of M. *baccata* with M. *domestica* may produce fruit sweet enough to be eaten off the tree, in which case, the fruit is sometimes called an apple crab.

Crab apples, which are based not only upon *Malus baccata* but upon several other *Malus* species as well, are divided into those grown just as ornamentals and those grown for harvesting a crop. The dividing line is drawn on the basis of fruit size alone. The fruit on trees classed as ornamentals, which may be less

Apples are among the best candidates for espalier. Although crab apples are seldom considered appropriate for this elegant pruning style, the crab 'Royal Ruby' vividly demonstrates its suitability at blossom time.

than half an inch wide, is painstaking to pick, although it is, like any apple, perfectly edible and will make a fine jelly. The pink- or magenta-flowering crabs known as rosyblooms are derived from M. *pumila*, native to the Tian Shan Mountains of Asia. Their fruit is orange-red and about an inch wide. The trees were introduced in 1920 by Neils Hansen, director of the agricultural experiment station at Brookings, South Dakota. Popular cultivars include 'Almey,' 'Makamik,' 'Radiant' and 'Royalty,' the last released by Percy Wright of Saskatchewan and distinguished by dark purple-green foliage. 'Thunderchild,' from Ottawa, has foliage that turns from green to red and is less susceptible to fire blight than 'Royalty.' As all of these cultivars were developed in places with harsh winters, they are reliably cold-hardy and may grow 30 feet tall even in prairie gardens. They and other crabs are good pollinators for domestic varieties of apples.

Most *Malus domestica* apples are confined to zone 5 or warmer, though a few cultivars are hardier and can be grown in protected corners in zone 4. In general, these trees are hardy to about minus 31 degrees F (-35°C). Lower temperatures will injure both fruit buds and wood and can kill the trees. The length of season required is an equally important consideration in the north. The popular Australian 'Granny Smith' ripens so late that it must be grown commercially in semitropical places such as California. Another long-season apple, although its name suggests otherwise, is 'Northern Spy,' which is also handicapped in the north by dormant fruit buds more tender than those of 'McIntosh.' Bill McKentley reports from St. Lawrence Nurseries in Potsdam, New York (USDA climatic zone 4), that the following cultivars either failed to survive his coldest winters or have not matured fruit: 'Baldwin,' 'Cox's Orange Pippin,' 'Granny Smith,' 'Idared,' 'Jonagold,' 'Jonathan,' 'Liberty,' 'Mutsu,' 'Northern Spy,' 'Red Delicious,' 'Rhode Island Greening,' 'Rome Beauty,' 'Twenty Ounce' and 'Yellow Delicious.' He writes in his catalogue: "Some might grow satisfactorily for years if we have a series of mild winters, only to be zapped when a test winter comes along. A few will even survive the test winters and bear fruit, but the fruit will not size or ripen."

While the general rule of thumb is that a gardener can grow anything proved hardy for his or her own climatic zone or a cooler one,

apples that excel in hardiness are not necessarily the best choices for growers in more benign areas. My own 'Norland,' an excellent new apple for the prairies, is so hardy that it sheds its leaves by mid-September, already gritting its teeth in preparation for a harsh Saskatchewan winter. It bears its fruit early too, in August. Early fruit is fruit that will not store well, and 'Norland' apples are an extreme example. They have to be picked when ripe, or they will decay on the tree within days. On the positive side, my tree began to bear the second year after planting and was compact and productive thereafter. 'Norland' is wonderful for gardeners who can grow nothing that requires a longer season, but gardeners in milder locations can grow better-quality fruit. Choosing cultivars from a nursery in your own climatic area will help you find the most satisfactory apples for your garden.

POLLINATION

An apple tree must have a pollination partner whose bloom time overlaps its own. Growing two trees is the most obvious way to provide cross-pollination. They must be different cultivars or different species. Crab apples, some of which are very ornamental, or spur-type trees that take up little room are a couple of space-efficient possibilities. Loren Tukey of Pennsylvania State University recommends 'Spur Winter Banana' as a pollinator. But the

APPLE ROOTSTOCKS

Apple trees are not all the same size. They come in several sizes, classified as standard, semistandard (or semivigorous), semidwarf and dwarf. The various sizes may result from cultivar or from climate—the colder the winters, the smaller the tree—but most variation comes from rootstock. Grafted to different rootstocks, the same cultivar may be full-grown when it is waist-high or when it is as tall as the eavestroughs.

The first classification, standard, is a full-sized, self-supporting tree that may exceed 30 feet in height. Standard trees should be planted 25 to 35 feet apart. Most seedling trees and trees on seedling rootstocks are standard, although the seedling rootstock Beautiful Arcade yields a semivigorous tree. Semivigorous trees, about 18 to 22 feet tall, produce their first crop a little sooner than standards but are otherwise very similar. They should be planted 14 to 18 feet apart. A semidwarf, at 14 to 18 feet tall, is decidedly earlier in first cropping than either of the two preceding classifications and may need staking. The trees should be planted 11 to 14 feet apart. Dwarf trees, which are the smallest of all, produce their first crop very early, are slow-growing and need to be staked. They are the best choice for espalier systems. Plant them 7 to 12 feet apart.

A list of the most common rootstocks follows. Those designated M are from the Malling program, and those labelled MM are the result of the work of two British stations, Malling and Merton; those designated elsewhere in this book as EMLA, for East Malling Long Ashton, also from England, are among the most virus-free available.

Beautiful Arcade: A seedling rootstock developed in Nova Scotia that produces a hardy, well-anchored, semivigorous tree.

M4: A fairly cold-tender rootstock that produces trees about 60 to 70 percent of the standard size.

M7: The most popular semidwarfing rootstock. Staking may be required. It is susceptible to crown rot and suckering.

M9: Produces a dwarf tree 25 to 30 percent of standard size. The tree begins fruiting early and requires irrigation on sandy soils. The rootstock is resistant to crown rot.

M26: Produces fairly hardy semidwarf trees that are 40 to 50 percent of standard size. It is highly susceptible to fire blight and crown rot and prone to burr knots, so it should be planted with the graft union only an inch or two above the ground. Bud break is retarded in spring.

M27: Produces the smallest tree of all, only about 20 percent of standard size. It must be supported, as it tends to lean.

MM106: A semidwarfing stock for trees somewhat larger than those on M7 but nonsuckering and much more productive. It is susceptible to crown rot and hardens off late in fall, so it can be damaged by early freezes.

MM111: Produces a semidwarf, fairly drought-tolerant tree about 65 percent of standard size. It accounts for almost half the trees now planted in Nova Scotia.

Mark: A 1980 release from Michigan State University, 'Mark' is a selection of M9 that produces a tree about 25 to 30 percent of standard size. For a dwarf rootstock, it roots well, is very winter-hardy, tolerates a variety of soil conditions and encourages early bearing and productivity. However, it is susceptible to woolly apple aphid.

Ottawa 3: From the Central Experimental Farm in Ottawa, it produces a dwarf tree 25 to 35 percent of standard size, very hardy but susceptible to fire blight. Trees, which should be staked, begin to bear in two or three years. Bud break occurs early in spring.

Robusta 5: Also from Ottawa, it produces standard trees that are very hardy until midwinter but do not reharden after a spring thaw, so should be considered only where winters are consistently cold. Bud break occurs early in spring.

Other stocks: A series from the Soviet Union called Budagovsky and a "P" series from Poland may be available from specialist nurseries, although they have not yet been shown to be superior all-round to existing rootstocks.

When selecting a tree, the gardener should have the desired size at maturity in mind. This semidwarf 'Northern Spy' is a good choice for the fairly temperate Ontario flower garden in which it grows.

gardener need not grow a second tree. If your neighbour has an apple or a crab within about 100 feet or if there are wild apples within the same distance, you will likely be fine. Another way to aid pollination is to graft a branch from a second variety onto the first, as described on pages 23 and 24. Or simply set a pail of water beside a tree whose buds are about to open, and fill it with almost-blooming branches of a wild apple, crab apple or domestic apple tree in need of a little pruning.

The overlapping of bloom times is normally not a problem, because the commencement of bloom of different varieties happens within a period of about a week. Only during cold springs might there be a gap between blossom drop of the earliest varieties, such as 'Vista Bella' and 'Idared,' and the blooming of the latest, including 'Northern Spy,' 'Macoun' and 'Golden Delicious.' It is more important to be aware of something called ploidy, which refers to the number of chromosomes within the plant cells. Most apples are diploids, with two sets of chromosomes. These are reliable pollinators, but the few apples that are triploids, with three sets of chromosomes, can pollinate only one another, not diploids. Triploids include 'Rhode Island Greening,' 'Baldwin,' 'Gravenstein,' 'Karmijn de Sonnaville,' 'Winesap,' 'King,' 'Mutsu,' 'Jonagold' and 'Spigold.' Triploids are often bigger trees with larger fruit. (Polyploids, with even more chromosomes, may have such big fruits that branches

break. There are no popular cultivars that are polyploids.)

As with other fruit trees, the future crop will be adversely affected by cold weather at bloom time. Areas that have frosts a couple of degrees below freezing after May 15 are marginal for apples, especially early-blooming cultivars, because if temperatures drop to 26 or 27 degrees F (-3°C) for an hour or more when the tree is in full bloom, the flowers will be killed. Also, any fruit that does set may be smaller or misshapen for two reasons: one is that the king blossom, the largest in each cluster of blossoms, is the one that will produce the largest fruit, but as it blooms first, it is also the most susceptible to frost injury; the second is that if the fruit is inadequately pollinated, one or two of the five compartments in the core will be devoid of seeds and the fruit will be irregularly shaped. If the spring weather is cold, bees may not fly at all or they may visit only the blossoms on the warm, sunny side of the tree. Few blossoms will be pollinated, and the fruit set will be low. It may be surprising to realize, however, that only about 8 percent of the blossoms need to set fruit in order for a tree to produce a good yield.

After pollination, fruit size is determined largely by the weather during the three or four weeks following blossom drop, when all cell division occurs in the developing fruit. Warm, sunny days will result in larger fruit than will cool, cloudy weather. If rainfall is slight, about an inch of water should be given the trees every week until at least midsummer, as a prolonged dry period will keep the fruit from reaching full size.

ALTERNATE BEARING

Some apples, including 'Baldwin,' 'Northern Spy' and 'Wealthy,' have a biennial, or alternate bearing, habit. Others, such as 'McIntosh' and 'Delicious,' will bear annually if properly tended but can be thrown into alternate bearing by heavy pruning or heavy cropping. Early cultivars are especially likely to ripen unevenly and have a tendency to bear large crops of smallish apples that encourage biennial bearing.

Thinning not only ensures that the fruit will be large and flavourful but also stimulates the tree to produce an annual crop. For apples, thinning begins at blossom time. Roger Way of Geneva, New York, who developed the apples 'Jonagold' and 'Empire,' says: "By taking off most of the crop at bloom time when you have too heavy a crop on the tree, you reduce the competition within the tree itself. Bloom for next year is already starting at the end of May. If you thin before the end of May and reduce the internal competition, the new blossoms will come on for the next year. By mid-June, when the fruits are an inch in diameter, it is too late, because next year's blossoms have already started."

Thinning should continue beyond blossom time, however, not to ensure blossoms for the following year but to encourage this year's fruit to be as large and of as high a quality as possible. The task of thinning fruit when it is small is made easier if one removes entire clusters with shears, rather than one or two fruits per cluster. There should eventually be about 30 leaves per fruit. Wayne Still thins his organically grown apples until harvesttime, removing any fruit that shows signs of pest infestation—the "coddlers," as he calls them. By scanning his trees for imperfect fruit, he also keeps abreast of any requirements for pruning or pest control.

ROOTSTOCKS

When selecting a tree, the gardener should have the desired tree size in mind, as apples are available in a greater variety of sizes than any other fruit tree. For one thing, different cultivars vary in their vigour and therefore in their ultimate size—mutant spur-type trees are especially compact, for instance, while the triploids, described on the previous page, are very vigorous. Also, climate is a great determiner of size. If you live in a marginal apple-growing area, you will have a dwarf or semidwarf whether you want one or not. In Beaverlodge, Alberta, Irene Wallace's 'Heyer 12,' tree is only nine feet tall, although it is 45 years old. But within a climatic zone, the variability in apple-tree sizes is largely a matter of rootstocks. (See information on page 101.) Gardeners in zone 6 or warmer have the largest choice of rootstocks, especially of dwarfing types. Seedlings are the choice of most orchardists, who often use 'Red Delicious' because they are fairly uniform. On the prairies, seedlings of crab apples such as 'Bedford,' 'Dolgo' and 'Columbia' are successful, the last being the hardiest.

Trees on dwarfing rootstocks are, by definition, less vigorous and less able to withstand climatic stress, and although they produce

A dwarf 'McIntosh' thrives although it occupies little space in a suburban backyard in Kamloops, where winters are mild enough to permit the survival of certain dwarfing rootstocks.

their fruit earlier, this apparent advantage may occur at the expense of the establishment of a strong tree. Another negative aspect of dwarfing rootstocks is that they are smaller and less fibrous and therefore less able to support the tree, so staking is required. Dwarf trees have a shorter life span around 30 years as opposed to 70 or more for a standard—and spring frosts may do more damage to blossoms because they are closer to the ground. Bart Hall-Beyer of Sursum Corda nursery in Quebec does not recommend dwarfing rootstocks for gardens in zone 5 or cooler: "In a cold climate, even a perfectly hardy variety, if grafted onto a dwarfing rootstock, may be winter-killed or, at best, linger season after season with minimal growth and no fruit. We have tested all of the dwarfing rootstocks here and have found them to lack the hardiness, vigour and disease resistance needed to thrive in our northern climate."

In slightly warmer places, dwarf trees have some advantages. They take up much less space, about a quarter as much as standard trees. Dwarfs require deep, rich soil and conscientious watering, but they can be planted just 6 or 7 feet apart, whereas semidwarfs should be 12 to 14 feet apart and standard trees 20 to 30 feet apart. For city gardeners, this compactness may make fruit trees possible where they otherwise would not be. The fruit may actually be larger, it will be within reach, and spraying and protecting against

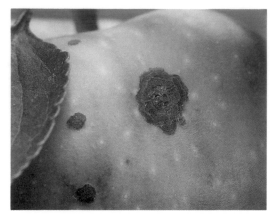

frost will be easier.

An interstem of a different variety—a piece grafted between rootstock and the desired cultivar so that it forms the lower part of the trunk—is sometimes used to increase compatibility between cultivar and rootstock or to confer a dwarfing effect. The dwarfing interstem can be compared with tightening a corset around the waist of the tree so that growth of the upper part is restrained, although the roots remain vigorous. The rootstock can be hardy, and the tree may not need staking. When a tree has a dwarfing interstem, the upper graft union should be above ground but the lower one several inches below the soil surface to prevent excessive suckering from the rootstock. Corn Hill Nursery of New Brunswick offers trees with Ottawa 3 interstems, which result in semidwarf, hardy, self-supporting trees. In catalogues, components of a tree are written from the top down: one designated 'McIntosh'/M9/MM106 is a 'McIntosh' with an M9 interstem and an MM106 rootstock.

In an extreme version, the interstem or rootstock may be a hardy variety that composes the entire trunk and sometimes even the scaffold branches. The desired cultivar is then grafted onto this sturdy framework, a system called topworking, framebuilding or stem building and recommended for areas with very cold winters. If the desired part of the tree does die, the hardier parts will remain and the tree can be grafted again. The hardy component of the tree also encourages the scions to enter dormancy earlier, increasing their ability to withstand winter weather.

DISEASE RESISTANCE

Another factor in tree selection is disease resistance. The consideration of diseases may seem discouraging at the outset of planning the home orchard, yet the apple grower is soon faced with a harsh reality: apples are notoriously vulnerable to various forms of microbial attack, and whether you intend to grow the trees organically or not, you should be aware of the most common diseases, the damage they cause and the options you have for overcoming at the beginning what might otherwise be a lifetime of difficulties.

The worst apple diseases are scab, fire blight, cedar-apple rust and powdery mildew. Although some of the heirloom varieties are disease-resistant, many impressive new varieties have arisen from programs that began in the 1940s and whose results have begun to appear only within the past decade. The PRI program, so called because it involves the universities of Purdue, Rutgers and Illinois (hence the "pri" in some cultivar names), released 'Redfree,' 'Jonafree,' 'Prima,' 'Priscilla,' 'Priam' and 'Sir Prize.' From the New York Agricultural Experiment Station have come 'Liberty' and 'Freedom,' and from Agriculture Canada, 'Macfree,' 'Nova Easygro,' 'Novamac' and 'Novaspy,' all highly resistant to scab and often to fire blight, rust and mildew as well.

Scab is named and best known for the rough spots and resulting cracks that appear on affected fruits. To some extent, these cosmetic defects can be overlooked by home gardeners, but they will affect long-term storage, and more seriously, the disease can cause premature fruit drop, early defoliation, weakened trees and reduced fruit-bud development for the next year's crop. This fungal disease is spread by spores that land on the new, green tips during wet weather in early spring. The warmer the temperature, the shorter the time the plant surface must remain wet for infection to occur; infection takes 48 hours at 32 to 34 degrees F (1°C) but only 9 hours at 58 to 76 degrees F (14° to 24°C). Scab is difficult to combat with sprays—commercial orchardists may spray fungicides seven or eight times during the growing season—but easily controlled if one chooses resistant trees.

Cedar-apple rust is caused by a fungus that attacks both apples and red cedars (a type of juniper). Apple trees are vulnerable if there are red cedars growing within two miles. On red cedars, symptoms of the disease are small, brown, inch-wide galls that sprout orange horns in spring. The spores blow from these horns to apple trees, where they produce greenish yellow lesions and, eventually, black dots within a reddish circle on the leaves. The rust causes premature defoliation and dwarfing and malformation of the fruit. The old way to control the disease was to cut down all junipers around the orchard, but now, resistant apples are available.

Powdery mildew, caused by a fungus that overwinters in the dormant buds, produces a white powdery coating on leaves and occasionally on blossoms, causing distorted terminal growth and sometimes a netlike pattern of russetting on fruit. Combat it with sulphur sprays or with disease-resistant cultivars. If powdery mildew is a problem in your area, avoid the very susceptible cultivars 'Idared,' 'Rome Beauty,' 'Jonathan' and 'Cortland.'

Cytospora dieback is also caused by a fungus. The spores enter cracks caused by winter damage. Most serious in severe climatic areas, it should be combated by regular pruning to remove damaged growth. John Davidson of Agriculture Canada says that where he works in Beaverlodge, Alberta, "Sooner or later, it gets everything." The station is fortunate, however, in that it experiences no fire blight, and "we're not about to introduce it." (Fire blight is described in the previous chapter because it is a more serious disease in pears. The symptoms and preventive measures are the same for apples.)

Crown rot, or collar rot, which attacks trees at or near the soil line, is most troublesome on the West Coast, where almost all soils are infected with the organism. The worst problems occur in soils that occasionally become waterlogged. Avoid susceptible rootstocks such as MM104, MM106 and MM111, which are no longer recommended for most of the Pacific areas. Also, do not allow the tree to produce heavy crops of fruit in its early years.

Young trees planted where old apple trees grew may suffer from a disorder known as apple replant disease, whose symptoms are slow growth both above and below ground. Trees on dwarfing rootstocks are most susceptible. If you are planting a new tree where an old tree recently grew, cover the ground in a three-foot-diameter circle around the new tree with plastic mulch, because the disease is caused by microorganisms in the top foot or so of soil. Once the roots grow below this depth, the tree will recover and grow normally.

Bitter pit and cork spot, or "corking," of apples, especially 'Imperial' and 'Red Delicious,' are not diseases but physiological problems caused by the application of too much nitro-

To renovate an old tree, encourage the growth of new wood and clean out the old while bringing the tree down to a manageable size. Here, an overgrown tree is reduced to a better height for tending and harvesting.

gen, which results in insufficient calcium being available to the trees. Spraying trees with 4 ounces of calcium chloride in 5 gallons of water will help to correct the condition. Russetting, which produces brownish, corky skin, is not considered a disease symptom, although it is associated with certain bacteria on the skin surface. Some apples naturally have this type of skin, while others become russetted if heavy rains occur two or three weeks after the blossoms drop. A boron deficiency, most common in the northeast, can be prevented with a spray of a quarter-pound of borax per tree every three years. On the West Coast, a thorough spray of 5 teaspoons of Epsom salts (magnesium sulphate) per gallon of water is recommended in early June, again to offset nutrient deficiencies in the soil.

PRUNING

There are directions on pages 17 to 19 and 25 for regular pruning and for espalier, which is suitable for slow-growing apples or those on dwarfing rootstocks. The renovation of an old tree calls for different tactics. Wayne Still says his trees were "very tall and overgrown when I took over the orchard. Any tree tends to grow at the top if you let it go. Over the last 10 years, I have been methodically cutting the tops from the trees to encourage lower growth. I can now pick all the fruit with a six-foot ladder, even though all my trees are stan-

The harvest may vary from fewer than 10 bushels on a dwarf or semidwarf tree to as many as 30 from a standard, right. However, all trees, whatever their height, will produce full-sized fruit.

dards." He cuts out the old branches and keeps only young, vigorous wood, including water sprouts, which are trained into positions closer to horizontal to encourage bearing. "That's how you get good-quality fruit."

PESTS

Unfortunately, the disease-resistant varieties, although very valuable, are just as vulnerable to pests as any other apples. And there are pests in abundance that love apples, one reason most organic apples are considered good for little but cider. Benign pest-control methods are discussed on pages 30 to 36. The worst pests of apples in most northern areas are codling moth, apple maggot and plum curculio.

It is said that the only thing worse than finding a worm in your apple is finding half a worm. Chances are, that half-worm is the remains of a larva of the codling moth, a European pest that arrived in the northeastern United States about 200 years ago and has been wreaking havoc on this continent ever since. (Codling is an old term for a small green apple.) Evidence of codling moth predation has been found on the remains of apples prepared for drying by prehistoric Europeans, and it is now the worst insect enemy of apples worldwide. The white larva with a brown head is all too familiar to apple growers who do not spray, but less well known is the adult, a greyish moth just under an inch long, which lays its eggs on the foliage and fruit shortly after they appear. In the northeast, moth flights are most numerous around early June. The larvae bore into fruit, fruit spurs or shoots, remaining there for several weeks to feed before they reach maturity. They overwinter in thin, spindle-shaped cocoons in the bark or in rubbish on the ground. In early spring, pupation begins, and the life cycle resumes. A dry, warm spring helps these insects thrive.

The apple maggot fly is about one-eighth inch long, black with yellow legs and a zigzag band across the wings. It lays its eggs just under the skin of the fruit, leaving a little scar that appears as a slight depression as the apple grows. After about a week, the eggs hatch, and the tiny white larvae tunnel down, leaving small brown trails through the flesh and causing mature apples to appear lumpy. The maggots spend about a month inside the apple. When the fruit drops, they burrow into the soil under the tree, where they remain until spring to resume the cycle of infestation. While sticky red spheres are the usual organic control method (described on page 32), picking up all fallen apples to prevent maggots from completing their life cycle can also dramatically reduce pest numbers. Orchardists Bart Hall-Beyer and Jean Richard of Quebec note that cooking apples seem less affected by apple maggot than are the sweeter dessert types.

Other pests that can be problematic, depending upon one's area, are aphid, plum curculio, various types of tent caterpillars, green fruitworm (a fairly large green caterpillar that can be sprayed with Bt), red-banded and oblique-banded leaf rollers (larvae that roll the leaves as they feed and later feed on fruit; again, Bt combats them), Oriental fruit moth and European apple sawfly, whose larvae are full-grown by about the time codling moth larvae are beginning to enter the fruit. Corn borers and stalk borers may enter the fruit if trees grow next to corn plants.

HARVEST

Apple trees begin to bear in 2 to 10 years, depending mostly upon rootstock, cultivar, climate and the gardener's pruning habits. A standard can continue to bear for more than a century. The harvest may vary from about 10 bushels on a dwarf or semidwarf tree to as many as 30 from a standard. Certain apples, such as 'McIntosh,' may fall from the tree before they are fully ripe, while others, like 'Cort-

Imperfect fruit need not be wasted, because small quantities can be used in jellies and butters and larger quantities can be set aside for the preparation of delicious cider.

land,' do not drop even when overripe.

Winter frosts may touch the fruit before it is picked. Roger Way of Geneva, New York, says: "It happens around here quite a lot with 'Rome Beauty,' a late apple that often freezes right on the tree. It reduces the storage life of that apple but doesn't interfere with the immediate consumption of it, so one of the instructions is, don't touch the apple while it's still frozen. Wait until midmorning or noon, until it thaws out, and then you can go ahead and harvest it." The more frequently an apple is frozen, the shorter its storage life becomes, until finally, it will decay on the tree. Late-ripening apples will tolerate temperatures as low as 29 degrees F (-2 °C) before internal damage occurs. Frost damage appears as discoloration, a water-soaked appearance and a spongy texture.

Apples vary greatly in their ability to withstand storage. In general, the earlier an apple is harvested, the shorter the length of time it will last in storage. 'Transparent,' ready to pick in early August around the southern Great Lakes, keeps for only a few days, while 'McIntosh,' picked in late September, keeps two to four months, and 'Idared' and 'Golden Russet,' both harvested in late October, keep at least four or five months in refrigerated storage at a temperature close to freezing. Bart Hall-Beyer of Quebec finds that 'Idared,' properly refrigerated, will keep until July. Many storage types will last a year in controlled-atmo-sphere (CA) storage, where levels of carbon dioxide and oxygen are carefully controlled by commercial growers. It is because of CA storage that 'McIntosh' apples continue to appear in supermarkets until spring. For prolonged quality in home storage, dip fruit in an 8 percent solution of calcium chloride (which is available in winter as a deicing material), dry the fruit, wrap it in newspaper, and store it in slatted wooden boxes or perforated plastic bags in a cool, dark place. Do not store imperfect fruit, and remember that fruit can be tainted in storage by leafy or root vegetables.

Only healthy, sound fruit should be saved for storage. Unfortunately, it is only after a few weeks in storage that apples will show signs of sunscald: bleached, bronzed or blackish areas on red fruit; bronze or reddish areas on yellow or green fruit. Sunscald, caused when hot, dry conditions follow cool weather, affects the part of the fruit facing the sun; the exposed side of the apple may be 20 Fahrenheit degrees (11 Celsius degrees) warmer than the shaded side. Scalded fruit should be eaten immediately, or it will rot.

A home gardener who has the space can grow early, midseason and late apples for fresh fruit from July or August until early summer. The cider, applesauce and jelly can last much longer. Such abundance comes only from the apple, a fruit that arrived in North America with the first human immigrants and will surely stay as long as we garden here.

Because there are so many cultivars, I asked a group of North American fanciers to recommend their favourite trees, ones they would choose for a small dream orchard in their own climatic area. As you read through these, take note of the climatic zone and area of the country of the apple's sponsor and compare it with your own, as you will likely have the greatest success with apples that have been found superlative in your own growing conditions.

'**Akane**': Crisp, tangy red apples similar to 'Mac' but with better keeping quality come from this 1971 Japanese cultivar. The fruit ripens in late August to mid-September. The foliage has a yellowish tinge, and the tree is resistant to scab and mildew. It is the first choice of Benowitz, who says, "A perfect summer apple for the organic grower."

'**Burgundy**': This early-fall apple was released from Geneva, New York, in 1974. 'Macoun' and 'Antonovka' are among its forebears. It is best known for an intense, almost blackish red skin that is smooth and glossy. The large round fruits are crisp with a slightly acid flavour and are considered very good for fresh eating. They will hang for three weeks on the tree when ripe but keep no more than a month in storage. Hall-Beyer recommends 'Burgundy' for zone 5: "Scab-tolerant, excellent, superb colour."

'**Chehalis**': From Washington comes a late-September apple that resembles 'Golden Delicious' in appearance and flavour but is larger and crisper. It is very scab-resistant and somewhat mildew-resistant. Benowitz writes, "Excellent for organic growers who like a big, sweet, yellow apple."

'**Cortland**': Although this 'Ben Davis' x 'McIntosh' hybrid was developed in 1915, the Geneva cultivar has stayed popular because the quality is better than 'McIntosh,' and the white flesh does not turn brown when cut, so it is excellent for salads and drying. The tree is relatively hardy, worth a try in sheltered corners in zone 4, and is a good pollinator. The large red-striped fruit will keep three or four months in cold storage. 'Cortland' is ready to pick approximately a week after 'McIntosh.' It is recommended by Craig.

'**Crispin**': See '**Mutsu**.'

'**Empire**': For an apple that was released just a generation ago, in 1966, this 'McIntosh' x 'Red Delicious' hybrid from Geneva has made a deep impression upon orchardists. Four of our experts (Quamme, Layne, Hall-Beyer and Tukey) listed it among their top five. The round red fruit is similar in flavour to 'McIntosh'—Hall-Beyer calls the flavour "superb"—but the texture is firmer, and the apple keeps much better, till about February. It has thinner skin yet doesn't bruise as easily. It ripens in early October near the southern Great Lakes and, like 'McIntosh,' needs cool nights to ripen properly; hot weather can turn it mealy. The trees, which are "easy to manage and train," says Quamme, are hardy to zone 4b or 5 and begin to bear annually and prolifically at a young age. It is susceptible to scab, moderately susceptible to powdery mildew and resistant to fire blight and cedar-apple rust. A new strain, 'Red Empire,' has redder skin.

'**Freedom**': The second disease-resistant apple released from Geneva, 'Freedom,' introduced in 1983, is well named, with resistance to scab, powdery mildew, cedar-apple rust and fire blight, although it is not as disease-resistant as its predecessor, 'Liberty.' 'Freedom' has red skin and a coarse texture. The tree is vigorous and very productive. The fruit ripens in early October around the southern Great Lakes and keeps till about January. Tukey recommends it, and Hall-Beyer suggests it for zone 5: "Excellent disease resistance, good flavour."

'**Gala**': One of the world's top nine apples, this 1960 New Zealand hybrid of 'Kidd's Orange Red' and 'Golden Delicious' produces fruit similar to 'Golden Delicious' in shape, texture and sweetness but with more flavour. The somewhat small fruit, which resembles a peach (orange blushed yellow), is considered outstanding for fresh eating. It ripens in mid-September and can be stored in plastic bags (to prevent shrivelling) until Christmas. It is very susceptible to scab and moderately susceptible to cedar-apple rust, fire blight and powdery mildew. Layne recommends it, and Tukey recommends both 'Gala' and its strains, which breeders have produced largely in the effort to give 'Gala' red skin: 'Royal Gala,' 'Imperial Gala,' 'Scarlet Gala' and several others.

'**Golden Delicious**': No relation of 'Red Delicious,' this West Virginia seedling found around the turn of the century was given its name by Stark Bros. Nurseries when they released it in 1914, after having been successful with 'Red Delicious.' 'Golden Delicious,' the most popular apple in Europe, is recommended by Craig and Layne and by Quamme, who explains its appeal: "This is my favourite if allowed to ripen to a golden colour on the tree

A relatively new apple that has quickly become one of the world's favourites, 'Gala' is similar in appearance to 'Golden Delicious,' one of its parents, but it has more flavour. It ripens in mid-September and can be stored for several months.

in October. It is poor if picked green, about mid-September on the West Coast, and unfortunately, most customers know only the immature version, because the tree-ripened fruit bruises easily and is difficult to handle in commerce. Home gardeners would not find this a problem." The fruit, of variable size, requires a long season to mature and will keep until March in cold storage. The vigorous, spreading tree is susceptible to most diseases. It sets heavy crops of fruit that should be thinned. Quamme adds, "The tree is not cold-hardy, and the fruit russets with heavy rain."

'Smoothee,' a recent mutation that exhibits less russetting, is recommended by Tukey.

'Golden Russet': A British heritage cultivar in existence for about three centuries, this brown-skinned favourite is one of the best for cider, but even when it is eaten as a fresh fruit, its distinctive tart flavour has many fans. The flesh is fine-grained, yellowish and crisp. The apples can be stored until March. The tree is vigorous and has a strong tendency to bear biennially, but crops ripen very late. Sherk writes: "Great flavour. My father grew it." Craig also recommends it.

'Idared,' which is harvested in October, is described as "the ultimate keeper" because it tastes best after Christmas and may still be in good condition in July.

'Greensleeves': A 1977 English release, one of whose parents is 'Golden Delicious,' this triploid has the colour and tartness of 'Granny Smith' but is hardy to zone 4 or 5. It is large and grass-green, turning slightly yellow as it ripens. It is recommended by Osborne, who calls it "very exciting."

'Hampshire': This new cultivar, not yet available to the public in 1991, was developed by Gould Hill orchard in Contoocook, New Hampshire. Lord writes: "Flavour and flesh firmness of the pleasant red fruits are exceptional—it is the best and firmest apple out of cold storage in December. The tree is easy to train and prune. Watch for this one."

'Idared': A 1942 hybrid of 'Wagener' and 'Jonathan' from Moscow, Idaho, this apple is very impressive for yield and storageability. "The ultimate keeper—till July!" writes Hall-Beyer. The medium-sized, spurry tree starts bearing its heavy annual crops when young. It is well shaped and does not need much pruning to keep it small, so it is a good subject for espalier. The tree blooms early and is susceptible to mildew and fire blight but becomes more resistant to fire blight after it begins to bear. Hall-Beyer reports that it is scab-tolerant and resistant to apple maggot. The bright red, bruise-resistant fruit, more than three inches wide, has firm, cream-coloured flesh that is tart when the fruit is harvested in mid-October but mellows and develops in storage. The fruit is best eaten after Christmas.

Hall-Beyer recommends it for zone 5.

'Jonagold': Recommended by more of this book's experts than any other apple, 'Jonagold' is relatively new, a hybrid of 'Jonathan' and 'Golden Delicious' released from Geneva in 1968. This triploid—it will not pollinate most other apples—has big, yellow, red-striped fruit. Quamme writes, "The flavour is good, the texture is crisp, and it is very juicy." The vigorous trees produce large annual crops that ripen fairly late. The fruit keeps till February in cold storage. It does well in cool areas but has a tendency to sunburn in warm climates and may fail where the weather is hot. High temperatures just before harvest mature the fruit without adding colour. The tree is susceptible to mildew and is less resistant to winter injury than 'Golden Delicious.' Craig and Layne recommend it, and Lord writes, "Excellent flavour and flesh quality. Does 'grease up' in storage." Tukey recommends 'Jonagold' and its strains, most of which have redder skin.

'Karmijn de Sonnaville': A 1971 release from Holland, this russet apple, brick-red over a yellow-green background, is a triploid hybrid of 'Cox's Orange' and 'Jonathan.' The flesh is firm, very flavourful, aromatic and slightly acidic when picked fresh but mellows after a month's storage. It ripens in mid-October on the West Coast. Recommended by Benowitz.

'Liberty': This 'McIntosh'-type apple with far better disease resistance was released from the Geneva experiment station in 1978. It is a 'Macoun' x 'Purdue' hybrid that is striped dark red, with pale yellow, crisp, juicy, slightly coarse flesh and a sprightly flavour that compares favourably with the best nonresistant types. The fruit, which browns readily when sliced, ripens in early October and keeps well in storage until January. The tree is a vigorous, spreading, highly productive annual bearer. It is recommended by Benowitz and Osborne and by Quamme for home gardeners who do not wish to use fungicide sprays, as it is highly resistant to apple scab, cedar-apple rust, fire blight and mildew.

'Macoun': A 1923 Geneva hybrid of 'McIntosh' and 'Jersey Black,' 'Macoun' produces medium-sized, flattened fruit that is flushed red over a light yellow background. The flesh is white, crisp, juicy, sweet and aromatic. The fruit ripens around late September, needs cool nights to ripen properly and must be picked when just ripe for best flavour. Thin the fruit for good size and to encourage annual bearing. It stores until December. Trees, which

'Golden Delicious,' Europe's favourite apple, should be allowed to tree-ripen fully before it is put into cold storage, where it should keep until about March.

grow upright and may need training to spread, are very susceptible to scab, fire blight and mildew but are resistant to cedar-apple rust. Lord writes: "From September 28 until October 20, this fruit is unbeatable. It is superdelicious and crisp—it explodes in your mouth. Not an easy cultivar to grow, it tends to be an upright grower and to bear biennially."

'**McIntosh**': Sherk recommends the apple discovered some two centuries ago by John McIntosh in Dundas County, Ontario. This classic ripens in late September near the southern Great Lakes and keeps for two to four months. Cool September nights will help it ripen properly; it turns mealy where summers are hot. Among its drawbacks are thick skin and disease susceptibility, especially to scab and fire blight. There are many similar apples that are more disease-resistant, such as 'Empire,' 'Novamac' and 'Spartan,' also described in this list. 'Summerland Red' is a dark red spur-type sport that is very popular with commercial growers on the West Coast.

'**Mutsu**': Released from Japan in 1948, this apple resembles one of its parents, 'Golden Delicious.' 'Mutsu' is a very large, triploid, yellow apple that ripens late—around the end of October near the southern Great Lakes—but is less susceptible to russetting, oversetting and storage shrivel than 'Golden Delicious.' It is, however, susceptible to blister spot, a bacterial disease which produces small green bumps on the fruit during July. These become purplish

black spots by harvesttime. Nevertheless, Layne recommends it, and Sherk calls it "my favourite eating apple." Lord writes: "Super flavour and stores well. This is a very strong 'repeat sale' apple with a devoted cluster of admirers." The name has been changed to 'Crispin' in New York and Europe.

'**Novamac**': A 1978 release from Kentville, Nova Scotia, this apple is much like 'McIntosh,' with similarly crisp, juicy, sweet-tart, creamy white flesh, although the fruit is slightly smaller, more aromatic and thinner-skinned. The tree produces large annual crops and is easy to train, a good espalier type for organic growers, as it is scab-free. Craig and Osborne recommend it. The latter writes: "We have never sprayed our 'Novamacs,' and they produce beautiful, unblemished fruit faithfully every year."

'**Novaspy**': The 'Golden Delicious' parentage of this 1986 Kentville release shows up in greenish yellow fruit with some red striping or blushing. The flesh is creamy yellow, crisp, juicy and slightly acidic. The fruit, ready to harvest in late October, stores well and is good for cooking and fresh eating. The moderately vigorous tree is upright and spreading, scab-resistant, fairly productive and crops annually. It is recommended by Craig.

'**Redfree**': A 1981 success from the New York State experimental program, this glossy red summer apple, which ripens in August or early September, has juicy, crisp flesh with a

111

Known to produce crops in cold and chinook regions where other trees fail, 'Heyer 12' is a smallish apple of Russian origin recommended for cooking.

mild flavour. The fruit ripens unevenly, so it may require two pickings; it will keep a month or two. The tree is upright, spreading and productive and tends toward biennial bearing, which can be discouraged by thinning. The tree is immune to scab and cedar-apple rust and moderately resistant to fire blight and mildew. Osborne recommends it, and Hall-Beyer suggests it for zone 5.

'**Spartan**': This 'McIntosh' x 'Newtown' seedling was released from Summerland, British Columbia, in 1936. It is a 'McIntosh'-type apple, but the tree is hardier (to zone 4) and quite scab-resistant. The fruit ripens in early October near the southern Great Lakes, tends to drop early and stores about four months. Quamme writes: "A 'McIntosh' type, bright red with white flesh, with better flavour; aromatic, with a good acid-to-sugar balance. The flesh is crisp, although the texture is fine. The tree is hardy but difficult to train, as the branches are wide and spreading, and often, the interior branches bear few fruits. The fruit tends to be small if not thinned heavily." Osborne also recommends it.

'**Spigold**': Late crops of large red-striped apples that have very firm, exceptionally high-quality flesh come from this 'Red Spy' x 'Golden Delicious' hybrid released in 1962 from Geneva. A triploid, it cannot be used to pollinate other trees. On young trees, a disease known as bitter pit can be a problem. Tukey recommends this for 'Northern Spy' lovers in climates a little too cool for the 'Spy.'

'**Yellow Transparent**': This very early apple, which ripens in July in warm places, is a Russian cultivar imported to North America in 1870. The tree is smallish, slow-growing, hardy to zone 3b and somewhat scab-resistant but susceptible to fire blight. The fruit, which is not a good keeper, has yellow skin that bruises easily and creamy white, tender, tart-

tasting flesh that is a frequent choice for pies and sauces. Catalogues may refer to it simply as 'Transparent.' Recommended by Sherk, who calls it "my favourite from childhood days."

HARDY APPLES

'**Breakey**': Introduced in 1935 from Morden, Manitoba, this upright, vigorous, hardy tree produces very large blossoms and heavy crops of two-inch fruit that is yellowish green, blushed red. It ripens in mid-September on the prairies, is good for fresh eating and processing and is recommended by Davidson.

'**Brookland**': This compact, hardy tree from Brooks, Alberta, produces annual crops of round fruit with crisp, coarse, sweet flesh. The fruit ripens in late August or early September on the prairies, stores well and can be used fresh or for cooking. Olsen writes: "Attractive red colour, medium size, good quality."

'**Carrol**': A hardy cultivar with 'Melba' parentage released from Morden in 1961, this dwarf-to-medium-sized tree ripens its striped red and green fruit in early September on the prairies. It is good for eating and applesauce and is recommended by Davidson.

'**Collet**': Named for the Manitoba man who discovered it, this streaked red and green cooking apple grows on a medium-sized tree. The fruit reaches up to three inches wide, ripens in early September on the prairies and keeps until the end of December. It is recommended by Davidson.

'**Fall Red**': For a prairie apple, this 'Duchess' x 'Haralson' hybrid released from Morden in 1986 has unusually good size and quality. It is about three inches wide, with dull red skin and white flesh. It ripens by mid- to late September and is worth a try in protected spots in zone 2. It is recommended by Davidson and by Olsen, who writes, "Large, good red colour, very good flavour, keeps well."

'**Garland**': This 'Melba' x 'Haralson' hybrid was released from Morden in 1961. It produces a medium-sized tree that yields large crops of three-inch fruit which is bright red over a light green background. It ripens in mid-September on the prairies and is considered excellent for eating, good for sauce and baking and a fair keeper. Hall-Beyer recommends it for zone 3: "Dark red, juicy, midseason, good flavour."

'**Goodland**': A vigorous 'Patten Greening' seedling from Morden, released in 1955,

Although 'Spartan' looks much like one of its parents, 'McIntosh,' it is hardier and more scab-resistant and the fruit tastier. It can be kept in cold storage for about four months.

'Goodland' produces large crops of two-to-three-inch bright red fruit with white flesh that is good fresh and for processing. It ripens in mid-September on the prairies. It is recommended by Davidson and by Hall-Beyer for zone 3: "Tender, aromatic, tasty, keeps two months, but susceptible to scab."

'Haralson': A very hardy, vigorous tree, worth a try in zone 2b, this 'Malinda' x 'Ben Davis' hybrid was released from the University of Minnesota in 1923. The trees produce big crops of aromatic, yellow, red-striped, white-fleshed fruit almost three inches wide that is ready to pick in October and keeps till March. The texture is fine, the taste mild and pleasant. Hall-Beyer recommends it for zone 3: "Good yield, good keeper, good to eat or to cook, late season (for the north)." Olsen writes: "Good quality and the best-keeping cultivar for zone 3."

'Heyer 12': Known to produce crops in cold and chinook regions where other apples fail, 'Heyer 12,' a Russian apple released from Saskatchewan in 1940, is described by John Davidson of Beaverlodge, Alberta, as "the one we can rely on the most." It is also recommended by Wallace, who writes, "Some of the newer varieties show promise of eventually replacing this one, but so far, it is still the standard." The very vigorous tree begins at a young age to produce two-inch yellow, red-streaked fruit that has juicy, acidic, moderately coarse, greenish white flesh good for sauce and pies but only mediocre fresh. The fruit does not keep well. It is ready to pick in mid- to late August on the prairies and is best picked slightly green, because it becomes soft and mealy when fully ripe.

'Mantet': Introduced in 1929 from Morden, this Russian seedling produces an upright, fairly vigorous tree whose mottled, three-inch red-over-amber fruit ripens in late August on the prairies. Hall-Beyer recommends it for zone 3: "Good flavour, scab-tolerant, keeps for a month."

'Norda': Distinctive, barrel-shaped fruit comes from this 1976 release from Beaverlodge, Alberta. The upright, spreading tree bears at an early age and is thereafter a consistent, moderate cropper. The red-streaked fruit, about three inches long, ripens in September on the prairies and keeps until February. It has creamy flesh that is very firm, crisp and juicy with an excellent, slightly sweet,

Best for many difficult areas, such as parts of the prairies, are the fruits that are smaller than a regular apple but bigger than a crab. So-called apple crabs such as 'Kerr,' right, will produce dependable crops of tasty fruit even where conditions are relatively harsh.

light flavour. In 1985, the Beaverlodge Agriculture Canada research station reported: "One of the largest and also the best-quality dessert apple for the prairies so far." Olsen writes: "Red or yellow fruit shaded like a 'Red Delicious' has good quality, and tree is very hardy."

'**Norland**': This 'Rescue' x 'Melba' hybrid was a 1979 success from a program known as the Prairie Fruit Breeding Co-operative, in which varieties were tried at several stations throughout the prairies. This, the earliest red apple from the program, produces annual crops that ripen from mid-August. The fruit, almost three inches wide, has green-tinted flesh that is similar to 'Melba' in flavour and quality. The tree is a natural semidwarf with a vertical habit. Quamme recommends it for the prairies. Olsen writes: "The best early apple. Good flavour but does not keep long. Moderately susceptible to fire blight." Davidson also recommends it, but in zone 2, Wallace cautions, "Along with other varieties from the Co-operative, these may replace the older ones because of improved size, colour and storageability, but it will take time to tell in this area."

CRABS AND APPLE CRABS

'**Dawn**': A heavy-bearing early-August apple crab released from the University of Saskatchewan in 1959, 'Dawn' has light crimson skin and yellow flesh and is considered good both fresh and cooked. It is recommended by Vick.

'**Dolgo**': This Russian seedling released in 1897 from Brookings, South Dakota, is a very hardy, vigorous tree that blooms early and produces large annual crops of inch-wide, oblong, sweet, delicious, juicy red fruit which makes a ruby-red jelly of excellent flavour and beautiful colour. Osborne writes that it has a "unique strawberry-pineapple flavour." The fruit ripens in early September. The upright, spreading tree is moderately susceptible to scab and slightly susceptible to fire blight but resistant to cedar-apple rust and powdery mildew. Also recommended by Vick, although in zone 2, the Beaverlodge Agriculture Canada station says it is only moderately hardy and requires protection.

'**Kerr**': A 'Dolgo' x 'Haralson' hybrid released from Morden in 1952, 'Kerr' has larger fruit than 'Dolgo,' almost two inches wide with creamy yellow flesh. It ripens in late September on the prairies. The scab-tolerant tree grows upright and spreading. The reddish purple fruit keeps until March. Olsen writes: "Best apple crab. When the fruit is preserved, it does not break down like 'Rescue.' "

'Osman': A 1911 release from the Central Experimental Farm in Ottawa, this very hardy, upright tree produces consistent, moderate crops of yellow, crimson-washed fruit less than two inches wide. The fruit, which is tart but good for canning and jelly, ripens in late August on the prairies. The trees are disease-resistant. Recommended by Wallace.

'Rescue': A seedling of 'Blushed Calville' released from Scott, Saskatchewan, in 1936, 'Rescue' has survived winter temperatures as low as minus 55 degrees F (-48°C). The tree yields beautiful big blossoms followed by large annual crops of dull red fruit about two inches wide; thin the fruits to ensure the large size. The flesh is yellowish white and sweet enough that the fruit can be eaten fresh or preserved. It is recommended by Wallace.

'Trailman': A hybrid of 'Trail' apple and 'Osman' crab from Beaverlodge in 1973, 'Trailman' yields consistent crops of egg-shaped fruit, almost two inches wide, that ripens in mid-September. The skin is golden with a reddish brown wash on the sunny side; the flesh is golden yellow, crunchy and juicy with an excellent, distinctive flavour that is good fresh and for processing. Upright, spreading trees are early-bearing, fire blight-resistant and rugged enough to be recommended for chinook and cold-winter areas. The research scientist at the Agriculture Canada station in Beaverlodge says: "It's an amazing apple, about as hardy as the Siberian crab but technically an apple crab." Wallace recommends it.

The experts who were asked to recommend cultivars for their own area:

Sam Benowitz, owner, Raintree Nursery, Morton, Washington (USDA climatic zone 8).

William E. Craig, tree-fruit specialist, Agriculture Canada Research Station, Kentville, Nova Scotia (Agriculture Canada climatic zone 6a; USDA zone 6a).

Dr. Campbell Davidson, research scientist, Agriculture Canada Research Station, Morden, Manitoba (Agriculture Canada climatic zone 3b; USDA zone 3b).

Bart Hall-Beyer, owner, Sursum Corda, Scotstown, Quebec (Agriculture Canada climatic zone 4a; USDA zone 4a).

Dr. Richard C. Layne, head, Horticultural Science Section, Agriculture Canada Research Station, Harrow, Ontario (Agriculture Canada climatic zone 7a; USDA zone 6a).

William G. Lord, extension specialist (fruit), University of New Hampshire, Durham, New Hampshire (USDA climatic zone 5b).

Paul Olsen, owner, Roseberry Gardens, Thunder Bay, Ontario (Agriculture Canada climatic zone 3a; USDA zone 4a).

Bob Osborne, owner, Corn Hill Nursery, Petitcodiac, New Brunswick (Agriculture Canada climatic zone 4b; USDA zone 4b).

Dr. Harvey Quamme, research scientist, Agriculture Canada Research Station, Summerland, British Columbia (Agriculture Canada climatic zone 6; USDA zone 6a).

Lawrence C. Sherk, formerly with Agriculture Canada, now chief horticulturist of Sheridan Nurseries, Georgetown, Ontario (Agriculture Canada climatic zone 6a; USDA zone 5b).

Dr. Loren D. Tukey, professor of pomology, Pennsylvania State University, University Park, Pennsylvania (USDA climatic zone 5b).

Roger Vick, curator, Devonian Botanic Garden, Edmonton, Alberta (Agriculture Canada climatic zone 3a; USDA zone 3a).

Irene Wallace, owner, Beaverlodge Nurseries, Beaverlodge, Alberta (Agriculture Canada climatic zone 2; USDA zone 2).

Harvest Dates
Apples

The range of dates refers to the approximate beginning of the harvest in the most popular fruit-bearing areas of the north.

Yellow Transparent	July 25-Aug. 10
Goodland	Aug. 25-Sept. 10
Akane	Aug. 25-Sept. 15
Gala	Sept. 10-20
McIntosh	Sept. 20-Oct. 5
Cortland	Sept. 25-Oct. 5
Macoun	Sept. 25-Oct. 10
Spartan	Oct. 1-10
Empire	Oct. 5-15
Liberty	Oct. 5-15
Jonagold	Oct. 5-15
Haralson	Oct. 10-25
Golden Delicious	Oct. 10-25
Idared	Oct. 15-25
Spigold	Oct. 15-30
Mutsu	Oct. 15-30
Golden Russet	Oct. 20-Nov. 10

A Matter of Curiosity

"The amateur of great fortune may be desirous, as a matter of curiosity, of having in his possession every known variety. It is our purpose to make a selection of what we esteem the best and which are most generally esteemed, adding something of the qualities of each."

– Thomas G. Fessenden, *The New American Gardener*, 1843

Many fruit trees can be overwintered indoors in pots or grown year-round in cool greenhouses, allowing gardeners in harsh climates to grow trees that would otherwise be killed by severe weather. A dwarf peach, left, blossoms outdoors in a large wooden container that can be moved if frost threatens.

It would indeed require a great fortune, not to mention acres of space, to grow every known variety of fruit. The result would be one's own personal botanical garden. But it takes very little money or space to grow one or two fruits that are unusual and worthwhile. There is something satisfying about managing to grow a plant that is not normally suited to your area, the sort of thing people used to call a curiosity.

I have one such curiosity, a potted 'Eureka' lemon tree destined by a drastically dwarfing rootstock to remain forever just a couple of feet tall; it produces anywhere from zero to half a dozen lemons a year. Passing the summers in the backyard and wintering in the dining room, it is decorative all year, with its shiny, dark green leaves and fruit that gradually swells and turns from green to yellow and, occasionally, back to green again. The spring blossoms, among the most fragrant in nature, fill the dining room with an almost ethereal perfume. After six or seven years of bearing, the tree probably still has not repaid my initial investment in terms of dollars, but fresh lemons in Canada are a delight that only those who have tasted them can know, and none of my strictly ornamental houseplants will pay me back a cent.

POTTED TREES

Citrus fruits are, of course, strictly out of bounds for outdoor planting in the north, yet some species are quite adaptable to pots, sturdy plants whose forebears have been moved indoors and out since at least the 17th century, when the Sun King admired a row of potted oranges in front of his palace at Versailles. Those trees were wheeled into a dim building known as an orangerie for winter protection, then wheeled out again when the

French climate began to approximate that of southern Spain or the Middle East, where the trees thrive outdoors year-round.

Other trees, too, are amenable to this type of treatment. As northerners develop a global palate, fruits with such romantic names as carambola, lychee and cherimoya will become available from nurseries on this continent. Bananas, figs and other delicacies can be had now. More common fruits too tender for the north are also candidates for growing in pots. Peaches, nectarines, sweet cherries and apricots become feasible in cold places if they are on rootstocks so dwarfing that the trees will crop when grown in containers. Some of these trees do require a certain amount of chilling, so they cannot spend all year in the dining room but must be kept in a cold but not freezing place, such as a basement, from fall till spring. A cool greenhouse can be an excellent permanent home for a small fruit tree or two, which could be trained against a back wall in the fashion of espalier, described on page 25.

These container or greenhouse plants give gardeners a chance to look beyond the hardiness ratings when shopping for trees. In fact, most plants on dwarfing rootstocks are by nature less adaptable to cold, so the best selections are offered by nurseries in the south or near the Pacific coast. Trees can be imported into Canada from the United States if they undergo the proper approval process. (See Sources at the end of this book for more information.)

Several years ago when I visited Ken Taylor, owner of Windmill Point Farm and Nursery near Montreal, he was growing oranges, kumquats, lemons, limes, figs and nectarines in pots. None of the trees, the oldest of which was a 15-year-old 'Ponderosa' lemon, was taller than five feet, and most were less than three. Some were growing on dwarfing rootstocks, while others were genetic dwarfs, trees that are small by nature. Taylor said of these: "They have such a beautiful growth pattern; their fruiting nodes are so close together that the tree is a mass of foliage—it's a bush, almost. They're just perfect for pots." Despite their small size, genetic dwarfs and trees on dwarfing rootstocks produce fruit of normal size, sometimes even larger than normal, the case with apples on the rootstock M27. Figs are the only standard-sized fruit trees normally grown in portable pots, where most cultivars will reach a height of about seven feet.

Deciduous trees such as
nectarines, left, require
lower temperatures after
their leaves fall in autumn.
They should be stored in a
cool basement or similar
place until the buds swell
in spring.

TENDING POTTED TREES

Growing a tree in a container does place more demands on the gardener than growing the same tree in the ground outdoors, because the gardener has to play the part of Mother Nature, making sure that all the tree's requirements—warmth, water, nutrients and pollination—are met. To compound the challenge, a fruit tree in a pot is more likely to suffer from temperature extremes, overwatering or drought than is a plant in the ground.

Make sure the pot is large enough to accommodate the roots easily, with little bending—a pot at least 18 inches across and just as deep, or one that takes about five gallons of soil, will suit most dwarf trees. Wooden containers have greater insulating value than those made of terra cotta, concrete or plastic, although plastic ones are lightest and thus easiest to move, an important consideration when you are dealing with a bushel or two of soil and an awkward and breakable plant. I have found that a basket with side handles, available in Oriental import stores, makes an attractive, lightweight container; it should be treated with a waterproofing stain to increase its longevity and lined with a garbage bag perforated on the bottom. Any pot must have drainage holes so that water can escape. To aid drainage, place about two inches of gravel or, for lighter weight, plastic peanuts or plastic-foam chunks in the bottom of the pot, and cover that layer with enough soil mix so that the tree graft will be just above the soil surface. Only figs and bananas lack such a graft.

Do not use potting soils alone for fruit trees; they are too lightweight and too low in organic matter. Compost alone is an excellent medium. If you have a small supply, mix it half and half with topsoil. For peaches, nectarines, apricots and cherries, lower the proportion of topsoil to one-quarter, and make up the remaining quarter with sand. Hold the trunk vertical, and fill in around the roots with planting mix. Fill the container, and firm the mix with your hands so that the pot rim extends about an inch above the soil and the tree is securely upright. Water the tree until water runs from the bottom of the pot. Taylor mulches the soil surface with bark chips "mainly for appearance but also because it keeps the top of the soil from drying out." The soil surface in pots also looks attractive decorated with small seashells or pretty pebbles. Because the pot will spend at least part of the year indoors, it needs to be able to sit inside a waterproof tray or pan.

Potted fruit trees outdoors fare best with a little shade to keep the pots from baking in the sun. The pots can be sheltered within hay bales or piled stones or partially buried in the earth. Even normally hardy trees, such as apples, will need protection in winter and careful watching in summer if grown in pots.

The type of fig grown in northern gardens requires no pollination. The small fruits that remain dormant all winter will swell unassisted when prompted by the warmer weather of spring.

Watering is especially important for small root systems confined above ground. Give potted trees a thorough watering whenever the top inch of soil is dry, which may occur every couple of days. A little fertilizer, in the form of an inch of compost or a fish emulsion prepared according to package directions, should be applied every spring around blossoming time.

INDOOR CARE

The care of fruit trees indoors depends, first, on whether they are evergreen (citrus fruits and bananas) or deciduous (all the other common fruits). Deciduous trees, which lose their leaves in fall, spend the winter in a dormant state, the horticultural equivalent of sleep, when they can withstand conditions of low light and temperature. As soon as their leaves fall, they are ready to be moved indoors. These trees actually need a certain amount of cold, in the range of 32 to 45 degrees F (0° to 7°C), to enable them to be fully productive the next year. A constantly cool basement or root cellar is a good place to overwinter a fruit tree, but a heated basement is not, nor is an outdoor shed, where branches, buds and roots might easily suffer frost damage. When the trees have had sufficient cold, usually in late February or March—a time signalled by bud swelling—they should be brought upstairs or into a bright place that is warm, not hot.

The evergreens are tropical plants adapted to warm temperatures year-round. These are easier trees to maintain indoors, as they can spend the winter in a living room, kitchen or anyplace where they have a good supply of natural light and the temperature does not fall below freezing. Still, temperatures should not be too high; around 50 to 65 degrees F (10° to 18°C) is best. These trees are apt to yellow and become pest-prone in the usual dry conditions indoors. They bask in a frequent misting with a room-temperature spray, and you should water them as carefully and as frequently as other houseplants, allowing the soil surface to dry between waterings. They can spend the entire year indoors, although fruit production is better with a summer outdoors.

Deciduous trees should begin to spend part of the day outdoors as soon as the foliage appears in spring. At this time, they should not be exposed to temperatures as low as a few degrees above freezing, which can destroy the developing buds and fruit. On cold days, play it safe by leaving the trees indoors. On warm days, put them outside in a sheltered place in full shade. Continue to move them outside every warm day, gradually increasing the time outdoors: an hour the first day, two the next, and so on, simultaneously increasing exposure to the sun, so that after several days, the tree is able to spend half of its outdoor time in the shade and half in the sun. This slow process of acclimatization, called hardening off, is necessary to prevent the tree's going into shock from the drastic change in its surroundings. Too rapid a change can cause blossom drop, leaf drop and even death. Finally, when nights are no cooler than about 50 degrees F (10°C), the trees can be left outdoors, but bring them inside whenever frost threatens. Obviously, hardening off is not a procedure for a neglectful orchardist. Fruit trees in pots require daily care. Keep the pots out of windy places, which can damage leaves, dry soil quickly and even topple the pots.

Both evergreen and deciduous trees, except the types of figs and bananas normally grown in the north, require pollination. If you have chosen a type of tree that does best with cross-pollination, the procedure is more complicated, as you will require two trees that blossom at the same time. (Fortunately, most of the tender trees that are best grown in pots are self-fertile.) When the blossom is newly but fully open, touch a small paintbrush or cotton swab to the pollen, and move it to the stigma—the tip of the post in the centre of that blossom or another blossom. Every day, pollinate each blossom that opens. I have found that while fruit will set this way indoors, it often drops if the tree is not exposed to outdoor sunlight soon after pollination.

Severely dwarfed trees should be given little pruning, but they can tolerate the usual removal or trimming of crossed, damaged or overly long branches. The fruit should be at least six inches apart, so thinning may be required for it to become full-sized and of good quality.

FIGS

The type of fig grown in northern containers requires no pollination. It is also one of the easiest container trees because it actually prefers to have its roots a little cramped, otherwise tending to run to foliage rather than fruit. In her book *A Joy of Gardening*, esteemed British gardener Vita Sackville-West writes: "A pot-grown fig, heavily hung with its fruit among its beautifully shaped leaves, is a thing to stand in summer on a paved path or beside a front door; it is decorative, and you can eat the figs."

In summer, a fig loves heat, so it can grow against a south-facing wall or in a sheltered, sunny corner outdoors. Figs are borne in the leaf axils on the tips of year-old and two-year-old branches. Pruning will lessen the crop, so heavy pruning should be done only during the first year or two and thereafter should be as light as possible. The small figs that develop in late summer will not mature unless the tree is in a warm greenhouse. Pick them off when the leaves fall, sparing only the smallest, pea-sized figs, which will remain dormant until spring. A container tree should yield one or two dozen figs in late summer. Figs are heavy feeders that should be fertilized monthly from March until October with a powdering of bone meal and a drink of seaweed solution mixed according to the package directions. It is most important that the soil never be allowed to dry out.

While gardeners in peach zones can grow figs successfully outdoors in sheltered places, especially if the trees are mulched and wrapped for winter, some northerners in cooler places are able to grow them outdoors by bending the trees to the ground and covering them with earth in fall or burying the trees in fallen leaves and wrapping them with plastic, in the manner of hybrid tea roses. Figs

Provided a fig tree is kept sufficiently warm, watered and fertilized, a crop of exotic fruit such as 'Brown Turkey' figs, left, can be the happy result.

can endure winter temperatures as low as 15 degrees F (-9°C), but they are best kept from freezing. Uncover or unwrap the trees as soon as the danger of heavy frost has passed.

BANANAS

The only edible-fruited cultivar of banana (*Musa* spp) that is suitably dwarf for container or greenhouse culture is 'Cavendish,' also called 'Chinese,' 'Dwarf,' 'Governor,' 'Dwarf Jamaica' or 'Ladyfinger.' In a pot, it will grow about six feet tall. This cultivar, like other commercial bananas, must be grown from a corm or cutting rather than from seed. Banana trees grown from seeds produce plants that are ornamental only, as the fruit is too seedy to be palatable. Plant 'Cavendish' in a half-barrel or a five-gallon pot filled with a mixture of equal parts topsoil, composted manure and peat moss.

As the banana will bear fruit only when winter temperatures stay above about 60 degrees F (15°C), the plant must overwinter in the house or a heated greenhouse. Bananas do best with the 10 to 12 hours of sunlight a day they would receive in the tropics, so indoor plants will do better if they are under bright lights. High humidity is equally important. Place the banana pot in a tray of gravel and water, and mist frequently with a spray of room-temperature water. As soon as the weather settles in late spring, the plant should

Oriental persimmons, right, are the type usually sold in supermarkets, but they are not as hardy as the American natives, which have smaller fruit.

begin to spend some time outdoors, starting in the shade, as described on page 120. In summer, bananas thrive in heat and high humidity, but they have large, fragile leaves, so they should be kept in a sheltered place out of strong winds. When the night temperature falls to about 50 degrees F (10°C) in autumn, begin to move the plant indoors, first for overnight and eventually for night and day.

Each banana plant produces just one crop of fruit, which it manages to do without pollination, a phenomenon known as parthenocarpy. The crop should begin to ripen about 1½ years after planting; bananas can mature at any time of year. A potted 'Cavendish' is capable of yielding 10 or 15 pounds of delicious four-to-five-inch fruit. Later crops come from suckers, daughter plants that begin to sprout from the corm when the plant is about six months old. Find the base of the daughter plant with your fingers, split it off with a knife, taking as many roots as possible, and give it its own large pot of rich soil. One sucker can be left beside the mother plant to replace the mother after the banana crop has been harvested. Pick bananas when they are fat and smooth but before they are fully ripe,

as tree-ripened bananas often split. Hang them indoors, where they will ripen fully in a few days.

CITRUS FRUITS

There are dwarfing rootstocks for all common types of citrus trees, which are the easiest of all indoor fruits. Trifoliate oranges (*Poncirus trifoliata*) and kumquats (members of a related genus, *Fortunella*) are the most tolerant of cool temperatures and shifting conditions as plants are moved indoors and out. The most popular indoor orange, often sold in florist shops, is the calamondin orange, a type of kumquat with sweet peel and sour fruit. Calamondins and kumquats produce small fruit best used for marmalades. Lemons are the most rugged of the large-sized citrus fruits, while sweet oranges, mandarin oranges, grapefruits and limes require progressively more heat and are thus more difficult to keep in the north.

While the hardiest citrus can endure freezing weather in December and January, all are best kept above 55 degrees F (13°C), their lowest temperature for growth. Bring them indoors in fall when frost is forecast, and take them out again on warm days until the weather becomes too inclement or your patience with the indoor-outdoor migration wanes.

Citrus trees begin to bloom as soon as days become brighter in spring. Blossoms should be hand-pollinated, although bees usually visit blooms that appear outdoors. The fruit matures slowly and, even when ripe, can be left on the tree for months, where it continues to look decorative throughout the winter, remaining in place while the tree blossoms anew. In chilly England, Samuel Pepys wrote in 1666 that on the first orange trees he had ever seen in that country, there were "some green, some half, some a quarter and some full ripe on the same tree; and one fruit of the same tree do come a year or two after the other." Pepys "pulled off a little one by stealth," only to discover that "it was just as other green small oranges are, as big as half the end of my little finger."

Citrus trees grown from pips will not produce the supermarket-type fruit that a gardener can obtain by buying a named variety from a nursery. The trees from pips are often much like their wild ancestors. Branches are thorny, and fruiting may not begin for years. Calamondin oranges, however, will often grow true to type from seed.

Avocados and mangoes are other fruits that many gardeners grow from seeds. In these cases, the trees are grown as ornamentals rather than for fruit. It is the rare gardener who can provide the warmth and pollination these trees require in order to set fruit.

Unpotted Curiosities

There are several kinds of fruit that are marginally hardy and little known in the north. Some, such as the jujube, or Chinese date (*Ziziphus jujuba*), can grow in the warmest parts of peach country. The jujube is hardy to about minus 10 degrees F (-23°C) and has one- or two-inch sweet, brown, figlike fruits. The attractive, slender tree, which grows about 30 feet tall, has furrowed bark, light green, glossy leaves and flowers that are small and greenish yellow. The fruit is very sweet when ripe and can be eaten fresh, dried or cooked. The tree is pest-free, drought-resistant and tolerant of alkaline soil, although it does best in good soil with ample moisture.

The pawpaw, custard apple or northern banana (*Asimina triloba*), a native of the south-

ern United States, is hardier, to minus 20 degrees F (-29°C). Another ornamental tree, it is about 25 feet tall, tolerant of shade and not bothered by insects. It has bright purple, fly-pollinated blossoms and large magnolialike leaves. The large, high-vitamin fruits have a pleasant fragrance, the texture of a banana and the flavour of a pear. The trees require no spraying and little pruning, although they will spread by suckers if growing contentedly in a fairly wet area. The fruits are ready to pick when slightly soft and should be allowed to soften a little more indoors before eating.

The American persimmon (*Diospyros virginiana*), another North American native, is hardy to minus 25 degrees F (-32°C). The edible, tough-skinned orange fruit, about two inches wide, remains on the tree long after the leaves have fallen. It can be eaten fresh when soft or can be peeled, mashed and frozen. The glossy leaves may be as long as six inches. Male and female flowers grow on separate plants, so the gardener will need two plants, a male and a female, and only the latter will bear fruit. The tree, which is usually pest-free in the north, grows about 25 or 30 feet tall and is slow-growing and attractive enough for espalier. Fruit is borne on new wood, so once branches have fruited, they can be removed as necessary. The more desirable Oriental persimmon (*D. kaki*), the species whose fruit is sold in the marketplace, bears larger, sweeter fruit that does not require pollination, but it is not hardy.

Kiwi

The genus *Actinidia* includes several vining fruits, most notably the kiwi (*A. deliciosa*, formerly *A. chinensis*), which grows with sporadic success as far north as the mildest parts of British Columbia, where the occasional cold winter sets it back. 'Hayward,' the foremost cultivar, requires temperatures above 5 degrees F (-15°C) and a long season of more than 200 frost-free days to mature its fruit. In an experimental program in Ontario, kiwi vines have been grown under winter cover, partnered with 'Granny Smith' apples and other finicky fruits such as peaches. Harvests have been large, but the system does require expensive winter heating of the greenhouse. Kiwi vines grown in a warm greenhouse do best if planted directly in the ground, not in pots.

Kiwi vines, which grow about 30 feet tall and require a trellis at least six feet high, are heavy feeders and drinkers that respond to generous treatment with robust growth and bigger crops of larger fruit. The vines should never be allowed to suffer from lack of water, especially after the plant has leafed out. Let them grow straight to the top of the trellis, then pinch them out. Train two lateral leaders to grow in opposite directions along a horizontal support; it is from these laterals that fruiting canes grow.

The fruit appears on only some of the vines, because actinidia plants are either male or female. The gardener must grow two—and not just any two, but a male and a female—in order to harvest fruit from just one, the female. The two must grow within about 35 feet of each other. Teaming them on opposite sides of a pergola or on nearby trellises is a possibility. The male flower entirely lacks a pistil, the female organ that normally protrudes from the flower centre. Female flowers have both stamens and pistils. Until actinidia plants flower, their gender cannot be determined. Seedlings flower in five to eight years and cuttings in three or four, but fortunately, nurseries sell plants already identified.

The recent success of *Actinidia chinensis* has turned gardeners' attention to a few cold-hardy cousins known chiefly as ornamentals, although their smaller fruit is just as edible and lacks the fuzzy skin of the kiwi. *Actinidia arguta* and *A. kolomikta* are the most dependable choices for northern fruit. The latter may be the hardiest member of the genus. It has been said to survive minus 50 degrees F (-45°C), although plants grown since the late 1960s at the Agriculture Canada Research Station in Morden, Manitoba, died after the winter of 1973-74, when temperatures plunged to minus 30 degrees F (-34°C). *Actinidia kolomikta* is decorative, with leaves that are metallic green in spring and splashed pink and white in summer. The fruit is very sweet, with a pineapple fragrance, and is the size of a currant or gooseberry.

Actinidia arguta, which has survived winter temperatures of minus 25 degrees F (-32°C), was known earlier in this century as the tara vine, bower vine or bower actinidia. In his *Landscape Decorating as Applied to Home Decoration* of 1911, Samuel T. Maynard noted that arguta "will cover an arbour or trellis more quickly than any vine we have." Ironically, it

The kiwi is one of the rare commercial fruits whose male and female flowers grow on separate plants. As only the female flowers will produce fruit but the male plant is required for pollination, the gardener who buys plants already identified has a head start.

was this very vigour that lessened arguta's popularity. In nurseries, the vine swamped less aggressive neighbours unless it was sold the first year or repeatedly pruned. Still, Maynard recorded an attribute of the species: "Some of the vines produce a small green fruit that one soon learns to like."

Three additional species, comprising *Actinidia callosa*, *A. melanandra* and *A. purpurea*, are also capable of producing edible fruit, although they are best known for their decorative foliage. *Actinidia purpurea* yields small purple-skinned fruit; *A. melanandra*, egg-shaped, inch-long, reddish brown fruit; *A. callosa*, yellow fruit. *Actinidia polygama*, known as a silver-leafed ornamental, yields the least palatable fruit. At the Royal Botanical Gardens in Hamilton, Ontario, it shares a pergola with a kolomikta vine.

In spring, as soon as the plants arrive from the nursery, set them in a sheltered position close to a support such as a trellis. Each vine should be allowed 10 to 15 feet of space all around. The vines are vulnerable to transplant shock, so disturb the roots as little as possible. Water them thoroughly as soon as they are planted and at least once a week during the first summer. Hardy kiwis will tolerate infertile soil, but none will do well in poorly drained soil. Protect the young plants from cats, as they contain some of the same chemical constituents as catnip.

Kolomikta blossoms can appear as early in spring as apricots, so they are vulnerable to frost damage, especially if they are close to the ground. Arguta blossoms appear later, around May, and fruits are ripe in September or early October. Provided they are not frost-damaged, hardy actinidias are bountiful, capable of producing hundreds of fruits per vine; most home gardeners would want only one male and one female. Michael McConkey, a former Canadian resident who specializes in hardy-actinidia culture in his garden in Maryland, knows one vine of an arguta-kolomikta hybrid planted in the 1970s that bore about 800 fruits in 1985. Actinidia fruit is best eaten when absolutely ripe and slightly soft. Then, Edward Goodell writes in *Arnoldia*, "I much prefer fresh arguta fruit to seedless table grapes because of its unique, sophisticated flavour."

Unique is the best word to describe all the fruiting curiosities. Peaches in Alaska, jujubes in Toronto, bananas in New York—many things become possible when a gardener embarks on a journey of horticultural adventure.

INDOOR PEST CONTROL

Fruit trees indoors are vulnerable to certain pests that are not such a problem outdoors, where harsh weather and natural predators can control them. The greenhouse provides a perfect environment for plants and pests alike. As a preventive measure, the first step is sanitation; do not bring unsterilized soil into the greenhouse. Either use purchased planting mixes, or sterilize your own soil by pouring boiling water through it until it drains freely from the bottom. Check any purchased plants for signs of aphids and spider mites, and make sure the plant is clean before bringing it indoors. This may mean spraying it within a plastic bag that will stay in place for a day. Thereafter, inspect plants daily. At the first sign of whiteflies or aphids, spray with a solution of mild dish detergent or with purchased insecticidal soap. Spray weekly, drenching all surfaces. After half an hour, the plants can be rinsed with room-temperature water. Scale, which commonly infests indoor citrus, can be removed with a toothbrush, either dry or dipped in a mild soap solution. Kill mealybugs and scale with a cotton swab dipped in alcohol.

For the greenhouse, some predatory insects are available from specialist suppliers. A population of these predators allows the greenhouse environment to approximate outdoor conditions more closely. The insect *Aphidoletes aphidimyza* parasitizes aphids, for instance, and syrphid flies will parasitize aphids, mealybugs and leafhoppers. Immature ladybugs consume aphids and scale. The whitefly predator *Encarsia formosa* needs warm temperatures to be effective.

The most benign of the pest-control methods described on pages 31 to 36 can also be used in the greenhouse. Use sticky yellow traps to catch whiteflies, placing the cards near plant leaves. Growing a few umbels, such as dill, in the greenhouse will give a home to many small predators.

Unusual fruits and fruits in containers

APPETIZING AND HEALTH-GIVING

*"Fruits freshly taken from the trees
or vines, with no injury from keeping
or from transportation, are much
more appetizing and health-giving
than those which are usually exposed
for sale. It should, therefore, be the
ambition of every owner of land to
cultivate fruits to some extent,
without regard to the question of
pecuniary profit."*

—W.C. STRONG, *Fruit Culture*, 1885

A homegrown fruit supply
means not only dessert
picked fresh from the tree
but also an array of possible
condiments, beverages and
preserves that may be
expensive to buy or
impossible to find in stores.

Those who eat the fruit of their own labour complete the cycle of work and just reward. The reward is the freshest fruit possible, and it may also be the safest if it is grown without harmful sprays. The harvest may be a modest return, especially when trees are young, or it may be bounteous, in the neighbourhood of 30 bushels from a standard apple tree, half that quantity of pears, plums, cherries or peaches. This is the kind of harvest that sets one to dreaming of ciders, pies, fruit wines and shelves heavy with jams and jellies.

Fortunately, these wonderful foods need not remain fantasies for long. Even a cook with the most basic skills can turn out perfectly good home preserves. Excellent ciders and wines are often made by those who think they lack the culinary equivalent of horticulture's green thumb. This chapter will list only the most important principles and measurements involved in the various types of fruit preservation; it will not attempt to offer the last word. After a certain point, creativity reigns. Those who want more guidance can find many books and government pamphlets dealing with fruit storage and cuisine.

"Europeans eat with their tongues; Americans eat with their eyes," says Roger Way of the Agricultural Experiment Station in Geneva, New York. He means, of course, that North Americans are too easily beguiled by colour and size when it comes to choosing food. Way developed a delicious red-blushed golden apple called 'Jonagold' that has been the object of a great deal of breeding energy from scientists intent on creating the very same apple but with red skin, a concession to nothing but visual preference. In considering fruit, both the home grower and the supermarket buyer must remember that beauty is only skin-deep. There is an exciting spectrum of fruit flavours and textures to be sampled once the buyer or gardener outgrows the habit of considering appearance alone. As a general rule, sweet fruits are best eaten out of the hand, but sour ones are better preserved, as their more complex flavours give them an advantage when married with sweeteners such as sugar or honey. These subtle qualities of flavour and texture were better known to our forebears, who had to depend upon what could be grown locally and who did most of their own preserving. They knew that the best-quality apples and pears were often the latest-ripening ones, while the tastiest apricots, peaches and cherries ripened during the hot

weather of mid- to late summer.

They knew, too, that the best flavour from most types of peaches, cherries, plums and other members of the genus *Prunus* comes from fruit that has ripened fully on the tree, a time signalled by fragrance, softness, flavour and colour. Most of these fruits are best eaten or preserved within a few days of picking. On the other hand, some apples and pears improve with storage, as described later. Gardeners who have the space can choose to grow both early and late cultivars to ensure an ongoing supply of fresh fruit.

Tasting is the most reliable way to judge when to pick the *Prunus* fruits. Fruit flavour is dependent upon a combination of sugars and acids, chiefly citric acid. As most fruits ripen, they become less acidic in flavour. Some acid, however, is needed to give fruit a pleasant taste. While flavour is a subjective issue, too much sweetness often makes fruit unappetizingly bland.

After fruit is fully ripe, the sugar content gradually decreases while substances formed in the fruit cause the texture to break down. Sweet fruit becomes starchy; crisp fruit becomes mealy; buttery fruit becomes watery.

Diners who know little about the subtleties of fruit flavours may be tempted to "eat with their eyes," but the largest, brightest-coloured fruit is not necessarily the tastiest.

This process may take days for peaches but weeks for late apples and pears and only after they are taken out of cold storage.

Harvesttime can also be judged to some extent by fruit colour. Young fruits are green because of the presence of chlorophyll, the same substance that colours leaves and stems and is responsible for photosynthesis, the manufacture of plant food by means of sunlight. Some fruits are yellow when young, while others turn yellow as they mature. The yellow colour, whose development is not dependent upon sunshine, comes from carotene or closely related substances. Red, blue or purple colours, which come from pigments known as anthocyanins, may or may not depend upon sunshine. The last stages of colour development in plums and cherries do not require sunlight, but the reddish blush on peaches and apples does, the reason the sunny side of these fruits is the most highly coloured. Dense foliage, shade or too much fertilizer can lessen any fruit colour. After fruit is picked, the amount of red pigment does not increase, but because the chlorophyll disappears — as it does in fall leaves — red and yellow colours become brighter.

While the fruits described in this book are edible, if not necessarily palatable, at all stages, the pits, twigs, bark and foliage of *Prunus* species should not be eaten. The only exceptions are the almondlike pits of the few sweet-pitted apricots. The leaves of cherry trees were once used to flavour puddings and sauces, but they are now known to release hydrocyanic acid in the stomach. Livestock and children have frequently been poisoned by eating the leaves or fruit pits of cherries or plums.

FRUIT STORAGE

Unlike the *Prunus* fruits, some apples and late pears taste best not when just picked but after a certain length of time in cold storage. These fruits require high humidity and low temperatures, but not too low; all fruit will freeze at a temperature a few degrees below freezing and will spoil rapidly upon thawing. The best temperature for storage is 32 degrees F (0°C) or a degree or two higher.

In an unheated basement, suitably wide, strong shelves can be constructed to hold a winter supply of boxes of apples and pears, as well as jars of preserves. In a heated basement,

Drying is an ancient and inexpensive way to preserve a large harvest of fruit in a relatively small space, although texture and flavour will be altered somewhat.

partition off a corner and insulate it—walls and ceiling—so that heat will not enter it and it will not cool the house above. There should be at least one closeable opening to the outdoors or the main basement for ventilation. A much smaller version of a cold room is a refrigerator with its thermostat set at the highest temperature level. A more ambitious and much larger version is an outdoor root cellar that is partly or entirely underground, insulated by soil and vented to the outdoors. A root cellar must be far enough underground or sufficiently insulated so the temperature within will not fall below freezing. The USDA suggests a design with masonry walls. Soil is banked around three walls, and the fourth is left exposed for an insulated door wide enough to admit a wheelbarrow.

In any storage room, keep fruits and vegetables separate, because fruits can absorb odours from vegetables. By the same token, do not store chemicals such as paint nearby. Pick over the produce, setting aside damaged fruit for early use and storing only sound, unbruised fruit. Pack it into perforated plastic bags, or wrap it individually in newspaper and stack it in cardboard or wooden boxes.

FREEZING

Small quantities of any type of fruit can be stored most easily in a freezer, although the crisp quality of the fresh fruit will be lost. To prepare fruit for freezing, wash, core, pit and peel it, as necessary. Then, if you want the fruit to come out in nicely separated pieces, spread it in a single layer on a tray and prefreeze before pouring into freezer bags or other sturdy, airtight containers. If you do not mind thawing an entire container of fruit at once, pour the fruit, cooked or raw, directly into the container. It can be frozen without sugar, but sugar will help to preserve the colour and flavour. Either pour sugar over the fruit or freeze it in one of the syrups described on page 132. If using a syrup, add the sugar to the water, heat the mixture, stirring to dissolve, let it cool, and pour it over fruit that has been loosely packed in containers. Fill the containers only about three-quarters full to allow room for expansion. Jams, preserves and stewed fruits can also be frozen, but again, leave a large space at the top of the container. If insufficient space is left, the containers will burst or lift their lids as the food freezes. Use packaging recommended for the freezer, or ensure that lids are tight, as otherwise, the food will desiccate and decline in flavour and texture fairly quickly. Frozen fruit should, in any case, be used within a year for best quality.

DRYING

Another easy way of preserving fruit is by drying, and in this case, the food can be stored at room temperature. To prepare fruit for drying, wash it and cut away any bruises. Peel and core apples and pears, halve small fruits, and slice larger ones no thicker than a quarter of an inch—the more surface exposed to the air, the better and faster the drying will be. The only fruits normally dried whole are prune plums, which are by nature so high in sugar and so low in moisture that they will dry throughout before they begin to decay. Prunes are made commercially by drying purple plums either artificially or in the sun. They are aged, or "sweated," for a few weeks, then glossed with steam, glycerine or fruit juice to produce sterile, shiny skin. Peaches and nectarines should be peeled before drying. Dip them into boiling water for 15 to 30 seconds, depending upon ripeness—riper fruit requires a shorter dip. Immerse the fruit in cold water until you can handle it, and the skins should slip off easily. Peel apples and pears with a paring knife. Apricots need not be peeled.

Some fruits, especially certain apples, pears and peaches, will discolour after they are cut unless they are treated with an antioxidant. Special products for this purpose are available, or use 1 teaspoon of ascorbic acid or 2 tablespoons of lemon juice to each cup of water. Dip the fruit before proceeding. You can also put the cut fruit into a solution of 2 tablespoons salt and 2 tablespoons vinegar in a gallon of cold water, but in this case, rinse the fruit in plain water before proceeding.

Commercial dryers are available and effective, but fruit can also be dried in an oven set at 150 degrees F (65.5°C) until most of the water has been removed, at which point the temperature should be lowered to about 100 degrees F (38°C) and the fruit stirred and inspected frequently to prevent scorching. Fruit can also be dried in the sun, but it must not be left outdoors overnight. If dew or rain falls on it, it will darken. Outdoor drying works best when the weather is consistently hot and dry. Spread the fruit in a single layer on a

Some types of fruit, such as certain peaches, should be dipped in an antioxidant solution of ascorbic acid, lemon juice or vinegar to prevent browning during canning or drying.

cheesecloth-covered screen, and cover it with cheesecloth to keep pests away.

To make fruit leather, cook fruit until soft, purée it in a blender or food processor, add sweetening and spices as desired, and spread the purée in a smooth quarter-inch layer on plastic wrap placed on a cookie sheet. Use an oven or a food dehydrator. The leather is ready to store when it is chewy and peels easily from the plastic wrap. Roll it for storage.

Fruit is dry when it is tough and leathery and returns to its original shape when bent or squeezed. Store dried fruits and leathers in plastic bags, plastic containers or lidded glass jars filled to the top and kept in a cool, dark place. If, after a few days, there appears to be moisture on the fruit or inside the container, remove the fruit for further drying. Fruit that is a little less dry, a consistency preferred by some people, can be stored in containers in a freezer. To reconstitute dried fruit, simmer it in water or apple juice for 10 to 15 minutes.

CANNING

Fruits are sufficiently high in acid that they can be preserved at home in purchased jars with airtight lids. Excellent whole or sliced fruit, jams, jellies, sauces, chutneys and pickles can be stored outside the freezer for an indefinite period of time, but most require some preparation. "Canning" is still the word often used, although metal cans are no longer em-

131

Homegrown fruit in the kitchen

Ripe, unblemished storage apples such as 'Jonagold' will retain their fresh quality for several months if preserved in bags or boxes at a temperature slightly above freezing.

ployed. The activity is better called processing. Processing can be done easily and safely at home, provided temperatures and timings are carefully observed, as this ensures that food is sterilized and kept in an air-free environment. A little special equipment is necessary, all of it sold in hardware stores and large supermarkets around canning time from summer through fall. The most common processing method includes a glass jar sometimes called a mason jar, in honour of John Mason, who invented the system 150 years ago. Nowadays, the jar is usually closed with a metal snap lid held in place by a metal screw band.

For processing, use only perfectly sound half-pint, pint or quart glass jars or their metric approximation. Sterilize the jars and lids by placing them in a large pot of boiling water for 20 minutes or longer until they are ready to be filled. I use a big canning kettle for doing the sterilizing and for processing the preserves. Use tongs or a pair of forks to take the jars out of the hot water.

Prepare the fruit as required for the recipe or in the same fashion as for drying it, as described earlier in this chapter. Always use equipment—including pots and spoons—that is galvanized or made of stainless steel or glass, as other metals can darken fruit and impart off-flavours. Again, fruit susceptible to discoloration by oxygen should be dipped in an antioxidant (described on page 131) before it is packed into the jars.

Fruits can be stored in water, in fruit juice, in a solution of water or fruit juice with honey or corn syrup or, most commonly, in a syrup made from white sugar and water. Although the syrup generally recommended and the best for retaining the natural fruit flavour is a 40 percent solution of sugar to water, the thickness of the syrup used is a matter of taste and diet and will depend in part upon the sweetness of the fruit. Prepare approximately 1½ to 2 cups of syrup for each quart or litre jar of fruit. Use 4 cups of water or fruit juice in all of the following syrups. Honey or corn syrup may be substituted for all or part of the sugar, but do not use artificial sweeteners:

Thin (30%)—2 cups sugar; yields 5 cups syrup
Medium (40%)—3 cups sugar; yields 5½ cups syrup
Heavy (50%)—4¾ cups sugar; yields 6½ cups syrup
Extra heavy (60%)—7 cups sugar; yields 7¾ cups syrup

Pack the fruit loosely into hot jars. Measure the sugar and water or juice into a saucepan, and heat the mixture to boiling, stirring until the sugar dissolves. Then ladle the hot syrup over fruit. This system is called cold-pack canning. In the hot-pack method, the fruit is puréed—applesauce, for example—or cooked in the syrup. The hot fruit-and-syrup mixture is poured into the jars before processing. A funnel that just fits into the jar opening helps a great deal in filling jars. This, too, is available where canning supplies are sold. Make sure there are no air pockets in the jar by inserting a clean knife down the inside walls.

You must leave an air space between the food and the lid so that the lid will seal properly. The smaller the jar, the smaller the headspace required. Half-pint jars should have about half an inch of space, quart jars an inch. Make sure the rim of the jar is clean before you put the hot lid in place. Then screw on the metal band so that it is just secure. Do not tighten after processing.

Some pickles, jams and preserves that call for high amounts of acid or sugar need no further processing, although it is safest to process even these foods. Other hot-pack and cold-pack fruit products definitely must be processed. The standard equipment is a metal pot large enough to hold several jars upright on

Most methods of fruit preservation require certain special equipment. A cider press is an investment that will prove worthwhile if large quantities of apples are grown or purchased.

a rack and tall enough to allow the jars to be covered by at least an inch of water. There are also steam canners on the market, but these have not been shown to maintain the high temperatures necessary for safe processing. Bring the water in the bath to boiling before you set the lidded jars in place. Cover the bath with a lid, and begin timing when the water returns to a rapid boil. The length of time the jars will remain in the bath depends upon the food product and the jar size:

Apples (hot pack): 15 minutes
Applesauce: 15 minutes
Peaches, pears, plums, cherries, apricots: raw pack, 20 minutes/pint, 25 minutes/quart; hot pack, 15 minutes
Jams, jellies, preserves: 10 minutes (½-pints and pints)
Pickles, ketchups, chutneys: 10 minutes/pint, 15 minutes/quart
Juices: 10 minutes/pint, 15 minutes/quart

Processing time also depends upon altitude — the boiling point is lower at higher altitudes. The times listed above are accurate for altitudes up to 2,000 feet. For any altitude over 2,000 feet, increase the time by one-fifth; for each additional 1,000 feet, add an additional fifth. For example, at 3,000 feet, a 20-minute recommended processing time would increase by 8 minutes (one-fifth of 20 plus one-fifth of 20) to 28 minutes.

When the time is up, turn off the heat, remove the jars from the hot water with tongs, and set them on a rack or dish towel on the counter, not touching and not covered. If you have used metal snap lids, you will hear each one pop as the air inside cools sufficiently to make the lid contract into its concave position. Screw bands that feel loose can be removed and used again. Let the jars cool for about 12 hours, then label them and store in a cool, dry, dark place. Warmth and light may cause colour changes in the food and will result in vitamin loss.

If a lid does not seal, put the jar in the refrigerator and use the contents within a few days, or put on a new, clean lid and process the jar again. Any preserved fruit that looks or smells suspicious should not be eaten, nor should anyone even taste food in a stored jar that has lost its seal. This is very important, as food preserved improperly is vulnerable to invasion by such toxic substances as botulins.

JELLIES

"The object in making jelly," says an Ontario Department of Agriculture booklet of 1915, "is to preserve the original flavour of the fruit as far as possible; to have the juice well jellied but not too thick, leathery or tough; and also to have a good clear colour." As any jelly maker knows, these objectives can be difficult to attain. Only if all measurements,

While European or prune plums are the best type for drying and for pies and preserves, Asian plums, right, are best eaten fresh or used in jams or jellies.

cooking times and temperatures are just right will the cook have perfect jelly.

In order to jell, fruit requires a certain proportion of both acid and pectin. Pectin is a type of carbohydrate that may come from a commercial source (liquid or powder) or may come from the fruit itself, although most northern tree fruits, with the exception of apples, crab apples and quinces, do not contain sufficient pectin. (The pectin content of apples is highest in the skins and cores. It is the breakdown of pectin, incidentally, that causes apples to become mealy when they are overripe.) Besides apples, other fruits high in pectin which can be added to low-pectin fruits to increase their jelling potential include cranberries, blackberries, gooseberries, Concord grapes, citrus fruits and currants (the berries, not the small raisins). The natural pectin content is highest in slightly underripe fruit. If you have purchased powdered or liquid pectin, follow the directions on the label.

To make jelly, wash the fruit, but do not pare it. Cook the fruit gently in as little water as possible, adding water only as necessary and cooking until the fruit is thoroughly softened —from about 15 minutes for soft fruit such as plums to about half an hour for apples. Stir to prevent sticking and burning. Mash with a potato masher, then pour the soft fruit into a jelly bag. Several layers of cheesecloth can be used, although this type of bag is difficult to recycle. (I have a recyclable bag made from an old cotton T-shirt. I sewed a line of stitches in a big U-shape from one bottom corner past the neck to the bottom again, then cut away the sleeves and neck.) Soak the bag or cheesecloth in water, and squeeze it drip-dry before pouring in the hot mashed fruit, or the fabric will absorb a great deal of juice. Tie the top of the bag together, and suspend it by a string over a glass, ceramic, plastic or stainless-steel bowl that will collect the dripping juice. Let the bag hang undisturbed until dripping stops, which may take as little as an hour or as long as overnight. Squeezing the bag will produce more juice, but the resultant jelly will be cloudy. The general rule of thumb is that a pound of fruit makes about 1 cup of juice, but of course, this depends upon the fruit and the amount of water used to cook it. Use the juice immediately, or store it in the refrigerator to use within two or three days. Scrape, rinse and wash the jelly bag before using it again.

For best results with jellies, prepare no more than 6 cups of juice at a time in a large, wide-bottomed stainless-steel or ceramic pot. Quick cooking means that maximum flavour is maintained. Add approximately ¾ cup sugar to every cup of fruit juice. Do not substitute honey, as it acts quite differently in the jelling process. Heat and stir the mixture until the sugar is completely dissolved, bring it to a full, rolling boil—the shorter the cooking time, the better the jelly—and do not stir again until after the jelly test: when the mixture reaches 8 Fahrenheit degrees (4.5 Celsius degrees) above the boiling point of water on a candy thermometer. If you have no thermometer, there is a mechanical test. Lift a little syrup from the pot with a dry metal spoon, cool it in the air for a few seconds, and pour the syrup off the side of the spoon. When two drops form on the edge of the spoon and run together to fall as one drop, the jelly is done. Immediately remove the pot from the heat. When boiling stops, skim off the foam, pour the liquid into hot, sterilized jars, and seal with a metal lid or paraffin, as described on page 135.

JAMS, PRESERVES AND BUTTERS

Jams, preserves and fruit butters are much more forgiving than jellies, and because they utilize the fruit pulp and sometimes the skin, the fruit goes further. If a mixture of fruit, sugar, water and perhaps pectin turns out thick, it can be called jam; thinner, it is a pre-

Home preservation in glass jars is an exacting practice but an easy one, provided the cook has the proper equipment at the outset and then times the processing according to established guidelines.

serve; and thinner still, a syrup or sauce for pancakes, waffles and desserts. Bill MacKentley, owner of St. Lawrence Nurseries in Potsdam, New York, makes a delicious plum sauce by putting 'Green Gage' fruit through a fruit press. Marmalades are jams or preserves that include some citrus fruit.

A butter is simply the thick strained or puréed version of a jam or preserve. To make fruit butter, cook the fruit until soft, strain or purée it, pour it into a pot with ½ cup sugar to every cup of fruit pulp, and cook the mixture, uncovered, stirring constantly to prevent scorching. When the butter is thick enough to hold its shape slightly, pack it into hot, sterilized jars, and process for 10 minutes.

Good recipes for jams, preserves and butters appear in most general-purpose cookbooks, and some cookbooks specialize in these foods. A few recipes are included in this chapter. Homemade labels add a finishing touch to gift jars.

Jams, jellies, butters and preserves can be sealed with lids and metal rings, as described on page 132, and either left unprocessed or processed, whatever the recipe recommends. These confections can also be preserved un-

der a thin layer of paraffin wax that seals all the edges of any sound, sterilized glass jars. Melt the paraffin in a tin can placed inside a pot of simmering water; do not melt paraffin directly over the heat, because it is flammable. Let the preserves cool for half an hour, then pour a one-eighth-inch layer of wax over the food, rotate the jars to seal the edges, let the jars cool overnight, and seal once again with another thin layer of paraffin.

PICKLES, CHUTNEYS AND KETCHUPS

Pickles, chutneys and ketchups are deliciously sweet-sour foods made from whole, sliced or puréed fruits preserved in a syrup made of various proportions of vinegar, sugar, salt and spices. Use pickling or kosher salt, as regular table salt contains additives that can darken the food. In chutneys, the fruits are often mixed with finely chopped vegetables such as onions or tomatoes. Sauces and ketchups are highly spiced and strained or puréed. Pickles, which consist of chunks of fruit or whole fruits, should be tender but not mushy. Although these foods contain such high levels

Soft apples not suited to long-term storage, such as 'Red Delicious,' right, are best for fresh eating but can also be used in juices and, mixed with more tart varieties, in ciders.

expansion during freezing. It may be desirable to add a certain amount of water to the juice before it is used. On the other hand, if juice is boiled down to one-quarter volume, it becomes a thick syrup.

WINES

Any type of fruit can be made into delicious wine, an excellent way to use windfalls and other damaged or bruised fruit. I have often turned to Mettja C. Roate's paperback, *How to Make Wine in Your Own Kitchen*, which includes such recipes as Golden Apple Wine, Apple-Pear Wine, Heavy Spiced Apricot Wine and Plain Plum Wine. Each recipe makes just a gallon of wine, and none requires the chemicals offered by wine-supply stores. The basic method involves cooking about 4 quarts of fruit gently in the same amount of water, mashing it with a potato masher and putting it through a jelly bag, which is squeezed dry. The warm juice is mixed with about 8 cups of sugar, a cup of chopped raisins and a small amount of yeast, then left, loosely covered, in a warm place to ferment for several weeks. The juice is put through the jelly bag again, covered, left to settle for several days and then siphoned into clean, sterilized bottles, which are corked and stored in a cool place. There are many other books on wine making, and they can be the inspiration for a summer-to-winter activity that is enjoyable in both the doing and the tasting.

CIDER

Making wine with any fruit other than grapes might be considered a questionable act by purists—I have a friend who refers to other fruit wines as "fermented fruit beverages"—but there is no question that cider is made from apples. I have yet to understand why there is not the fully developed cider industry in eastern North America that there is in England, where excellent, regionally varied ciders, syrupy sweet to lip-puckeringly dry, are sold in the neighbourhood pubs. Certainly, the eastern states and provinces provide some perfect country for apple growing. In the West, there is a modest selection of local ciders, but Eastern growers continue to turn their attention to wine grapes that can be grown better elsewhere.

Part of the answer is undoubtedly a lack of demand. North Americans generally think of

of acid that processing is not always recommended, they are safest if given metal lids and screw bands and processed in a hot-water bath (10 minutes for pints, 15 minutes for quarts).

JUICES

Any of the fruits in this book, except bananas, can be made into juice, either on their own or blended with others. Some flavours—apricot with apple or peach with orange—blend especially well. The fruit can be pressed in equipment such as a cider press, put through a juicer or cooked gently until soft in just enough water to prevent sticking and burning, then strained through a jelly bag, as described earlier in this chapter. All processes except the last result in a cloudy juice. Commercial packers use an enzyme to clear juice, but there is no good reason, other than aesthetic, for rejecting juice that is cloudy. In any case, some of the solids will gradually settle to the bottom of the containers during storage.

If juices are not to be refrigerated and used very soon, they must be processed to prevent fermentation. Add sugar or other natural sweetener if desired, heat the juice almost to boiling—200 degrees F (93°C)—and pour into sterilized jars, leaving adequate headspace, as described on page 132. Seal, and process for 10 minutes. Juice can also be stored in airtight jars or plastic containers in the freezer. Fill the containers only three-quarters full to allow for cider as brownish apple juice, not a beverage that varies greatly in flavour and alcohol content. However, ciders, still or crackling, hard (alcoholic) or soft (nonalcoholic), can be prepared at home. The secret of a good cider is the blend of apples used. What is "good" is, of course, a matter of opinion. The USDA standards of quality for cider dictate 50 to 60 percent medium-acid apples, such as 'McIntosh,' 'Northern Spy,' 'Cortland' or 'Spartan'; 30 to 40 percent high-sugar apples, such as 'Golden Delicious' or 'Red Delicious'; 10 percent (maximum) high-acid apples, such as 'Winesap,' 'Duchess' or 'Rome Beauty'; and 5 percent (maximum) astringent apples, such as crabs. This makes a fairly sweet cider, whereas the Old World palate often prefers a cider with a greater proportion of high-tannin apples, such as russets and crab apples. 'Rhode Island Greening,' 'Roxbury Russet,' 'Golden Russet' and a Canadian apple, the 'Snow,' or 'Fameuse,' are venerable cider apples that are still easy to find in nurseries.

If you have an orchard and intend to make cider seriously, you will need a cider press, a piece of equipment that squeezes the fruit into pulp, releasing the juice into a pan underneath. For cider, use ripe, reasonably sound apples but not windfalls, which harbour the bacteria that turn juice into vinegar. Scabby fruit is fine. Wash the apples, then store them indoors for about a week to soften and mellow before pressing. Very hard apples such as crabs should be put through a hand grinder before they are pressed. Collect and store the juice in containers made of plastic, stainless steel, earthenware, glass or clean wood, as other materials may give the juice off-flavours. Either pasteurize or begin the fermentation process immediately, as the juice will otherwise attract insects and moulds.

Cider is made alcoholic, or hard, through the conversion of sugars into alcohol by yeast, a process that will gradually take place in soft, unpasteurized cider even if it is stored in the refrigerator. When all the sugar is used up, the yeasts die. A second type of fermentation, which occurs later, results in a smoother cider. For a full description of this process and the preparation of various ciders, look for a good guide such as *Sweet and Hard Cider: Making It, Using It and Enjoying It* by Annie Proulx and Lew Nichols. The authors write, "Once your palate has accepted the unique savour and zest of cider, you will always want a dozen bottles of the tangy liquor in your cellar."

The range of colours and flavours available in wines can also be had in ciders. The best consist of a blend of variously flavoured apples, including some crabs.

Vinegar

Vinegar, from the French *vin aigre* — "sour wine" — sometimes seems all too easy to make. Leave fermenting fruit juice sitting out uncovered for several weeks, or try to make cider in a barrel once used for vinegar, and you will end up with vinegar, the result of acetobacter (acid-producing bacteria) at work on the alcohol being produced in the juice. Fruit flies are often the agents that bring the acetobacter to the juice. To make vinegar intentionally, place a container of juice covered with cheesecloth in a cool, dark place. Adding a little vinegar to the juice will speed the process and help ensure that the final product is tasty. Fruit vinegars vary in quality, with the sweetest fruit making the most acid vinegar. Vinegar that is too strong can be diluted with water.

Homemade vinegar should not be used in pickle making unless you know its acetic-acid content. The flavour and storageability of pickles are generally dependent upon the type of vinegar sold in the supermarket, which has an acetic-acid content of 5 percent.

Vinegars, like wines and hard ciders, can be stored without processing in clean bottles with corks. These, too, can take their place in the root cellar or cool basement beside the pears and apples and the jars of jams and jellies, all of which will bring rewards that continue long beyond the last picking of fruit.

Peaches are incomparable when freshly picked from the tree, and any that remain can be enjoyed dried, frozen, canned or in jams, jellies and even marmalades.

APPLESAUCE

Pour enough peeled, cored apples into a large pot to fill it about three-quarters full, and add just enough water to cover the bottom of the pot. Simmer, stirring frequently and adding more water if necessary to prevent sticking. When apples are soft, put them through a sauce cone for the smoothest consistency, or press with a potato masher for a chunkier but easier sauce. Add sugar, if desired. Pour into sterilized jars, leaving a half-inch headspace, adjust lids and process for 15 minutes.

APRICOT, PEACH OR PEAR NECTAR

Wash, drain, pit and slice fruit. Treat for darkening, if desired. To each 4 cups of prepared fruit, add 1 cup water, and simmer until tender. Put through a sieve. For every 2 cups of sieved fruit, add 1 Tbsp. lemon juice and ½ cup sugar. Pour into hot pint or quart jars (leaving headspace), lid, and process for 15 minutes in a hot-water bath. When serving, add water to the desired consistency.

PEACH MARMALADE

6 quarts (10 pounds) ripe peaches
8 oranges
Sugar
Juice of 1 lemon

Blanch peaches by dipping into boiling water for 15 to 30 seconds, depending upon ripeness. Plunge into cool water, peel and slice. Squeeze juice and pulp from oranges; chop rind very fine. Add 2 cups sugar to every 2½ cups of the peach-orange mixture. Cook until clear, stirring frequently. Add lemon juice. Cook 5 minutes longer. Pour into hot, sterilized jars, lid and process for 10 minutes.
Makes 14 pints.

PEAR CHUTNEY

2½ cups fresh pears, diced
2½ cups fresh or canned tomatoes, quartered
½ cup white seedless raisins
½ cup chopped green pepper
1 cup sugar
½ cup white vinegar

1 tsp. salt
½ tsp. ground ginger
½ tsp. powdered dry mustard
⅛ tsp. cayenne pepper
¼ cup chopped canned pimento

Remove skins from pears and tomatoes by simmering the whole fruit in boiling water for 15 to 30 seconds, then plunging it into cold water. Combine all ingredients except pimento in a saucepan. Bring to a boil, and simmer till thickened, about 45 minutes, stirring occasionally. Add pimento, and cook 3 minutes longer. Pack into clean, hot, sterilized jars, leaving headspace. Adjust lids. Process in boiling water for 10 minutes. Set jars upright, several inches apart, on a wire rack to cool. Serve with chicken, pork or hamburgers.

Makes 3 or 4 half-pint jars.

Plum Pie

Pastry for a 2-crust, 9-inch pie
½ cup brown sugar
1½ Tbsp. quick-cooking tapioca
¼ tsp. nutmeg
¼ tsp. cloves
⅛ tsp. salt
12 to 16 prune plums, pitted and quartered
1½ tsp. lemon juice
1 Tbsp. butter

Line pie plate with pastry. Combine dry ingredients, and mix with fruit. Turn into pie shell, and sprinkle with lemon juice. Dot with butter. Adjust top crust, seal and flute edges, and cut steam vents. Bake 40 to 45 minutes at 425 degrees F (218°C).

Pickled Crab Apples

6 lbs. crab apples
4 cups cider vinegar
2 cups sugar
1 Tbsp. whole cloves
2 sticks cinnamon, broken into pieces
1 Tbsp. ground ginger

Wash crab apples, and steam until soft but not broken. Place in preserving kettle with vinegar, sugar and spices. Slowly bring the mixture to the boiling point and cook gently for about 10 minutes. Pack apples in hot, sterilized jars, cover with syrup (leaving headspace), lid, and process for 15 minutes.

Makes 12 half-pint jars.

Some European pears can be kept in cold storage in the manner of apples, but all can be preserved in delectable chutneys and other preserves or made into a distinct version of cider known as perry.

Sour or Nanking Cherry Jam

4 cups cherries, pitted
8 cups sugar

Wash and pit cherries, and pour into a saucepan. Crush cherries, add sugar, and boil uncovered until thick, about 10 to 12 minutes. Pour into sterilized jars, adjust lids, and process in boiling-water bath for 10 minutes.

Makes 10 half-pint jars.

Cherry Olives

3 lbs. ripe sweet cherries with stems
2 cups cider or white vinegar
2 cups cold water
2 Tbsp. salt
2 Tbsp. sugar

Select and wash fruit, leaving the fruit whole but clipping stems to 1 or 2 inches long. Pack into clean, sterilized jars. Combine remaining ingredients, and pour cold over cherries in jars. Seal, and process for 10 minutes.

Makes approximately 4 pints.

These recipes are reprinted from several government booklets, including *Jams, Jellies and Pickles* (Agriculture Canada publication 992) and *Home Canning* (Alberta Homedex 1151-1).

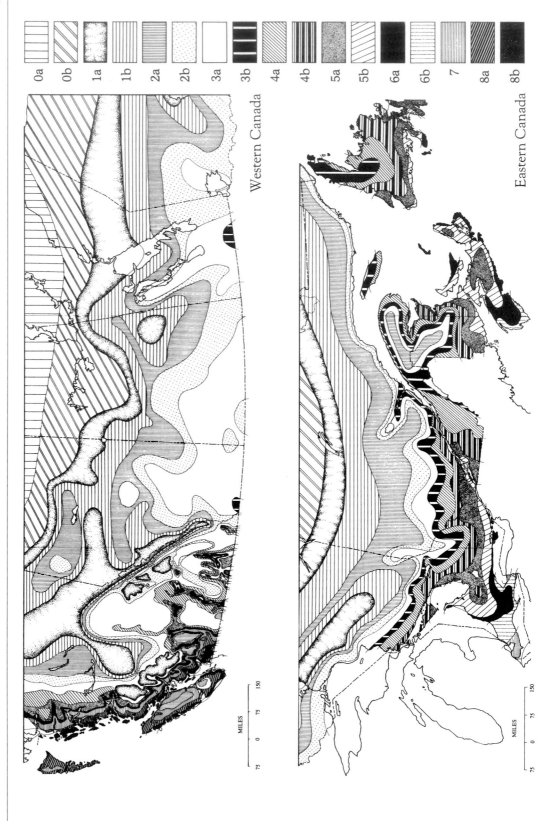

0a 0b 1a 1b 2a 2b 3a 3b 4a 4b 5a 5b 6a 6b 7 8a 8b

Western Canada

Eastern Canada

MILES
75 0 75 150

MILES
75 0 75 150

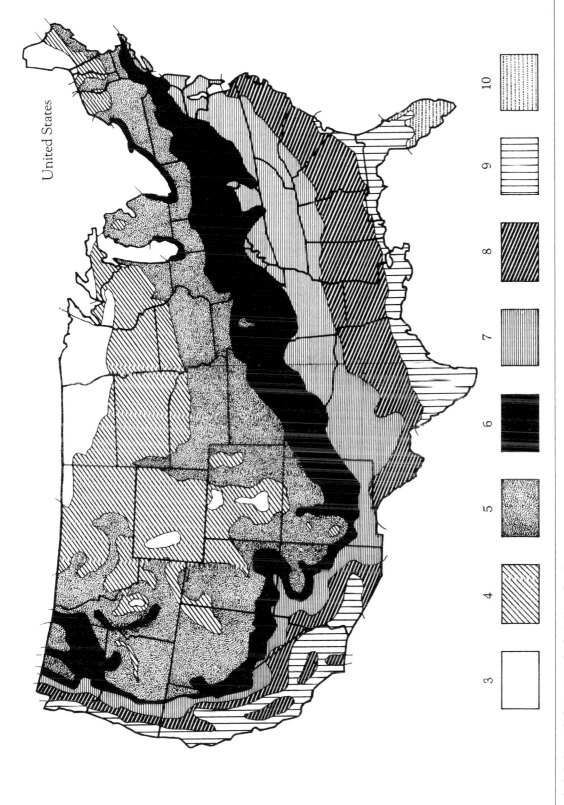

USDA Climatic Zone Map

United States

10

9

8

7

6

5

4

3

The U.S. Department of Agriculture Climatic Zone Map that appears here is a simplified version of the USDA's latest map. While the text refers to more complex zone gradations, readers will be able to identify their zone by referring to the general category—for instance, refer to box 3 to locate zone 3a. Readers should also be aware of the climatic changes caused by local topography as well as year-to-year variations in temperatures and obtain regional maps for reference.

Records

Cultivar: _____ Year of Purchase: _____

Location: _____

Pruning Record: _____

_____

Harvest dates: _____

_____

Description of fruit: _____

Pest or disease treatment schedule: _____

_____

Cultivar: _____ Year of Purchase: _____

Location: _____

Pruning Record: _____

_____

Harvest dates: _____

_____

Description of fruit: _____

Pest or disease treatment schedule: _____

_____

Cultivar: _____ Year of Purchase: _____

Location: _____

Pruning Record: _____

_____

Harvest dates: _____

_____

Description of fruit: _____

Pest or disease treatment schedule: _____

_____

The Orchard Checklist

EARLY SPRING (before bud break)
- Plant trees.
- Prune (dormant pruning will remove unwanted growth, encourage new growth and delay fruiting), including removal of winter-killed wood. As soon as apricots, peaches and nectarines attain blooming age, delay pruning until after bloom.
- Spray dormant oil.
- Apply early fungicide sprays.
- Fertilize lightly, if necessary.

BUD BREAK
- Spray fungicides and pesticides as necessary. Set up and monitor pest traps.
- Weed and mulch the clear area around the base of the trunk.

- Prune apricots, peaches and nectarines soon after bloom.

SPRING AND SUMMER
- Monitor traps and treat for pests as necessary.
- Water weekly, if required.
- Summer-prune (to remove unwanted growth, discourage new growth and delay fruiting). In cold areas, do not prune any later than a month before the first fall frost. Do not prune apricots, peaches and nectarines after June.
- Thin fruit as required.

AFTER LEAF DROP
- Remove fallen leaves and fruit.
- Apply trunk protection for winter.
- Bring tender container trees indoors. Citrus and banana trees do not drop their leaves, so bring indoors as soon as frost threatens.

Cultivar: _____ Year of Purchase: _____

Location: _____

Pruning Record: _____

_____

Harvest dates: _____

_____

Description of fruit: _____

Pest or disease treatment schedule: _____

_____

Cultivar: _____ Year of Purchase: _____

Location: _____

Pruning Record: _____

_____

Harvest dates: _____

_____

Description of fruit: _____

Pest or disease treatment schedule: _____

_____

Records

Cultivar: _____ Year of Purchase: _____

Location: _____

Pruning Record: _____

_____

Harvest dates: _____

_____

Description of fruit: _____

Pest or disease treatment schedule: _____

_____

Cultivar: _____ Year of Purchase: _____

Location: _____

Pruning Record: _____

_____

Harvest dates: _____

_____

Description of fruit: _____

Pest or disease treatment schedule: _____

_____

Cultivar: _____ Year of Purchase: _____

Location: _____

Pruning Record: _____

_____

Harvest dates: _____

_____

Description of fruit: _____

Pest or disease treatment schedule: _____

_____

Cultivar: _____ Year of Purchase: _____

Location: _____

Pruning Record: _____

_____

Harvest dates: _____

_____

Description of fruit: _____

Pest or disease treatment schedule: _____

_____

Cultivar: _____ Year of Purchase: _____

Location: _____

Pruning Record: _____

_____

Harvest dates: _____

_____

Description of fruit: _____

Pest or disease treatment schedule: _____

_____

Cultivar: _____ Year of Purchase: _____

Location: _____

Pruning Record: _____

_____

Harvest dates: _____

_____

Description of fruit: _____

Pest or disease treatment schedule: _____

_____

Cultivar: _____ Year of Purchase: _____

Location: _____

Pruning Record: _____

_____

Harvest dates: _____

_____

Description of fruit: _____

Pest or disease treatment schedule: _____

_____

Cultivar: _____ Year of Purchase: _____

Location: _____

Pruning Record: _____

_____

Harvest dates: _____

_____

Description of fruit: _____

Pest or disease treatment schedule: _____

_____

Cultivar: _____ Year of Purchase: _____

Location: _____

Pruning Record: _____

_____

Harvest dates: _____

_____

Description of fruit: _____

Pest or disease treatment schedule: _____

_____

Trees–Canadian Nurseries

B.C. Certified Budwood Assn.
Research Station
Summerland, British Columbia
V0H 1Z0
Budwood in season. Send a SASE for information. Canada only.

Boughen Nurseries Valley River Ltd.
Box 12
Valley River, Manitoba R0L 2B0
Organically grown, prairie-hardy fruit trees such as apples and cherry plums to Canada only. Catalogue free.

Campberry Farm
RR 1
Niagara-on-the-Lake, Ontario L0S 1J0
Specialists in nut trees but also carry persimmon, pawpaw and hardy apricots. Price list $1.

Corn Hill Nursery
RR 5
Petitcodiac, New Brunswick E0A 2H0
A good selection of fruit trees hardy to at least zone 4b, including plums, pears and heirloom and disease-resistant apples.

Golden Bough Tree Farm
Marlbank, Ontario K0K 2L0
A small selection of fruit trees hardy to zone 5. Catalogue $1.

V. Kraus Nurseries, Ltd.
Carlisle, Ontario L0R 1H0
Fruit trees for orchardists and home gardeners. Retail catalogue $1.

Lakeshore Tree Farms Ltd.
RR 3
Saskatoon, Saskatchewan S7K 3J6
A small selection of prairie-hardy tree fruits. Catalogue $3.

Le Reveil de la Nature
206, RR 1
St-Philibert, Quebec G0M 1X0
A slim French-language catalogue of fruits hardy in Quebec. Catalogue $1.

McConnell Nurseries Inc.
Port Burwell, Ontario N0J 1T0
A small selection of hardy fruit trees. Catalogue free.

McFayden Seeds
Box 1800
Brandon, Manitoba R7A 6N4
A small selection of prairie-hardy fruit trees. Catalogue $2.

Morden Nurseries Ltd.
Box 1270
Morden, Manitoba R0G 1J0
A good selection of prairie-hardy fruit trees. Catalogue free.

Northern Kiwi Nursery
RR 3, 181 Niven Road
Niagara-on-the-Lake, Ontario L0S 1J0
A good selection of hardy kiwis. Price list free.

Keith Somers Trees Ltd.
10 Tillson Ave.
Tillsonburg, Ontario N4G 2Z6
A small selection of fruit trees. Catalogue $2.

Sursum Corda
Scotstown, Quebec J0B 3B0
A good selection of organically grown fruit trees from a zone-4 nursery. Catalogue $2.

Tsolum River Fruit Trees
Box 68
Merville, British Columbia V0R 2M0
Extensive list of organically grown apples, pears, plums and crab apples. Also Asian pear, medlar, quince. Catalogue $3.50.

Western Ontario Fruit Testing Association (WOFTA)
Agriculture Canada Research Station
Harrow, Ontario N0R 1G0
Membership of $15 per year brings a thrice-yearly newsletter and the opportunity to buy new, sometimes as yet unnamed, fruit trees. Budwood and seeds available to nonmembers.

Windmill Point Farm & Nursery
2103 Boul. Perrot
N.D. Ile Perrot, Quebec J7V 5V6
An extensive list of organically grown apples and other fruit trees including cherry species, kiwi, figs. Catalogue, in either French or English, is free.

TREES–U.S. NURSERIES

Many U.S. nurseries will not ship beyond the continental United States, as noted in the following listing. Those that will ship to Canada require an import permit, obtainable from the Plant Protection Division, Agriculture Canada, Ottawa, Ontario K1A 0C7. All the nurseries in the following list will ship to Canada unless it is stated otherwise. Note that *Malus*, *Prunus* and *Pyrus* species cannot be imported into Canada. *Prunus* species also cannot be imported into California, Washington or Arizona.

Burnt Ridge Nursery & Orchards
432 Burnt Ridge Road
Onalaska, Washington 98570
Unusual fruit trees. Send a business-size envelope and an International Postal Reply Coupon for price list.

Edible Landscaping
Box 77
Afton, Virginia 22920
Jujubes, persimmons, bush cherries, crab apples, kiwi and other unusual fruits. Catalogue $2 to the U.S., $2.50 to Canada.

Garden of Delights
14560 S.W. 14th Street
Davie, Florida 33325
Rare fruit trees. Catalogue $2 (U.S.).

Henry Leuthardt Nurseries, Inc.
Montauk Highway, Box 666
East Moriches, Long Island, New York 11940
Specialists in dwarf and semidwarf fruit trees, including espalier. Price list free, although an espalier handbook is $1 refundable. Accepts U.S. orders only.

Hidden Springs Nursery
Route 14, Box 159
Cookeville, Tennessee 38501
Unusual fruits including jujube, kiwi, persimmon, quince and disease-resistant apples. Price list free.

Hollydale Nursery
Box 26
Pelham, Tennessee 37366
Common fruit trees including an excellent selection of peaches. Price list free.

Kelly Nurseries
Box 10
Louisiana, Missouri 63353-0010
Catalogue free, to the continental U.S. only.

Lawson's Nursery
Route 1, Box 472
Yellow Creek Road
Ballground, Georgia 30107
Popular tree fruits and heirloom apples. Catalogue free.

Lawyer Nursery Inc.
950 Highway 200 West
Plains, Montana 59859
Fruit trees and a good selection of rootstocks. Catalogue free.

Living Tree Center
Box 10082
Berkeley, California 94709
More than 90 unusual varieties of fruit trees. Catalogue/journal $7 (U.S.) refundable, to the U.S. or Canada.

Long Hungry Creek Nursery
Red Boiling Springs, Tennessee 37150
Disease-resistant apples. Price list free, to U.S. only.

Mellinger's Nursery
2310 W. South Range Road
North Lima, Ohio 44452-9731
A comprehensive catalogue offers a limited but interesting selection of rootstocks and fruits including quince, kiwi, native fruits and dwarf citrus. Catalogue free to the U.S., $2.10 (U.S.) to Canada.

J. E. Miller Nurseries, Inc.
5060 West Lake Road
Canandaigua, New York 14424
A full-colour catalogue including all popular tree fruits and a good selection of heirloom apples. Catalogue free, to the U.S. only.

New York State Fruit Testing Co-op Association
Box 462
Geneva, New York 14456
An excellent selection of many of the newest tree fruits, especially those developed at Geneva. Also some antiques. Catalogue free, membership $5 (U.S.).

Newark Nurseries, Inc.
Box 578
60397 CR 681
Hartford, Michigan 49057
Many of the newest cultivars; specialize in supplying commercial growers. Catalogue $5 (U.S.).

Northwood's Nursery
28696 S. Cramer Road
Molalla, Oregon 97038
Popular tree fruits including good selection of citrus, figs, persimmons and Asian pears. Catalogue free.

Oikos Tree Crops
721 North Fletcher
Kalamazoo, Michigan 49007-3077
Native fruits such as pawpaw, persimmon, American plum, beach plum and crab apple. Catalogue free.

Pacific Tree Farms
4301 Lynwood Drive
Chula Vista, California 92010
An impressive list of unusual fruit trees. Catalogue $2 (U.S.).

Rocky Meadow Orchard & Nursery
Route 2, Box 2104
New Salisbury, Indiana 47161-9716
Custom propagation of fruit trees. Catalogue $1, to U.S. only.

St. Lawrence Nurseries
RR 5, Box 324
Potsdam, New York 13676
An excellent selection of hardy fruit trees grown organically. Catalogue $1 to the U.S., $3 to Canada.

Southmeadow Fruit Gardens
Box SM
Lakeside, Michigan 49116
More than 500 types of "choice and unusual" tree and small fruits. Price list free. Descriptive 112-page catalogue $8 (U.S.). U.S. orders only.

Stark Bros. Nurseries & Orchards
Louisiana, Missouri 63353
A full-colour, informative catalogue listing all popular fruit trees, including a good selection of dwarfs. Catalogue free, to continental U.S. only. Toll-free number 1-800-325-4180 (in Missouri, 1-314-754-4525).

SUPPLIES AND ASSOCIATIONS

Supplies can be imported into Canada, provided duty and GST are paid where applicable. Canadians can legally import 500 g. or 500 ml. of any pesticide for personal use.

Harmony Farm Supply
Box 460
Graton, California 95444
Books and equipment for all types of horticulture, agriculture and orchardry; bird netting, pruning shears, grafting supplies, sprayers, insect traps, organic pesticides and fungicides. Catalogue $2 (U.S.).

Ladd Research Industries, Inc.
Box 1005
Burlington, Vermont 05402
Traps for apple maggot, codling moth, leaf roller and plum curculio. Price list free.

Land Steward
434 Lower Road
Souderton, Pennsylvania 18964
Nontoxic insect traps. Price list free.

North American Fruit Explorers (NAFEX)
Tom Vorbeck
RR 1, Box 94
Chapin, Illinois 62628
An association established for and dedicated to discovering, cultivating and appreciating superior varieties of fruits and nuts, NAFEX publishes the quarterly journal *Pomona* for its members and offers fellowship, advice and annual meetings. Write for current membership information.

Orchard Equipment & Supply Co.
Box 540, Route 116
Conway, Massachusetts 01341
Equipment for commercial orchardists, but some items here will be of interest to small growers, such as hand-operated cider presses. Catalogue free.

Ringer
9959 Valley View Road
Eden Prairie, Minnesota 55344-3585
Garden tools and supplies, including organic fertilizers and Safer's organic pesticides (now owned by Ringer). Catalogue free.

ALTERNATE BEARING—Also called biennial bearing, describes a tree that bears heavily one year and sparsely or not at all the next. Some **cultivars** are naturally more prone to biennial bearing than others, but the habit can be encouraged by allowing a particularly heavy **fruit** set, which inhibits the growth of **buds** for the next year's crop.

BACILLUS THURINGIENSIS (Bt)—A bacterium that kills larvae of members of the insect order Lepidoptera (moths and butterflies). This is an organically approved **pesticide**, available as a powder or spray, for caterpillars such as codling moth and tent caterpillar.

BIENNIAL—See **alternate bearing**.

BORDEAUX MIXTURE—A fungicide invented in France for use on grapes, consisting of varying proportions of copper sulphate, lime and water. It is approved for use in organic orchards.

BUD—When used as a verb, describes a type of **grafting** in which a single dormant bud and its surrounding bark are placed on the **cambium** of the **stock**, which is usually a different **cultivar** or **species**. As a noun, refers to a vegetative structure containing an embryonic **flower**, leaf or flower cluster, usually protected by overlapping scales. The terminal bud is the one at the tip of the shoot. Many buds do not develop, remaining latent until natural tree wounds or **pruning** activates them.

CAMBIUM—A layer of cells directly under the bark of a tree. This layer is responsible for increases in the girth of the tree both inside and outside the cambium. When **grafting**, the cambium layers of both **stock** and **scion** must be united for new growth to occur.

CLIMATIC ZONE—An area of Canada or the United States defined by climate and given a number. The zones are used mainly to indicate what plants are suitably **hardy**. The lower the number, the colder the winter; thus, fewer plants can survive there. See pages 140 and 141.

CLING, or CLINGSTONE—A *Prunus* fruit in which the flesh adheres to the pit or stone. The opposite of **freestone**.

CLONE—A plant or plant part grown vegetatively from a mother plant and thus genetically identical to the mother. Clonal **rootstocks** are generally more expensive than **seedlings** and may carry virus diseases but offer predictability in the qualities they confer.

COMPOST—As a noun, indicates fertile organic matter decayed in the presence of oxygen. As a verb, the process of making this topsoil amendment.

CULTIVAR—An artificially created variety or a named **seedling**, thus a *culti*vated *vari*ety. 'McIntosh' is the cultivar name of a type of apple.

DIPLOID—A tree with two sets of chromosomes. Because the chromosomes divide evenly, these trees are good pollinators, unlike **triploids**. Most apples are diploid, as are sweet cherries and some plums. Sour cherries are tetraploid, with four sets of chromosomes that again divide easily for good **pollination**.

DRUPE—A fruit that has a fleshy layer surrounding a pit or stone, which in turn protects the true seed within. Cherries, plums, apricots and peaches are all drupes. They are related, too, as members of the subfamily Prunoideae, which belongs to the rose family Rosaceae.

DWARF—A plant that is less than one-half the usual, or **standard**, size.

ESPALIER—A verb meaning to **prune** severely to create a two-dimensional tree that is grown against a wall or trellis. Espalier is also an adjective to describe these trees. In its strictest sense, it refers to only one style of two-dimensional pruning in which there are several horizontal branches.

FERTILIZATION—Occurs within a **flower** after **pollination**, when two sexually different plant cells fuse inside an ovule to form the embryo of a seed capable of producing a new plant. When fertilization is successful, hormones are released that allow the **fruit** to swell.

FESTOON—To **prune** a **fruit** tree by tying young branches to the stem, usually the very flexible new branches of a freshly planted plum tree. The term and technique are more common in Britain than in North America.

FLOWER—In the angiosperms, or flowering plants, this is a plant structure which is composed of modified leaves, the perianth, surrounding the sexual organs. The perianth typically has two parts: an outer circle, or calyx, of small green leaves, the sepals, and an inner showy ring, or corolla, of small, bright coloured leaves, the petals, which attract pollinating insects and help protect the sexual organs in the flower centre. The innermost part, the pistil, is made up of the female organs; a postlike style topped by a sticky stigma and, at the base of the style, the ovary, which contains ovules, destined to become seeds if **fertilization** occurs. The pistil is surrounded by stamens, the male parts, each of which consists of a threadlike filament topped by a pollen-bearing anther. Most temperate fruit trees have so-called perfect flowers, such as those just described, with male and female organs present.

FRAMEWORK—The trunk and main branches of a tree. The framework may be a different **cultivar** or **species** than the desired variety, which is **budded** onto the branches of the framework variety. For instance, to confer fire blight **resistance** on 'Bartlett' trees, 'Bartlett' **buds** can be **grafted** to the **scaffold** branches of the resistant **cultivar** 'Old Home,' a technique known as **topworking**.

FREESTONE—A *Prunus* fruit in which the flesh does not adhere to the stone or pit. The opposite of **cling,** or **clingstone**.

FRUIT—The seed-bearing capsule of a plant, not necessarily fleshy or edible but usually both.

GRAFT—To attach a piece of one plant, the **scion**, to another, the **stock**, so that their **cambium** layers are securely in contact and growth can take place. Virtually all fruit trees consist of a **scion** of the desired **cultivar** grafted to a different **rootstock**. Grafting is also commonly done to introduce an additional **cultivar** or to help the tree survive severe wounds.

HARDEN, or HARDEN OFF—To acclimatize a plant slowly to a different environment by gradually increasing its exposure to the new surroundings. Hardening must be done, for instance, when a container tree is moved from indoors to outdoors in spring or back indoors in fall.

HARDY—A relative term that describes a plant's ability to survive low temperatures.

INTERSTEM—A section of the central stem or trunk that is a different **cultivar** from either the **rootstock** or the **scion**. In a designation of the **cultivar** name, it is the middle term. For example, 'McIntosh'/Ottawa 5/M5 describes a 'McIntosh' tree with an Ottawa 5 interstem and a Malling 5 **rootstock**.

LEADER—The topmost or outermost growth of a tree. Usually the topmost growth is a continuation of the central leader, the stem, or trunk, of the tree.

MYCOPLASMA—A minute, viruslike organism, recently discovered, that lacks cell walls and can cause diseases.

PARTHENOCARPY—The ability of **fruit** to set without **fertilization**. Parthenocarpy is sometimes a sign of a long period of cultivation. The most palatable types of figs and bananas, for instance, produce **fruit** parthenocarpically. These plants must be propagated vegetatively.

PECTIN—A type of complex carbohydrate in certain **fruits** that causes jelling when cooked with the right amounts of sugar and acid.

PESTICIDE—A substance used to kill insects (insecticide), fungi (fungicide) or weeds (herbicide). Some pesticides are approved for use in organic gardens and orchards.

PIPPIN—A **fruit** tree, especially an apple or pear, grown from a seed, or pip. This is the cheapest way to grow **fruit** trees, but production of **fruit** is late, and the quality of tree and **fruit** is unpredictable. Today's **cultivar** names that include the word "pippin" describe trees which were not themselves grown from seeds but whose ancestors were **seedlings**.

POLLINATION—The transfer of pollen (dustlike grains containing male sex cells) from anthers at the tips of the stamens of a **flower** to the stigma at the tip of the pistil of the same or a different **flower**. Honeybees are important factors in this transfer, but pollination can also be done by hand, with a small paintbrush or by removing stamens from one **flower** and touching the anthers to the stigma of another **flower**. Cross-fruitfulness, or cross-pollination, occurs when the pollen of one **cultivar** or **species** causes the setting of **fruit** of another. **Self-fruitful** describes plants whose **fruit** will set with pollen from their own **flowers**.

POME—A **fruit** with a core, such as the apple, pear and quince, all of which are members of the subfamily Pomaceae in the rose family Rosaceae. The fleshy, edible part of a pome is the floral cup, which expands after the blossom is fertilized. The thin, papery layer around the core, enclosing the seeds, is the ovary wall.

PRUNE—As a verb, to remove unwanted parts of a plant to either encourage or restrict growth. As a noun, refers to a type of purple plum and the dried **fruit** made from it.

RESISTANT—In describing disease susceptibility of plants, indicates a certain ability to remain uninfected. Compare with **tolerant**.

ROOTSTOCK—The **species** or **cultivar** that forms the roots of a **fruit** tree, to which the top of the tree, the **scion**, is **grafted**. Rootstocks may be **seedling** or **clonal**.

RUSSET—Adjective describing brownish, rough-textured **fruit** skin, especially of certain apples and pears. Some **cultivars** are identified by skin that always russets—in the case of apples, they are known as russets—while other **cultivars** will russet in certain climatic or disease situations or when sprayed with sulphur. Russetted skin is thick but perfectly edible.

SCAFFOLD—A main, load-bearing branch of a tree, usually growing almost horizontally. The main objective of early **pruning** is the development of strong scaffolds. Ideally, the scaffolds are fairly evenly spaced around and up the tree, with about six to a **standard** tree.

SCION—Part of a tree that is removed and **budded** or **grafted** to another. This is the **fruit**-bearing or preferred part of the tree, as opposed to the **stock** or **rootstock** on which it grows.

SEEDLING—A tree or **rootstock** grown from a seed. Seedling **rootstocks** are relatively inexpensive, **vigorous** and virus-free in comparison to **clonal rootstocks**, but their results are usually less predictable and sometimes less impressive.

SELF-COMPATIBLE—See **Self-fruitful**.

SELF-FRUITFUL—Describes a plant that can produce **fruit** with its own pollen, by means of a process called self-pollination. If viable seeds are produced, the plant is also termed self-fertile, or self-compatible. Plants that do not produce **fruit** with their own pollen are called self-unfruitful, or self-sterile. See also **pollination**.

SELF-POLLINATION—See **Self-fruitful**.

SEMIDWARF—A relative term that describes a tree neither as small as a **dwarf** nor as tall as a **standard**. It is at least half the size of a **standard**.

SHUCK-FALL—The time when the final remains of the base of the blossom drop off, exposing a tiny, immature **fruit**. This period is important in timing sprayings and may be mentioned on **pesticide** labels.

SPECIES—A class of related plants that have common attributes and are potentially capable of interbreeding.

SPORT—A mutation that occurs unpredictably, sometimes as a branch or single **fruit**. The nectarine, for example, occurs occasionally as a natural, fuzzless sport on a peach tree. New **cultivars** are sometimes discovered growing as sports, which are then propagated by **grafting**.

SPUR—A small, knobby growth on apple or pear branches that develops from a **bud** and supports several blossoms. An apple spur may be fruitful for 10 to 20 years.

STANDARD—A tree that attains the full size it would if it grew from a **seedling**.

STOCK—The plant part that forms the base for the **scion**, the desired **cultivar**. In the process of **grafting**, the **scion** is brought to the stock.

SUCKER—A vertical, vegetative shoot that arises from the roots. It should be removed close to the base, because it is identical in **cultivar** or **species** to the **rootstock**, not the **scion**, and will compete with the latter as it grows.

TENDER—Describes a plant that is susceptible to damage from cold or frost; the opposite of **hardy**.

THIN—To remove a certain portion of the **fruit** crop when young to increase the size and quality of the remaining **fruit** and to help ensure a crop the next season.

TOLERANT—In describing disease susceptibility of a plant, indicates that it may become infected with the disease but is likely to survive. Compare with **resistant**.

TOPWORK—To **graft** a desired **cultivar** to a **framework** consisting of another **cultivar** or **species**. This is sometimes done in areas marginally too cold or otherwise too severe for the desired **cultivar**, where the **framework cultivar** is **hardier** than the **scion**.

TRIPLOID—A tree with three sets of chromosomes. Because the chromosome number is not divisible by two, these trees cannot be used as pollinators. The extra set of chromosomes means, however, that the trees may have larger **fruit**, so some desirable **cultivars** are triploid. Common triploid apples include 'Jonagold,' 'Mutsu' and 'Rhode Island Greening.'

VIGOUR—Refers to the ability of a tree to grow relatively large and relatively quickly. **Dwarfing rootstocks** lessen the vigour of a tree.

WATER SPROUT—A vertical, fast-growing branch on a **fruit** tree, named for its succulence and suppleness. If left to grow vertically, such a branch will seldom produce **fruit**, but it can be trained to grow more horizontally and can then become a useful branch. Water sprouts usually arise just below the cuts that occur when a tree is damaged or **pruned**.

WHIP—A year-old **grafted** tree, little more than a single central **leader** with a few **buds**. It may also be called a maiden.

WINDFALL—A traditional name for an apple that falls of its own accord. Such apples are now more commonly called drops.

ZONE—See **climatic zone**.

Credits

p.4 Joanne Pavia
p.6 Jerry Howard, Positive Images
p.7, p.13, p.27, p.41, p.53, p.63, p.73, p.83, p.97, p.117 p.127 Illustrations by Lori Richards
p.9 Jerry Howard, Positive Images
p.10 Jennifer Bennett
p.11 Walter Chandoha
p.12 John Scanlan
p.15 Gary Holscher
p.16 John Ruskay
p.17 Gary Holscher
p.18 Jennifer Bennett
p.19 David Cavagnaro
p.20 David Cavagnaro
p.21 David Cavagnaro
p.22 David Cavagnaro
p.23 Cosmo Condina
p.24 Jerry Howard, Positive Images
p.25 Jerry Howard, Positive Images
p.26 Zig Leszczynski, Earth Scenes
p.28 Runk/Schoenberger, Grant Heilman Photography
p.29 Wendy Neefus, Earth Scenes
p.30 Donald Specker, Earth Scenes
p.31 Jennifer Bennett
p.33 David Cavagnaro
p.34 John Ruskay
p.35 Chris Thorpe, OMAF
p.36 Charlie Palek, Animals Animals
p.37 D. Overcash, Bruce Coleman Inc.
p.38 Dwight R. Kuhn
p.40 Jerry Howard, Positive Images
p.42 Walter Chandoha
p.43 P. Fletcher, Focus Stock Photo Inc.
p.44 Val Whelan, Valan Photos
p.46 Thomas Eltzroth
p.47 Carl Hanninen, Photo/Nats
p.48 Gary Holscher
p.49 Gary Holscher
p.50 David Cavagnaro
p.52 Walter Chandoha
p.54 Cosmo Condina
p.55 Morden Research Station, Agriculture Canada
p.56 Morden Research Station, Agriculture Canada
p.57 Thomas Eltzroth
p.58 Sylvia Schlender
p.59 Eldon L. Reeves, Tom Stack & Associates
p.60 Jennifer R. Kemp, Valan Photos
p.62 Walter Chandoha
p.64 Dennis Barnes
p.65 Agripress, Focus Stock Photo Inc.
p.66 Thomas Eltzroth
p.67 Thomas Eltzroth
p.68 Cosmo Condina
p.69 Walter Chandoha
p.70 Jennifer Bennett
p.72 Cosmo Condina
p.75 Walter Chandoha

p.76 John Lynch, Photo/Nats
p.77 Thomas Eltzroth
p.79 Gary Holscher
p.80 Thomas Eltzroth
p.82 Walter Chandoha
p.84 Rosalind Creasy
p.85 Walter Chandoha
p.86 Walter Chandoha
p.87 Walter Chandoha
p.88 Rosalind Creasy
p.89 Walter Chandoha
p.90 Rosalind Creasy
p.91 Larry Lefever, Grant Heilman Photography
p.93 Walter Chandoha
p.94 David Bedford
p.96 Grant Heilman Photography
p.98 Larry Lefever, Grant Heilman Photography
p.99 Malak
p.100 Jennifer Bennett
p.102 John Scanlan
p.103 Jennifer Bennett
p.104 Runk/Schoenberger, Grant Heilman Photography
p.105 Lee Foster, Bruce Coleman Inc.
p.106 E.R. Degginger, Bruce Coleman Inc.
p.107 Rosalind Creasy
p.109 Thomas Eltzroth
p.110 David Cavagnaro
p.111 Thomas Eltzroth
p.112 Jennifer Bennett
p.113 Clara Parsons, Valan Photos
p.114 Morden Research Station, Agriculture Canada
p.116 Thomas Eltzroth
p.118 Jerry Howard, Positive Images
p.119 Rosalind Creasy
p.120 Lefever/Grushow, Grant Heilman Photography
p.121 Thomas Eltzroth
p.122 David Cavagnaro
p.123 Thomas Eltzroth
p.124 Linda Gilkeson
p.126 Barry L. Runk, Grant Heilman Photography
p.129 Sylvia Schlender
p.130 David Cavagnaro
p.131 David Cavagnaro
p.132 Gary Holscher
p.133 David Cavagnaro
p.134 Charles Marden Fitch
p.135 Thomas Hovland, Grant Heilman Photography
p.136 Thomas Eltzroth
p.137 Barry L. Runk, Grant Heilman Photography
p.138 Thomas Eltzroth
p.139 Thomas Eltzroth
p.140-41 Maps by Marta Scythes